Praises for *The Strategic Treasurer: A Partnership for Corporate Growth*

"The Strategic Treasurer is a must read for anyone looking to break away from the transactional Treasurer role and take the Treasurer position to its rightful place as a strategic business partner. Jeffery gives the insights needed to view the big picture as required in this new role, while providing the practical concepts needed to move along this new path."

—Arthur P. Lorenz, CTP, CPA, Treasurer,
Hunter Douglas North America

"Today's dynamic businesses need treasurers who do more than shave points off debt rates. Businesses need treasurers who are visionary partners on the executive team, directing smart financial management throughout the enterprise. From 'boot camp' basics to sophisticated relationship building and financial risk management, Craig helps treasurers break through yesterday's silo mentality to deliver more value in creative ways."

—Robert J. Warren, CPA, CMA, VP Corporate Development &
Finance, (Formerly VP & Treasurer 20 years),
Diebold, Incorporated

"As a client of Craig's, I found the same systematic approach to the Treasury function in his writing that I did in working with him during his engagement. He has encapsulated the Treasury function as a process that defines of one of the most critical aspects of any business–the ownership and stewardship of cash. This is a great read, while providing guidance, for both those aspiring to assume a leadership role in Treasury as well as those who are currently in leadership and seeking ways to improve their current process."

—Ward Allen, VP Finance, WinWholesale Inc.

"Craig Jeffery makes a strong case that recent market turbulence greatly increases the importance of the Treasurer position as steward of a company's liquidity and manager of its financial risk. The book abounds with practical guidance, but never loses sight of the larger picture. Treasury is an integral part of a financial process that permeates the entire organization. The strategic treasurer looks beyond his functional boundaries and sees disparate activities and controls as part of a single process . . . Jeffery shows you how."

—Dennis Sweeney, Deputy Treasurer,
General Electric Company

"Craig makes it clear that mere technical expertise does not a strategic treasurer make and challenges us to look past our traditional zones of influence. The technical aspects of the treasurer's job remain, and Craig reasserts the critical ones with insight into how their application and utility can sometimes be distorted in the real world environment. This book is a valuable resource for the neophyte as well as the seasoned professional in the trenches looking to get re-grounded on what is most important."

—John Beattie, VP & Treasurer, Spectrum Brands, Inc.

"Like anything in business, beyond the academic and the theoretical, the practical approach to a discipline ultimately governs both the planning and the successful execution to the enterprise. Craig has been able to capture this in print."

—Mark Henry, Treasurer, SVP Global Tax &
Risk Management, Infor

"*The Strategic Treasurer* serves as an excellent reference tool for corporate finance executives. Craig Jeffery distinguishes the role of Treasurer from that of Controller and shows how the treasury function is about much more than cash management."

—Thomas A. King, Treasurer, Progressive Insurance

The Strategic Treasurer

The Strategic Treasurer

A Partnership for Corporate Growth

CRAIG A. JEFFERY

John Wiley & Sons, Inc.

Published by John Wiley & Sons, Inc., Hoboken, New Jersey.

Published simultaneously in Canada.

For general information on our other products and services, or technical support, please contact our Customer Care Department within the United States at 800-762-2974, outside the United States at 317-572-3993 or fax 317-572-4002.

Wiley also publishes its books in a variety of electronic formats. Some content that appears in print may not be available in electronic books.

For more information about Wiley products, visit our Web site at www.wiley.com.

Library of Congress Cataloging-in-Publication Data:

Jeffery, Craig, 1963-
    The strategic treasurer: a partnership for corporate growth/Craig Jeffery.
        p. cm.
    Includes bibliographical references and index.
    ISBN 978-0-470-40777-6 (cloth)
    1. Corporate treasurers. 2. Corporations–Finance. 3. Cash management.
I. Title.
HG4026.J44 2009
658.15–dc22

                                                                2009010853

Printed in the United States of America

10 9 8 7 6 5 4 3 2 1

Contents

Preface

Market turbulence has created quite a ride for Treasurers in recent years. This has emphasized the need to better manage risks and to achieve a level of visibility to liquidity and the risks to liquidity that was never before imagined. Accordingly, the need to perform all of these duties has to be met in Internet time versus financial reporting time. It is time again for Treasurers to show their value. This has not always been so obvious.

Long before double entry accounting was conceived as an idea, the function of Treasury existed. The function as well as the job title of "Treasurer" was part of ancient governments many millennia ago. In corporations, the Treasurer title has existed for many decades, filling a role that is distinct from the Controller. However, Treasury is not generally thought of as a discipline for which one says "When I grow up, I want to be. . ." and goes to school for specific training. The skills necessary to execute the Treasurer role sometimes overlap other positions in finance but often are quite unique to this function. The areas of responsibility include capital structure, cash management, stewardship of assets, foreign exchange management, interest rate risk management, corporate finance, and debt and investment management. A solid understanding of accounting has consistently been a prerequisite for the role.

Here in the twenty-first century, however, the Treasurer's role encompasses much more and includes additional responsibilities in the areas of working capital management and more broad coverage of financial risk management. And no longer can Treasurers work in isolation when fulfilling their duties.

Addressing these added responsibilities has become possible due to the development and now the extensive use of various technology tools and services. Indeed, technology now allows the Treasurer to more accurately and efficiently measure risk, protect regional and global assets, optimize working capital, manage investments, and leverage external and internal relationships effectively. The increase in responsibility over time has made the Treasurer's role more interesting. But that is not all that has made it more interesting.

With the expanded role of today's Treasurer, the imperative now is to go beyond the basic expectation of managing the cash conversion cycle to becoming a strategic business partner. Thus, the concept of *Strategic*

Treasurer was born out of this author's belief that the Treasurer's role in today's global organizations requires a new definition and focus, lest it give up its rightful territory and shrink to a mere bookkeeping or transaction-oriented function.

Strategic has in the past years found its way into the business lexicon as the term that adds value to a chore, simply by its utterance. For the Strategic Treasurer, however, merely using a new word and following a roadmap comprised of a series of tasks and checklists will not get the job done.

Being strategic is basically having the ability to view the big picture, to assess suitable options, and to act on one's best judgment. Being strategic requires thinking and ordering one's thoughts and then taking appropriate action. Consider a regiment occupying a mountain pass, where a few people can hold off a giant army. Being strategic will allow just that—holding the vast armies of lower priority items at bay and attending to the urgent ones. It is a case of negating the items that can defeat and render the role of Treasurer less valuable.

This is not to say that protecting one's job or turf is the priority. It is much more than that. The Treasurer must proactively act as a strategic business partner with other units, bringing their specific skills and insights to the table to add corporate value and focus. By thinking and acting as Strategic Treasurers, today's Treasurers have an opportunity to bring far more meaning to their efforts by contributing to a greater level of organizational success.

This book is designed for those on the path to becoming a Strategic Treasurer and for those already there but wanting to refine their goals and skills to more effectively act as a business partner of the organization they support. The book is divided into 19 chapters, which will be summarized briefly in the Chapter Overviews. For Corporate Directors and others in senior management who are strapped for time, a suggested prioritization of chapters follows.

Treasurers Deserve Equal Time

Currently, numerous books exist geared toward the roles of the Chief Financial Officer and Controller, with more being published almost monthly. The Treasurer is largely limited to some excellent periodical resources, with very few books on the general subject of Treasury or Treasurers.

Books that exist in the fields pertaining to Treasury are heavily weighted toward general reference on cash management or are core materials related to professional designations. Specific volumes on cash management, international cash management, foreign exchange risk management, hedging and hedge accounting, investment management, and investor relations cover the majority of the other materials available to Treasurers and Treasury professionals.

It is interesting that several large international banks have more cash and Treasury management books produced in-house available than what seem to be in print from public sources. This could easily provide an argument for having more material available to the Treasurer and those who need to care about that role.

Treasurers have seen a regular and consistent increase in their responsibilities. Board members and the CEO have recently been recognizing the value that a Strategic Treasurer brings to their organization.

This book is intended to add to the resources that are available to the Treasurer. Additionally, it can be a tool to provide guidance and provoke thought for those who have been Treasurers for years, are new to the role, or are contemplating becoming a Treasurer someday. However, a number of important areas of which the Treasurer must be aware are not covered in this book in depth or at all, since other materials are readily available for those areas.

Chapter Overviews

Chapter 1, "Building the Case for Being a Strategic Treasurer," outlines the key arguments for the value of the Treasurer and the necessity of that role being filled with one who acts in a strategic manner.

Chapter 2, "First Things for the New Treasurer," provides guidance to those starting this role in an organization. It outlines many of the most important steps that should be initiated as quickly as possible.

Chapter 3, "Being a Partner, Not a Vendor," lays the intellectual framework and reasons for why Treasurers must act as a business partner and use their unique strengths to help the business.

Chapter 4, "Managing Relationships," provides reasons and guidance for being systematic and formal about managing bank and other key relationships. Organizations need relationships that provide advice and capital, and Treasurers must be deliberate about this responsibility.

Chapter 5, "Owning Cash and the Five *O*s of Treasury," details key reasons why Treasurers must act as the owners of corporate or entity cash. It describes what owning cash means and provides some prescriptive steps for moving to that position.

Chapter 6, "Cash Boot Camp for Treasurers," provides a practical and accounting-oriented approach to understanding different perspectives of cash as well as how accounting and Treasury can live in harmony at the point where their cash-recording lives intersect.

Chapter 7, "Owning Working Capital," discusses the importance of having the Treasurer either own or oversee working capital for the organization. Traditional and alternative formulas are covered, and examples highlighting various working capital optimization methods are provided.

Chapter 8, "Differences between a Process View and a Silo View," presses the case that Treasury must understand and help optimize an entire *process* rather than a single department.

Chapter 9, "Financial Risk Management, Part One: Considering Risk Through the Eye of the Beholder," details a framework for viewing and assessing the financial risks organizations face. This chapter was written by contributing editor David Stowe.

Chapter 10, "Financial Risk Management, Part Two: Altering the Risk a Company Faces to Match the Risk It Desires," provides intellectual and practical guidance for managing risks according to your plan. This chapter was written by contributing editor David Stowe.

Chapter 11, "Losses and Fraud: What Can Keep Treasurers Awake at Night," touches on several key areas where losses can occur from action, or inaction, and offers advice to ensure more peaceful sleep for the Treasurer.

Chapter 12, "Communication: Mars and Venus," begins to document the variety of ways the Treasurer and Controller see things differently. The reason behind these differences is described and discussed, allowing for understanding between these two crucial financial players.

Chapter 13, "Building and Developing the Treasury Team," shares perspectives on forming and reorganizing a Treasury team. It details how having the right team is more important in Treasury than in many other areas of an organization.

Chapter 14, "Understanding and Maximizing the Use of Treasury Technology Tools," describes portions of the vast technology landscape and the opportunities that exist to employ these tools to help the Treasurer and the organization fulfill their respective missions.

Chapter 15, "Advice from Various Treasury Leaders," offers a range of quotes and summarized information, from various Treasury leaders of organizations in high concentration.

Chapter 16, "Volatility and Liquidity Management," describes various recent situations that have made the Treasurer's job particularly exciting. It describes the market situation and government interventions that prove reality is not as stable as theory. It enforces the activities and perspectives that a Treasurer must perform and maintain to protect an organization.

Chapter 17, "Achieving Visibility to Your Liquidity," provides guidance, perspectives, and analysis to enable the Treasurer to possess a clear view of the organization's liquidity as well as the various areas and events that can impact that liquidity. Chapters 16 and 17 were written during the financial upheaval in late 2008 and early 2009.

Chapter 18, "Envisioning Treasury in the Future," takes a look at and makes predictions about what the future holds for Treasuries. It explores what will remain the same and what will change across several categories.

Chapter 19, "'Not-to-Do' List for the Treasurer," offers an assortment of ideas to move Treasurers toward success by being more selective in what they and their group do and do not do. With this guidance, Treasurers will be able to more clearly focus on the areas where they can best invest their time and thinking.

Corporate Directors

This book is targeted for those in or pursuing the role of Treasurer. However, others in senior leadership positions and members of the board of directors will want to be more familiar with some of the core responsibilities and perspectives of this role, and they may benefit from many of the chapters. There are also areas that pertain to survival of the business related to liquidity management and financial risk management that should be of particular value to board members. While much authority and responsibility may be delegated downward in the organization, there are a few key areas where every board member will want to have a reasonable sense of risks and roles as well as how excellent organizations can manage these properly. The following grid is intended to prioritize these chapters, with the understanding of real time constraints.

The recent market turbulence has impacted every organization in some manner. Every organization needs to understand and manage its risks and also ensure it has adequate and protected liquidity. Accordingly, many readers will initially turn their attention to the Financial Risk Management and Controls and Liquidity Management chapters of the book.

Category	Focus Chapters	Specialization or Application
Core Treasurer Responsibilities and Perspectives	Chapter 4, "Managing Relationships"	Chapter 1, "Building the Case for Being a Strategic Treasurer"
	Chapter 5, "Owning Cash and The Five *O*s of Treasury" Chapter 7, "Owning Working Capital"	Chapter 2, "First Things for the New Treasurer" Chapter 6, "Cash Boot Camp for Treasurers" Chapter 8, "Differences between a Process View and a Silo View"

(Continued)

(Continued)

Category	Focus Chapters	Specialization or Application
Financial Risk Management and Controls	Chapter 9, "Financial Risk Management, Part One: Considering Risk Through the Eye of the Beholder" Chapter 10, "Financial Risk Management, Part Two: Altering the Risk a Company Faces to Match the Risk It Desires" Chapter 11, "Losses and Fraud: What Can Keep Treasurers Awake at Night"	
Liquidity Management	Chapter 16, "Volatility and Liquidity Management"	Chapter 17, "Achieving Visibility to Your Liquidity"

Acknowledgments

When finishing the manuscript of a book a number of feelings and thoughts stream to the front of one's mind. Relief is the dominant feeling that replaced the earlier feelings of anxiety about deadlines and other commitments. Appreciation and thankfulness are two other thoughts that are increasingly vivid and important.

David Stowe, who originally counseled against writing a book at such a hectic time, provided much help in ensuring its completion. This help included writing two chapters on risk management and providing critical guidance in key areas. His help and intellectual curiosity have been immensely helpful with this book and with growing the firm.

When looking back on all of the people who have coached, guided, taught, challenged, and encouraged me in my life, career, and even with this book, I owe quite a debt of gratitude. It has now become apparent to me that as others coached and taught me, my level of acceptance of that guidance and teaching varied dramatically over time and in different situations. I have learned much from all of my managers, coworkers, and those I have had the privilege of managing over the years, and I acknowledge their help, professionalism, and patience.

My older brother, Scott D. H. Jeffery, who joined the Treasury profession after me, has been an enormously positive influence on my life as well as my career. He was instrumental in providing the impetus to get my business, Strategic Treasurer LLC, off the ground and has provided wise counsel through the years. In all the ways he has helped or encouraged me, none speaks more loudly than seeing grace under pressure modeled in his life. He has modeled that well and consistently. I loudly acknowledge his support, guidance, love, and encouragement over the years.

Henry L. Waskowski led the Wachovia Treasury & Financial Consulting group for years before forming Treasury Performance Group in 2004. Most people may not realize that my former manager is the individual who has most influenced the profession over the past two decades. He has done so without fanfare or self-promotion. He has influenced people new to the profession as well as the leading thinkers in this space in such a quiet and thoughtful manner that those of us who have been challenged and influenced by him think about the content of his ideas and not the person who delivered them. Henry has been a great mentor, supporter, intellectual provocateur, and friend for almost a decade. Many of the good ideas and concepts in this book bear the mark of his fingerprints.

Over the years I have had managers who have taught, challenged, and put up with me. I am grateful and appreciative for all they have done.

Bob and Carl Roehrich taught and modeled much about the value of hard work, logistics, and general business sense. Lois Bradgon, Nick Mason, and Dan Doty taught many useful concepts that mainly I learned years after the fact. Nancy Deyette Romppainen, Don Waggaman, Rich Garrett, and Jim McAuley provided me with many finance, Treasury, and business opportunities to challenge my thinking and expand my experiences and advance my career. Ward Gailey loved business strategy and was not afraid to try new things, and Don Shaurette loved the art of the deal and of networking.

Many colleagues and friends at various banks have continually challenged my thinking on Treasury, change management, communication, and planning, including Doug Hartsema, Ranjana Clark, David Trotter, Joni Topper, Linda Cascardo, Bryon Null, Joe Schneider, Maria D'Alessandro, Kevin Peak, Diane Quinn, Ron Chakravarti, and many others.

Every one of our clients has taught me and our team valuable lessons and perspectives. I especially appreciate those who taught us the most while graciously pretending to receive tremendous value from our work together. We are particularly indebted to you in so many ways.

For all of those at Strategic Treasurer LLC who put up with my distraction and other shortcomings, which were exacerbated during the period of time when I was writing—thank you. Thank you for picking up the slack and adjusting to rapid priority changes. I further acknowledge those who helped with the document editing, graphics, and organization, including Jane Jeffery, Ellen Heffes, and Christy Cook. I would also like to thank my editors at John Wiley & Sons: Stacey Rivera, Development Editor; Sheck Cho, Executive Editor; Lisa Vuoncino, Production Editor; and other staff: Helen Cho, Editorial Coordinator and Debra Bowman, Professional Indexer. Either this book project or I would have died without their help.

Finally, I acknowledge my family for their support, prayers, love, and patience. I further thank and acknowledge my dear wife, Suzanne, publicly for her friendship, encouragement, and unswerving support over the years, without which the Strategic Treasurer LLC consulting firm would not have been created or this book written. She encouraged me to form and pursue dreams, when taking a Treasurer position would have seemed to be a far safer alternative to establishing a consulting firm.

Sources, where directly attributable, have been referenced in this book. Furthermore, where an idea or a major component of an idea or concept was created and introduced by someone else, we have made efforts to ensure that the proper person is either credited or acknowledged.

Various articles and books have influenced my thinking over time or provided a base of understanding. There are many other conference presentations and discussions that have become part of my thinking, and therefore this book, in some shape or form.

Errors and misunderstandings of others' concepts remain my responsibility.

CHAPTER 1

Building the Case for Being a Strategic Treasurer

A successful Treasurer must not only manage traditional funding and relationship activities, but also must possess an integrated and strategic view of the organization and broadly manage risk, add value by effectively partnering with key business players, and manage complex technologies and relationships. To do less jeopardizes the company and significantly limits their career.

—Henry L. Waszkowski, Managing Director,
Treasury Performance Group

When going through a period of tremendous market turbulence and upheaval, as we have experienced recently, Treasurers have two primary thoughts. The first thought centers on their responsibility of protecting their organization for the next situation that will arise. They plan and prepare themselves for the next event, so that they will be able to respond quickly and properly to protect their organizations. Their second thought, during a lull in the storm, is about how exciting it is to be a Treasurer during this time. There has never been a better time to be a Treasurer than now. The equivalent of many years' worth of learning can be crammed into weeks or days.

With market turbulence at an unprecedented level, this environment will hone some Treasurers' skills and identify opportunities to improve their preparedness. For other Treasurers, it will point out significant gaps in their thinking and plans. Some will look for positions other than that of Treasurer—on their own initiative or out of necessity.

As increasingly broad financial difficulties have emerged, there has been marked improvement in the perceived value of the Treasurer. During long periods of relative stability in the liquidity markets, it is easier for senior management and board members to become complacent about the importance of Treasury for the health and well-being of the organization. Strategic Treasurers bring value to the organization in ways beyond securing the necessary capital and protecting the organization's balance sheet. They identify and manage a range of risks, assist the organization in making better decisions with analytical rigor, and partner with other departments to improve processes and performance.

A Strategic Treasurer brings great value to the organization and has a strong sense of career fulfillment. The fact that Treasurers continue to develop marketable skills and intellectual capabilities is an added benefit.

There is much a Treasurer can learn both from history and the more recent variety of events and from issues that continue to emerge. The thoughtful Treasurer will not only learn from the specific situations. She will understand with alacrity how to apply principles already learned to new and different situations.

It is an exhilarating time to be a Treasurer. And being a Strategic Treasurer has never been more highly valued.

Volatility and Turbulence as Opportunity

Different surfers have different reactions as they head out into the ocean as the waves build up ahead of a hurricane that is bearing toward shore. Some think, *I must be crazy putting myself at such great risk.* Another response is a smile at the thought of what a great time it will be navigating in the new and uncharted surf. The level of focus that is required in the extreme environment is exhilarating. The surfer's skills will be refined. This difficult environment provides a testing ground that will make regular surfing seem far easier than ever before.

Now, not everyone really wants to head out into dangerous surf, but there are times when even the most prudent will find themselves in situations that have emerged in which a response is needed. For example, the events of 2007 and 2008 have created extreme financial risk management situations—some of which possibly could have been predicted, but most of which could not have been prevented.

Those Treasurers who have mastered the basics and have prepared for dealing with a variety of situations can respond most rapidly and can quickly improvise when needed to adjust for changing conditions. Extremely challenging events will make some quit, break some, or make some stronger and better able to handle the next situation. Appropriate, continuous preparation will help bring about the third result.

Resiliency, Diversification, and Due Diligence

Organizations need to be resilient. They must be able to weather multiple storms, absorb multiple hits, and survive. No single event should put a company out of business or imperil its very survival.

No area in the company plays a larger role than Treasury in helping the organization be resilient. Securing and sustaining adequate liquidity may be simple in good times and nearly impossible when times are challenging.

The Strategic Treasurer will ensure liquidity and resiliency through a variety of means. This resiliency requires careful planning, diligence monitoring, and quick analysis and responses to changing conditions.

Building resiliency also means diversification, even though that appears to add costs to the organization during more stable times.

Diversification alone is not sufficient. Treasury will need to perform due diligence with various counterparties and providers as a matter of course. For example, in the 2007–2009 economic climate, due diligence requires more intense focus—especially when blue chip companies are failing, rating agencies' information is suspect, and no one is quite sure how the government will respond to the latest situation.

The Strategic Treasurer will communicate both how and why he is building resiliency into the business. The Strategic Treasurer will also recognize that the world of second-guessers—who have the benefit of 20/20 hindsight—will always question actions and point out what could have been. The Strategic Treasurer will stay the course, even if the true value of what he is doing takes three decades to be recognized by the board and senior management.

At the end of 2008, the Bernard Madoff Ponzi scheme scandal came to light. The fund was enormous, long lasting, and highly restrictive regarding who could invest in it. Warning signals that were released beginning in 2000 were essentially ignored or buried for more than eight years. Some individuals lost their entire personal worth as a result.

This disaster came to light over just a few days, and its impact was not just confined to individual investors. Several charities lost all of their invested assets, which had been held with Madoff, and many had to shut down. Other charities were gravely impaired by losses or by the loss of big donors whose financial position had suffered greatly. Such situations are sad but instructive. Whether for-profit, governmental, or not-for-profit, organizations should have a level of resiliency that allows them to handle any type of financial surprise or environmental disaster. One bad situation or counterparty should not be able to put an organization out of business.

Being a Strategic Business Partner

Treasury is never effective when it acts in an insular manner—disconnected from the organization's business. Treasury needs to be proactive in seeking to help the organization fulfill its mission and to help specific departments achieve their goals efficiently and thoughtfully.

Treasury brings a unique set of skills to the organization, skills that need to be brought to the table and put to use. The Treasurer's analytical rigor can help every area of the organization. Her ability to understand the broader environment and her ready access to external advisors allows the Treasurer to employ the dialectical method and challenge the status quo when it needs to be challenged.

Most Treasurers have an inherent fiscal conservatism that helps prevent their company or organization from entering into overly risky situations. They provide an intellectual and financial framework of stability that is essential for survival and confidence.

Chapter 3 discusses in greater detail the value to the organization and Treasury when the Treasurer acts as a strategic business partner.

It Is Good to Be Needed

During the years and even decades when much in the world that impacts Treasury is stable, the organizational view toward Treasury has ranged from bare tolerance to general acceptance. But when extreme volatility hits the markets, the organization's need to survive creates a strong realization of how important it is to have a great Treasurer. Such Treasurers not only help the organizations survive, but also help the various business units improve their processes. And, as Treasurers and their department help the organization make prudent decisions about investments and risk, they will be viewed as increasingly valuable.

Strategic Treasurers set proper expectations of their role. They also recognize the need to explain their role to the organization, and they realize that communication must be a recurring activity. Astute Treasurers recognize that communication and education are not a single event. Relationship and expectation management are vital to the organization and for Treasury. Chapter 4 covers this topic in more detail.

Technology Has Improved

Treasurers, in order to marshal all of the resources at their disposal, need a clear view of the battle and the resources available. The technology tools and services that are available have recently seen significant advances on many fronts. There are software tools that can make it far easier and more complete than ever before to gather information and identify issues and exceptions to policies. These tools allow Treasury groups to devote far more time to analysis and strategic issues.

Indeed, services are now available to medium and small firms that were once exclusively the domain of the largest multinationals. These services are available through banks and various technology vendors.

The movement to Internet-based services has been dramatic. For most companies, these application service providers (ASPs) offer an ever-expanding level of capabilities with a fraction of the overhead of the previous technology platforms. The functionality of ASPs, also known as Software as a Service (SaaS) providers, benefit many organizations. They offer a pay-as-you-go method of using technology, which means a lower capital outlay and automatically updated software. This method also avoids the major challenges of owning the necessary hardware, which is leading to faster and more complete implementations. Reducing the amount and magnitude of the technical headaches and operational activities is welcome relief.

Strategic Treasurers will take advantage of these new and improved technologies to support their goals of owning cash, managing working capital effectively, and helping to ensure that risks are managed and mitigated appropriately. Having a clear Treasury information and technology plan remains important and is now easier to implement and will better support the business processes and goals that Treasury must achieve.

Chapter 14 on Treasury Technology describes the opportunity and necessity of leveraging this technology in more detail.

Summary

Clearly, going through major market and governmental turbulence is the best time to be a Treasurer. Perhaps, as never before, one's plans and skills will be tested. The resilience and strength of organizations depend on what the Treasurer has done and how she will respond.

The Treasurer who acts as a strategic business partner, instead of being simply a dispassionate vendor to the organization, will serve her organization far more effectively, enjoy the work more thoroughly, and stay gainfully employed far longer than those who focus solely on operational and tactical matters.

Being a Strategic Treasurer requires a strong technical background and the ability to communicate effectively with various financial and nonfinancial people in a way that makes sense to each. The Treasurer must have an especially strong ability to identify and manage risks. He must be or become the clear owner of cash and liquidity and will be either the overseer or owner of working capital. The health and survival of the organization depends, in large measure, on how well the Treasurer manages its business, counterparties, and relationships.

Boards of directors and senior management now understand, more than ever before, the value of having a highly capable Treasurer. This is the time of the Strategic Treasurer.

CHAPTER 2

First Things for the New Treasurer*

Plan your work and work your plan.

—Vince Lombardi

By nearly all accounts, honeymoons are wonderful. They are the mystical time carved out at the start of a relationship before reality sets in. Neither party can do any wrong. All is bliss. Life is easy. Then the honeymoon is over, and the part of a relationship that requires ongoing work begins.

After becoming Treasurer, there is a brief period that must be used wisely. Although there are usually urgent and immediate demands on the new Treasurer, there is always a bit more tolerance and understanding during the period immediately after the hire date. Without question, the first few months are the optimal time for the new Treasurer to get his mind around the organization and determine Treasury's initial needs and goals. After this time is over the pressures increase dramatically, and the expectation levels rise.

Taking over the reins of a smoothly running organization is, perhaps, a rare luxury. Turbulent economic times, combined with challenges that face the organization, can make the reality of grabbing the reins of control both exhilarating and intensely focusing. While urgent matters at hand may require an enormous amount of time and dedication to manage, the Treasurer still must ensure that certain activities are done and plans put in motion. And, while some of those activities do not need to be done specifically by the Treasurer, some will indeed require direct involvement.

---

*All quotes in this chapter are from personal interviews.

Most Treasury organizations are thinly staffed, which requires a greater emphasis on how the Treasurer puts the group together and how she develops the people within that team. No matter what level Treasury is staffed at, Treasurers have the responsibility to fulfill their mission without fail. Given the fact that Treasury must secure adequate liquidity and manage a wide variety of risks, forming the typically small team to accomplish this effort is a top objective.

Beginning this new role requires a reasonable approach and ordered thinking. Exhibit 2.1 shows the conceptual progression of activities from the start of the process through to action steps taken to achieve your new vision and fulfill your duties as Treasurer.

Study the Business

While some in Treasury view their role as separate and apart from the details of the business, this is not a mature perspective. The Treasurer, and in fact everyone in Treasury, needs to have a solid understanding of how the business works. Joni Topper, Senior Vice President (SVP) and Regional Director of Government and Institutional Banking for Wells Fargo, based in Los Angeles, takes that point and emphasizes that excellent Treasurers make the efforts to ensure that the Treasury department as a whole has a good understanding of the entire business end of the organization. She states,

> It is very important for the Treasurer to really understand the details of the business. And, they need to recognize that there are some people in every organization or business that are really good in some areas. They may understand the production side, for example, but may not know too much about other aspects. Their knowledge may be compartmentalized. Great Treasurers find ways of synthesizing the various facts that individuals know in order to put together a department that understands their business more completely.

The Vice President and Treasurer of Honeywell, John Tus, points out the need to have a broad comprehension of the business in order to perform Treasury duties: "The leader must understand how the Treasurer fits into the organization to create value. Where is cash being generated, built up and invested?" A danger that looms larger for Treasurers arises due to the role they play in the organization. "Treasury can be viewed as part of an insular function versus the Controller or someone heading up Financial Planning and Analysis. Those roles have more automatic interaction with the business areas and the business itself. Treasury is focused more externally: banks, credit arrangements and agreements, and overall liquidity management."

While the rationale for studying and understanding the business has been addressed, the description of how a new Treasurer would go about

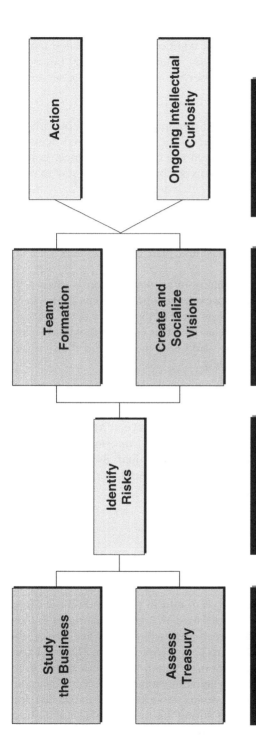

Action

Ongoing Intellectual Curiosity

Team Formation

Create and Socialize Vision

Identify Risks

Study the Business

Assess Treasury

BASELINE UNDERSTANDING

- Identifying business drivers and perspectives
- Business plans and history
- Treasury structure
- Relationships
- Services used
- Organizational and staff understanding
- Treasury processes
- Treasury systems

RISK IDENTIFICATION

- Determining diversification needs and exposure
- Reviewing and understanding various financial risks in the organization
- Instrument risk
- Settlement risk
- Transaction risk
- Liquidity risk

COMMUNICATION AND TEAM

- Determining resource needs
- Forming the Treasury team
- Communicating Treasury's role, vision, and plans
- Helping others understand the risk management framework
- Laying the foundation for the working capital council

PERFORM

- Executing the action plan
- Preparing for likely and unexpected events
- Ensuring Treasury staff is actively engaged with departments/business units
- Establishing opportunities for staff development and continuous learning

EXHIBIT 2.1 Conceptual Progression of Activities

9

this work has not. And, while this book will not go into a detailed recommendation of how to study your business, a few thoughts may be useful. These have been provided based on observation and analysis of successful Treasurers.

- **Reading list.** Financial and general newspapers, business periodicals, and broad economic journals make up the most mentioned items for a reading list. The intent is to stay on top of treasury/finance, general business, and the specifics related to your business and to stay mindful of the broader issues developing.
- **Internal discussions.** Systematic internal discussions about the business and how Treasury can help are held either by Treasury alone or with various departments that Treasury supports. Discussing the ramifications of events or the business plan helps to keep Treasury intellectually sharp.
- **External dialog.** The internal dialog in an organization is often a bit too predictable. Actively engaging external parties, such as bankers and consultants, can create a whole new level of thought by those who are more willing to challenge the status quo. This external input aids many good Treasurers to learn via the dialectical method and then engage other internal areas more effectively.

The work of studying the business is a major event at the beginning of the time a Treasurer serves at an organization. However, it must be viewed as an ongoing process and not merely as an isolated event. At the end of this chapter we make mention of ongoing intellectual curiosity, which would encompass knowledge about the business but would also involve other areas, including Treasury. To begin the process of understanding Treasury, a formal time to assess the department is necessary.

Assess Treasury

Understanding Career Stages

The prerequisite to assessing Treasury is to refresh your mind on the career stages for Treasury professionals. Rick Moss, SVP and Treasurer of Hanesbrands, divides up the Treasury career into two stages. "The first is the foundational stage where you build up your technical skills. There is exposure to many different areas of expertise within your profession. Some people do themselves a disservice by avoiding some of the less glamorous areas of treasury." He makes further points about the need to interact successfully with others at the same level during this building phase of a career track to Treasurer. "If you can't deal with the technical questions, you will not have the credibility to address the really big questions. The foundational phase is really important and some people try to rush through it too quickly and do not have a firm enough footing." Excellent Treasurers need to be generally well rounded from a business standpoint and must have more detailed understanding of their organization's activities and environment.

Moss identifies the second half of the Treasurer's career as the strategic phase. Having the proper foundation laid is of critical importance for success to be sustainable at this level. Some people try to rush this process too quickly and "... do not get as firm a footing as they need to. There is something to be said for broad experience ...," Moss points out. If you are contributing to the organization as a strategic business partner, ensuring strong knowledge about the particular business you are in is important. And having at least a fundamental knowledge of marketing, sales, human resources, and so on will allow the Treasurer to relate to her colleagues within the context of their particular organization. By understanding the business and the organization, the groundwork is laid for understanding needs of others in senior management. For the Treasurer to add insight and value to the organization in terms of analytical rigor and business acumen, and to help to better identify and manage risks, several activities are appropriate. These include an in-depth assessment of Treasury and interviews and assessments of other areas. These assessments will be instrumental in the risk identification and risk management activities understanding of the organization and will need to be done at the time of taking on the title of Treasurer and at periodic intervals afterward.

Start Your Assessment

Depth perception is far more effective and easier when using two eyes. The same is true for assessing Treasury and other departments. The second eye can come from a source other than the Treasurer. This could be from a highly experienced practitioner from within Treasury, Audit, or the ranks of senior Treasury consultants.

Begin your assessment by looking at the Treasury department first. Jeff Wallace, the Managing Partner of Greenwich Treasury Advisors, makes the case for using the audit staff and existing documentation as a starting point of an assessment process, "Have internal audit review Treasury's internal controls. It is a good way to become familiar with the controls and the operations. Sarbanes-Oxley documentation is another good source of material to help you understand Treasury." Supplement that information with other documentation related to Treasury, including policies, strategic planning documents, system maps, Treasury reports, and relationship plans.

The documentation and assessment are intended to capture the current state of Treasury processes and systems. The dialog with the Treasury staff will help you to better understand the status of personnel as well as gain a sense of what the mission and vision statements really mean to this organization. Having this baseline understanding will allow you to further refine your vision for the future and make the plan to connect the current state to that aspirational future view. Treasury assessments can be made by the Treasurer alone or with an outside consultant.

The documentation portion will need to include a financial inventory component. The financial inventory will include cash, bank accounts, debt, investments, intercompany loans, and hedges. Many inventories will also include cross-border flows, volumes, and more detailed information on bank accounts, signers, and counterparties. Depending upon the complexity of the company, the level of historical decentralization, recent activities, and acquisitiveness and control mindset, this effort can range from manageable to very challenging. Keeping this data current and organized will usually require the use of various automation tools to build this control into the process. Chapter 14 provides some additional information on this process and how to minimize the amount of rework and version control problems that can arise.

Not performing an assessment when taking over the Treasury group or every three to five years is akin to skipping your annual or biannual physical. While getting the physical is never pleasant and you may have some uncomfortable moments, it is always better to get the feedback earlier in the process while you have time to work on it.

As you complete the review of Treasury, you will find that it provides a good basis for understanding the other business areas more deeply. Assessing areas outside of Treasury can occur at various levels of depth. While one may choose to start at a surface level to gain a sense of context, there are pros and cons to this approach. The benefit of this approach is that it will be less time-intensive for all parties involved. The negative aspect is also practical. You do not always have a second chance to assess an area. Going in the first time and gathering only a high-level perspective may create friction when you attempt to go back for a more thorough assessment. Either approach may achieve the benefit desired if the Treasurer has thought through and communicated the plan and approach to the other departments.

For a less-detailed review or assessment, normally the Treasury group will perform this function on a solo basis. When a more detailed assessment is appropriate, engaging experienced resources is always beneficial. The resource should have experiences that include assessments, Treasury, the order-to-pay process, and the order-to-collect process. Other levels of experience may be needed based upon what you hope to accomplish. This may include additional depth related to systems or accounting.

Treasurers must be ever vigilant in managing risks, and part of any Treasury-driven assessment should help accomplish this effort. These risks may exist within Treasury, in another business area, or in the dangerous space between departments where handoffs exist.

Identify Risks

Anyone moving into the role of Treasurer understands that she is responsible for managing a variety of risks. When taking on this role, it is important to identify as many risks as possible right from the beginning of your tenure as Treasurer. Your assessments are a crucial way to rapidly identify various risks that exist within your organization and it serves to provide a baseline perspective that coincides with your assumption of this role. The risks are many. Exhibit 2.2 shows a sample of risks that a Treasurer will ensure are inventoried and managed. The boxes at the top identify some of the traditional risks that Treasurers manage. The risks in the table below the traditional risks highlight some risks that organizations have experienced during the recent market turmoil.

Operational Risks

"In hindsight, major operational problems are obvious. Treasurers who avoid understanding Treasury operations put themselves and their organizations at an unnecessary disadvantage," says Wallace. By using your assessments as a way to understand the areas of Treasury you can improve, you have the perfect opportunity to identify operational risks. The risks that have been identified may require a range of responses to address them in groups or individually.

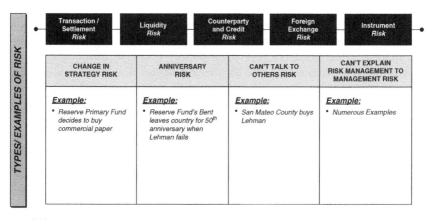

EXHIBIT 2.2 Risk Chart

Internal Control

Small Treasury groups often have some built-in segregation of duties and coverage problems. Dealing with enormous fund transfers—which can occur instantly and irrevocably—requires excellent controls and an alert Treasury. Wallace points out the need to find and fix any control issues promptly: "If there are internal control weaknesses, you want to find them as soon as possible. Because after a while they will become your internal control weaknesses."

Treasury is busy, very busy. However, that excuse will not carry much weight if a major problem erupts on your watch. Wallace again: "The problem with Treasury is that Treasury mistakes are easily quantifiable and easily prevented with twenty-twenty hindsight. People sometimes forget that ten fingers were already filling in ten other holes in the dike. One thing that Treasurers try to do is prevent the obvious mistakes." Performing the assessment, regular thought and analysis, networking with other Treasury professionals, and working to fix known issues all represent important steps to maintaining your internal control.

Very few auditors and internal audit departments can perform an effective Treasury audit. This may seem good at first, since they can ask only a relatively short list of questions and carry out a limited number of tests. However, they represent one group internal to your organization that can help Treasury get better. Many good Treasurers find that it is well worth the multiyear effort to train this group to understand Treasury. The value of an effective internal audit department is significant for Treasury over time, even if it means more short-term pain.

Socializing Your Assessment

Once you have made an assessment of Treasury or other areas, it is important to share this information with the proper people. It should be shared in a manner appropriate for your organization. Every organization seems to have a different culture and style for sharing information. What is viewed as "open and direct" in one organization may be viewed as "rude and unprofessional" in another. And what is said "tactfully" in one place is treated as "too nuanced" to gain any traction. The goal is to increase organizational knowledge of what you are responsible for, gain acceptance and understanding of Treasury's vision, and secure support for any plans you have to make Treasury a more effective business partner to the organization. Your presentation will likely include:

- Key items and issues identified during your assessment
- Treasury responsibilities

- Issue list of items that were found during the assessment
- Treasury vision, mission, roles, and responsibility
- List of risks to be managed

John Tus, Vice President and Treasurer of Honeywell and recipient of two consecutive overall Alexander Hamilton Awards, points out a common knowledge gap with senior management about Treasury. He rightly indicates that this gap of understanding can arise from different causes but it is Treasury's responsibility to help fill that void. For instance, "the CEO and CFO in some organizations may not understand Treasury responsibilities since the group can be viewed as part of an insular function versus the Controller's group or Financial Planning and Analysis." This view typically arises since Treasury has key responsibilities that deal with those outside of the organization, including banks and other credit and service providers. It is vital for the Treasurer to understand that the challenge will be devoting enough energy and attention to helping the internal organization excel while not diminishing their effort and performance with their externally facing duties.

It is absolutely critical that the Treasurer be a public face of Treasury. At the start of your time as Treasurer, be intentional, deliberate, and even systematic about building relationships and meeting others in the organization.

Put Your Team Together Like a Puzzle

Building the Puzzle

The Treasury department needs to support the organization properly, and this requires the right staff. Accordingly, the Treasurer must ensure that the staff formation allows the department to execute this responsibility well. While there are many different ways to look at staffing the Treasury group, its limited size and the critical role that each person plays makes every position and person important. One person out of place becomes more obvious than would be the case with larger departments. And, this out-of-place person presents the overall organization with a greater level of risk.

The Treasurer of Hanesbrands says that meeting staffing needs is like solving a puzzle. Moss says, "You have to think of an organization like a puzzle. Too often we think of organizations in the form of a traditional organization chart where you're looking for boxes and lines. There is some merit to this, as an organization chart is a helpful way of communicating some aspects of the business." People are not perfectly round or square, and when they are put together on a Treasury team, it is prudent to ensure that they are complementary. Thought needs to be given to understanding and addressing the strengths and weaknesses of the various people in Treasury in order to provide good coverage. When you begin your work at an organization, you often start with a set of puzzle pieces that may or may not fit well together. However, those are the pieces you have to work with at the start. One important early step for the new Treasurer is to determine what the puzzle should look like and then ensure that Treasury has the right pieces.

The Need for the Right Pieces

The Treasurer must be strategic, and this requires some assistance in order to make time available to think. Jiro Okochi, the co-founder and CEO of Reval, identifies the requirements necessary to meet this key objective. "The Treasurer has to build an organization where they can delegate the tactics and operations so they have a chance at being strategic. It is largely about getting the right people on the bus. If you do not have the right people on the bus, then you can't be as strategic as you want to be. Get the right people who can execute and to whom you can delegate." Though Okochi's example of bus riders differs from the puzzle-piece analogy, the principle of needing the right resources is emphasized. Additionally, he brings out the need and desire to have people who have some measure of flexibility, which is ideal in constantly and rapidly changing business and economic environments.

Since the organization changes over time, there is a strong possibility that staff will need to change accordingly. Some staff will be able to adapt, and others will need to find a better fit outside of the organization. A well-respected Treasurer discusses this challenging situation and quickly addresses it head on. The problem is very hard, but it is not personal. "Treasurers will sub-optimize their organization rather than make those decisions." This process is substantially easier if the Treasurer has an institutional focus on developing staff. If that development is effective, the person who needs to move on will often recognize that before the manager does.

While sometimes people and organizations change and may no longer fit together nicely, frequently the work can be adjusted and moved around to fit the staff that you have. This may require some rework of your organization chart and perhaps some job descriptions. In the scale of things, that is a small effort to make if it will help you optimize your organization while retaining good-quality staff.

Reworking the Puzzle

Organizations change over time. Their need for various staff also changes. This is an exciting situation since it involves changes and another level of challenges. It also can be a somewhat sad situation as certain people may no longer fit with the organization and adjustments need to be made.

New situations or events can cause new needs to arise that show a hole in your puzzle that should be filled. Other events may decrease the need for some puzzle pieces. Moss says, "Organizations are very organic in the sense that they really are a living, breathing, growing, changing, morphing entity." Not every puzzle piece or person is completely adaptable, and initially hard decisions will have to be made by the Treasurer. Sometimes it is appropriate to part ways. Few Treasurers want to make those necessary adjustments. And those who continually put off these decisions do their employees and their organization a great disservice. A seasoned Treasurer noted that "one of the biggest mistakes that senior managers make is to be unwilling to make difficult personnel decisions as organizations evolve. By that I mean, what was the right structure in the past, might not be the proper structure." Sometimes it is appropriate to part ways. More discussion of the topic of staff development and staffing is found in Chapter 13.

Creating and Socializing the Vision and Plan

Once you have understood the business, assessed Treasury and other departments, identified risks, and formed or reformed your team, you will have created a draft plan and have some idea of the vision you have for Treasury. The best vision and most well-thought-out plan will not work if they stay embedded in your mind or safely kept in a three-ring binder. The plan and the vision must be *socialized*. By this term we refer to the process of sharing information around the organization. This socializing may have the goal of seeking input, or it may simply be communicating the changes you will make.

People need to understand what is being done, and many enjoy knowing the reason for changes or for a new direction. Not only may other departments not support your efforts if they do not know what or why Treasury is doing something, but they also may actively oppose your work.

Treasury needs to have a clear vision. Part of having a clear vision is being able to articulate and defend it. Crista Binder, the assistant Treasurer of the City of Los Angeles, makes a strong case for having a compelling vision as this will drive other activities of the organization, "How do you make something work when everybody else may not think like Treasury? The most important step is to set the overarching vision right up front. This vision becomes where we have to go, not just where we want to go." Taking ownership to ensure that the vision is properly established will help with the other decisions and work that needs to be done. As the vision is socialized, others buy into how the vision will help the overall organization.

They become champions and help to accomplish the overarching goals. Binder notes, "People from various departments become part of a project and make enormous contributions in helping the overall project succeed. This helps the City achieve our vision. And, those individuals build a track record of accomplishments that are valuable."

Socializing the vision is rarely easy. Usually it is extraordinarily difficult. Joya De Foor, the Treasurer for the City of Los Angeles and Binder's manager, makes a few observations: "Treasurers and those in Treasury need particularly thick skins because they so often need to push change hard to move the organization forward." People in almost every organization resist change, unless they are the ones advocating it. Change management does not always require securing buy-in for every decision. However, effective change management means that others are brought along. De Foor comments further about perspectives on bringing change to organizations: "You approach these positions as you would a general in battle. You need to be strategic most of the time and tactical when you must. You want to promote good change. You have to look at what you are doing—every decision—to see if it is promoting the change you are advocating. And, there will be times where you have to be tactical and make a decision to get something done. But, in general, I think you need to be strategic and forward thinking."

Socializing the vision and your plan means being visible in the organization. As Jiro Okochi states, "If no one knows who the Treasurer is, then it is hard to be strategic."

A Time for Action

Harvard Business Review, other periodicals, and numerous management books regularly write about formulating appropriate strategies and then taking effective steps toward accomplishing your mission and achieving your vision. The effective Treasurer will make use of those resources to help Treasury excel. And excelling requires wise thoughts, appropriate words, and diligent action. The best Treasurers have a clear plan and ensure that all actions and activities move them along the path toward their goals. Extra action that does not move the organization forward toward the right destination is eliminated. Specific accountability is as crucial as it is obvious. John Tus recommends assigning specific responsibility and turning your staff loose on a problem. His definition of *loose* has a feedback loop. Here is his list to ensure that the right advances are made on a systematic basis:

- **Focus on key processes.** Assign accountability according to processes.
- **Identify the world-class standard for each area.** Determine what data is needed; what processes and systems you need; the goals you will set from a productivity and return on investment (ROI) standpoint.

- **Hold annual group reviews.** Each manager must describe to the others in Treasury the future state, and explain the path to get there by creating a process, system, and people roadmap.
- **Determine the financial payback.**
- **Review last year's accomplishments and progress.**
- **Look at next year's expectations.**

Tus views the Treasurer as a facilitator of the process and describes how the team makes the individuals better. "The group will question each other to drive better value into each person's area. We leverage the group's knowledge to challenge and vet ideas. We will look at a delineated set of future steps and action items. For example, the U.S. and global processes may need to be standardized so every region isn't performing their activities in a separate and different way. As part of the weekly status meeting, there will be progress reports and we will monitor progress against our roadmap."

Ongoing Intellectual Curiosity

All excellent Treasurers seem to have a strong intellectual curiosity about Treasury, the business, and the economic environment. They range from disciplined to voracious readers. They are constantly looking for input and debate on various ideas and topics. They will meet with bankers and consultants to share ideas and learn. Meeting to understand and dialogue with internal departments is done in a disciplined manner.

The actions employed to learn about the business (from the chapter introduction) are used broadly as well. Treasurers seek to know what is going on in Treasury, of course, but also in the broader economic environment and beyond. They seek to know how these various items and trends can impact other areas. They seek to synthesize these various ideas into actionable ideas.

The best and most Strategic Treasurers never lose their intellectual curiosity, no matter how much data and knowledge they have in their gray matter.

Summary

For the Treasurer, the first few months on the job represent the best opportunity to understand the business and what needs to be done first to ensure that Treasury can perform its role effectively before other challenges set in.

The Treasurer must ensure that he understands two aspects of the organization as a prerequisite to success. He needs to (1) gain a reasonable knowledge of the business itself and (2) understand Treasury in detail. There are no shortcuts to gaining this knowledge, but there are some ways to make it far less painful.

Because of the size of the group and the level of risks that must be managed, the Treasurer must be particularly thoughtful and careful in this effort. Since there is less flexibility, this should be done with more care than other finance and operation areas need to exercise. Forming the team as one would put a puzzle together, versus filling out an organization chart, will better ensure complementary results. Ensuring diversity of thought, skills, and experience for a group focused on risk management is vastly superior to hiring an army of mental clones.

Intellectual curiosity is a requirement for all who are or who seek to be Treasurer. This will include a plan to actively seek out knowledge and analysis covering leadership and broad business learning, as well as focused technical understanding.

After assessing the situation carefully and creating a plan, action is required. To be optimally effective, the Treasurer needs to be able to telegraph this plan and how Treasury will execute it. The vision, plan, and rationale for both must be shared consistently and broadly.

CHAPTER 3

Being a Partner, Not a Vendor

The Strategic Treasurer must take a view of thinking like a partner and not like a vendor.

—James Newfrock, Senior Director and Treasurer of
Booz Allen Hamilton Inc.

Sometimes a simple phrase can resonate so loudly that it can organize one's thinking more than an entire series of management courses or 20 pages of Sarbanes-Oxley internal control documentation.

I was leading a panel discussion for *Treasury & Risk* magazine on being a Strategic Treasurer. During a preparatory call, James Newfrock, the Treasurer for the consulting firm of Booz Allen Hamilton, provided a quote that has resonated well in finance. He said that to be relevant, to be strategic, it is essential that the Treasurer be "a partner and not a vendor." A partner is one who supports the overall mission of an organization, and thus helps others to achieve their goals in support of that mission. A partner is someone who is sought out by others in the organization, who pursues ways he can provide insight and bring his unique abilities to help others in the organization in reaching common goals.

A vendor, however, is someone who happens to be on staff and is basically used to secure certain services. In the Treasury realm, this individual may secure funding, order bank services, or execute letters of credit. And, similar to an "external" vendor, such individuals will perform what is necessary to keep the business functioning. They remain focused on managing the capital structure and ensuring adequate liquidity over the near term. Additionally, they act in such a manner that the proper operational bank services are procured and delivered at a level of service that is acceptable.

Beyond overall liquidity and bank structure and service considerations, vendor-treasurers are not sought out for advice. They are brought in once the real business issues are decided to simply take the order. Not much is known about what they do or why it is done. Others may simply tolerate a vendor-treasurer since they do provide a needed service. However, their work is viewed as of little worth, and they are not treated as part of the core team; there is no seat at the table for the vendor-treasurer.

Treasurers with a vision of adding great value to their organization will make plans and take specific steps to become and be recognized as a strategic business partner. Those Treasurers who act as strategic business partners have greater longevity in an organization and enjoyment in their positions than those who perform as disconnected parties. Both partners and vendors really last only as long as they are essential and useful to the organization.

A strategic partner will be vital to an organization's health and mission, while the perceived value of a vendor can change quickly. This is true of the vendor-treasurer as well, and some of the displacement and dissatisfaction of those filling that role typically stem from others having a diminished perception of the value they bring to the organization. Treasurers need to see that their group is adding significant value to the organization and that the perception of their group mirrors the level of impact they are having. Managing a department's perception is an important activity that should not be confused with office politics. Office politics is a separate matter entirely. Being a good politician can only delay the inevitable if the Treasurer acts as a vendor.

Avoiding Inevitable Pitfalls

Sometimes getting to where an individual wants to be involves avoiding wrong turns and errors. For a Treasurer, it is easy to become viewed as a vendor. Indeed, getting out of that dead end can take some tricky driving and good navigation. Exhibit 3.1 shows seven key attitude pitfalls to avoid.

Once a view is formed that someone is essentially an outside party, it is hard to overcome. In describing his company's Treasury group, a highly successful sales executive from a business line said, "All they do is tell us we can't open up all of these bank accounts that we ask for. Yet, we need to get them open and get the assets flowing in here. We have to escalate this. They can't just prevent sales because they have a hard time with change."

In this case, it was not a matter of doing a better job explaining to the sales executive the strong rationale and benefits to the firm in preventing

- Myopic focus on your own concerns.
- Don't reach out to others systematically.
- Don't seem to understand their objectives, challenges, and needs.
- Be a bureaucrat—use your position and power to stop things.
- Treating communication as an event, not a process.
- Taking the perspective that because you have unique skills and intellectual capabilities that those are all that truly matter.
- Forcing others to conform to your Treasurer language.

EXHIBIT 3.1 Attitude Pitfalls

the unrestrained proliferation of bank accounts would bring. Nor did it matter that what the salespeople were proposing was unworkable. What they needed was a solution that would work. And it had to be a solution that would work for sales, Treasury, and accounting. Regaining the trust and confidence of the executive sales leadership while maintaining the integrity of a rational account control structure takes a significant amount of work—on both the project and the relationship.

Keeping in Between the Two Lines

There are a variety of ways to become a better partner. The following examples aim to help the reader think about this more clearly. This is more than a list of to-dos.

Put on Some Scrubs: The Ohio State University Example

When James Nichols, Treasurer for the Ohio State University, took over responsibility for the organization's hospitals, he realized he needed to do something to get his mind around this new business. They do not teach you how to be the finance head of hospitals in "Treasurer School" (naturally, there really is not a "Treasurer School"!). Nichols knew that he needed to understand what was important to those at the hospital, and to do that required familiarity with what the business was all about.

So he started by visiting the hospital. He visited different areas, at different times, since the hospital has three shifts. He described observing surgery on the third shift as a unique experience. Those at the hospital seemed to remember that this was the first time that the finance head had come to observe surgery—and at night. Nichols attributed his focus for learning the hospital management issues to better understanding of what they needed and where his group could both assist and partner with the hospital.

Hospital management saw someone make the effort, and at inconvenient times. This helped them to trust and respect him as a partner who cared. This action granted Nichols far more openness and access than any finance head would normally receive.

The same Treasurer served on the hospital's board of governors for many years. Since the board was comprised of leaders from the student body and the faculty as well as the head of the university, it addressed issues from a multitude of perspectives. It was and is a truly multifunctional organization.

To many in finance, that sounds like a good responsibility to avoid—at all costs! What could be more annoying or boring? However, Nichols sought it out, and not because he thought it would be boring or political. He believed that by being part of the core workings of his organization, he would be exceptionally well-prepared to help the organization achieve its objectives. Being associated with the various constituencies on a regular basis would also provide a good context for building the relationship as a strategic business partner. It certainly achieved that objective for him, as Treasurer, but more importantly, it helped the overall organization to have an effective Treasury—effective, in the sense of being a great business partner. It is obvious in this case that Treasury, at the Ohio State University, is viewed as a partner and not as a vendor.

One may not need to don hospital scrubs to find out what is really going on in the business. Perhaps it is a hard hat or a concierge uniform. And, whether one wears the uniform or not, the Treasurer who truly seeks to be a better business partner will have to get closer to the business—and get involved. Treasurers need to get outside of their comfort zone. If it is a situation that creates unsettled feelings, such as observing surgery, perhaps you can avert your eyes during the tough parts. The staff will appreciate the effort. It is especially important to remember for the ongoing relationship that getting close to the business is not a one-time event; it is a pattern and practice.

Getting Close/Keeping Some Distance

Near or far? How close to or how far should one physically be from business partners, especially when there is a choice? Many have long believed that the model of closer is always better. While that is most often the best choice, it is not the single best practice.

ATTRIBUTES OF "NEAR" Being in close physical proximity makes it possible to easily catch up on various matters. The natural increase of connections and interactions is typically an enormous benefit to all parties involved. There are numerous strategies for making sure there are enough connections.

However, WinWholesale, an Ohio-based wholesaler that owns, or jointly owns, a distribution network of hundreds of plumbing and electrical stores, takes being close to a very high level.

Everyone who has worked on a trading floor understands the value of quick communication and the benefits of overhearing nearby conversations. Such proximity provides for an informal and unplanned way of keeping communication current—and eliminates many meetings in the process.

At WinWholesale, the CFO and two of the top finance staff sit in three "fake" offices. In this case, *fake* means that while each has a door to the outside, there is no door between the offices. A waist-high wall extending just a few feet provides an illusion of a separate office. This works great for keeping communication flowing smoothly among the finance areas. Conversations are surely overheard and trigger appropriate follow-up.

But that is not the main reason for this structure. The close proximity, without a wall blocking access, means that the head of finance can turn her head and address two other finance leaders without running into two separate offices or setting up a meeting.

At a Midwestern wholesale company, the CEO practices intentional "wandering around" and asking intelligent questions. He does not wander around and ask questions just to see what is going on or just to make others believe he is interested and engaged. While that could be useful, he is doing something far different. He often asks, "What are you working on?" Immediately after the response, which contained some general comments about improving working capital usage, he asks a follow-up question, taking what was said and layering in several other points about the buying spree that purchasing recently made and asking how this would be addressed. It was quickly apparent that he could have made these statements only if he already had good information on what big issues the department was addressing. After experiencing this level of questioning from the CEO, employees were better prepared for the next encounter.

ATTRIBUTES OF "FAR" While being close to the areas an individual supports is far more effective than having a great physical distance, there are ways distance can work. Indeed, greater distance can often work better in certain instances, if the right mitigating steps are taken. Such a move to a separate location (for the Treasury function) is most effective when it is deliberate and those involved know it is being done for a purpose. Again, it is important to know the boundaries of one's comfort zone.

An example of gaining perspective from a distance took place at Colorado State University, where Treasury had the opportunity to move either close to another business area or to a completely different location across the campus. It chose the latter since it wanted to avoid the disadvantages of being close. The university was highly political, and there was always some event *du jour* that would distract the staff with useless water cooler chatter.

In this case, the Treasurer felt being close to such day-to-day details as gossip would be a huge detriment to her group and to the department's overall mission. Additionally, the Treasurer wanted to make sure that real issues would be taken seriously and focused on when they were about cross-functional issues. Having other areas make a trip out of their area to Treasury's site, or vice versa, made everyone focus on the topic of importance. Also, there were far fewer interruptions and other distractions.

To compensate for the distance, the Treasurer ensured that Treasury took steps to remain connected and in touch. This required focus and planning with the schedule. It also required some flexibility for quick cross-campus drives. In this case, the Treasurer believed that Treasury—being separate in their environment, and with their intentional outreach plan—had the optimal arrangement.

This is a case of the Strategic Treasurer keeping staff at the right distance from the business partners.

Forming a Strategic Alliance for Excellence: A Major City Example

A large U.S. city's Treasury had the common issues of political infighting, big egos, and functional orientation—traits that are common with nearly every city and major corporation in the United States. In this situation, few were asking what was right for the city. Instead, they were effectively asking what was right for "me (individually)" or "my department." Naturally, this led to systemic problems, since optimizing part of the process often suboptimizes the whole.

Over time it seemed that the lack of restraint had led accounts and systems to proliferate. For example, there were dozens of fixed asset systems in place. Processes needed more than just updates, they needed a major overhaul. Some areas were cutting checks to themselves and depositing them into a sister account to fund electronic funds transfer (EFT) disbursements and create the initial accounting entries. This was not being done to support the full employment act, but because Treasury, controllers, finance, information technology, and other departments acted as separate islands. Historically, partnerships between areas did not exist. In order to make a change, everyone had to be in agreement; any one person could stop the best of efforts of an entire group. Sadly, few people were asking the question about what would be the correct thing to do for the organization and not just what would help them.

Treasury became frustrated with poor processes and dysfunctional internal and external relationships. Accounting, in the same boat, was always fighting to try to do the right thing, to streamline and consolidate. Due to budget pressures and leadership from its head, IT had some fresh ideas and was charged with reducing the number of systems the organization had to support. Finally, a common purpose emerged, and, like many alliances, the second step was conversations about those common goals.

Relationships between the Treasurer, the head of IT, and the controller began to form, and their vision to work together as a team began to emerge. They met as a group to formulate a vision as the city's finance process group. They created a formal vision statement and a mission statement. They became increasingly energized. They started creating vision-supporting strategic and tactical statements that would help them move forward.

They partnered with a new bank. Then they started attacking the system. They challenged other departments that did not want to change from the old, ineffective processes and systems. The change group sent a message: "There are problems here, and the process needs to change." The change group was direct in questioning both content and resistance. They asked questions such as these:

> "Is your reluctance to do what is best for the city based on good business practices or what is best for your department?"
> "Let me get this straight, you are convinced that lockboxes—which have been around nearly 50 years—aren't a proven concept yet?"

The multidiscipline team worked well together in probing deeply, almost like intervention, but their manner was encouraging, and they found good responses. Initial resistance would change when questions were asked such as, "Is this best for our customers?" or "Is this best for our organization?"

Essentially, this team formed an alliance. The common mission and tactics allowed them to truly partner and start moving the rest of the city toward an effective and efficient finance vision. The leaders served as the steering committee for process redesign and internal consulting. Furthermore, they oversaw the entire project of improving the financial processes and systems in the city. Treasury does not need to go it alone. Working in tandem with other departments can be an ideal way for Treasury to act as a strategic business partner.

Know What Is Important to the Organization and to Its Partners

In becoming a strategic business partner, it is crucial to understand what is important to the organization's clients: Who are they, what is the organizational objective, and how do the clients help fulfill it? How will they be supporting the objective, and what can you—as a Strategic Treasurer—do to help them support it? Understanding their business and what they are trying to do is the price of admission. Generating additional ideas and bringing intellectual rigor and financial discipline to the table and discussions is a crucial role the Treasurer must play as a partner.

Providing great services, helping the organization to be efficient, and bringing a risk mindset that is unique to finance to the rest of the organization are all basic components. While looking at activities or processes in light of risks and ensuring a rigorous business process mentality is maintained, partners recognize what each party brings to the table and what role they all should play. See Exhibit 3.2 for indications that Treasury is acting either as a vendor or as a partner. To be a Strategic Treasurer requires that the role have the word *partner* embedded in it. Otherwise, people may have the title, but they will be merely operational Treasurers.

These examples may indicate that you are on the right track and you need to continue the pace going forward. Continue to evaluate yourself. And ask for feedback on how you can be a better partner.

AMONG THE INDICATORS THAT YOU ARE A VENDOR

- You are brought in at the last minute of a project, and the sales website, which is going live Monday, needs to accept credit cards.
- People ask you to just "go get funding and leave us alone."
- You receive calls asking you to just get them a service, and they get frustrated when you start to ask questions . . . so you stop.
- Over the past six months, the only contact initiated with you has been customer service-related: "Please follow up on this issue with the bank or the card provider."

AMONG THE INDICATORS THAT YOU ARE A PARTNER

- You are invited to attend part or all of another department's semi-annual planning meeting.
- Over lunch, the head of another division asks if you will have time to brainstorm about some business opportunities with them.
- Your Assistant Treasurer is called into a planning process early on—well before any major decisions are made—to get support and input.
- Another group reschedules a brainstorming session because you are already booked at another off-site planning event.

EXHIBIT 3.2 Vendor or Partner Indicators

Summary

In order to be strategic, Treasurers must act as business partners. They must provide their internal customers reasons to call regularly and seek their input, guidance, and help. To be a business partner requires an understanding of the other departments' needs and knowing in what ways Treasury can best assist them in accomplishing their goals. Treasury must understand their role and unique perspectives.

Being a vendor is a simple and unrewarding activity. Treasurers who act as vendors will secure the necessary financing and services and remain aloof and disconnected from the mission of the organization. They will find minimal enjoyment in this position and hold it until the board of directors or CFO realizes what the organization is missing.

For the Treasurer, being a partner means bringing analytical rigor and external perspectives to the table. It requires being able to identify and mitigate risks in a way that protects the organization and can help the other internal parties.

To be a partner requires being intentional in how you connect with other areas. Being intentional in your meetings, and even how you determine physical proximity, can have an impact on how well you will be able to partner effectively.

To be a strategic business partner will require clarity of thought, hard work, and taking the initiative with some activities that may be outside of your comfort zone. In the end, being a strategic business partner will create a much larger comfort zone for the Treasurer and for the organization.

CHAPTER 4

Managing Relationships

Use your advisors, your bankers and consultants. They can add significant value. Pay attention to those partners and use them as a secondary piece of your Treasury staff. We operate pretty leanly and our partners provide us more resources.

—Ward Allen, Vice President Finance, WinWholesale

It is a common thing to find someone networking hard and fast—trying to make up for lost time—immediately after being displaced from a position. Executive staffing professionals wisely advise finance folks to build such networks before they are needed.

Managing relationships is a foundational activity both for individuals and organizations, and it is reasonable and appropriate to be thoughtful and proactive when network building. When times are tough, there are usually too many distractions to start the process for building effective relationships. The challenges of tough times often create a high level of distraction, so it is much better to take a more intentional and methodical approach to managing a Treasurer's many relationships. As Timothy Hart, Senior Vice President and Treasurer of First National Bank of Nebraska, states, "You can't wait to develop relationships when you have to have them. You need to begin developing those relationships earlier. Having an idea of what your balance sheet needs to look like 36 months in the future will help you better prepare."

Organizations, too, manage relationships. Every firm has a relationship plan. These plans are either formal or informal. Indeed, all great companies have a relationship management plan that is thoughtful, formal, simple, and well understood by key members of the organization.

A relationship plan documents both management's perspective and the process by which the relationships between the organization and its key partners are managed. Treasury should know and understand this plan thoroughly, and in many cases it will be the group that moves the relationship management plan into the formal realm. The Chief Financial Officer needs to clearly understand the perspectives and general working aspects of this plan and be able to articulate them automatically.

Relationship plans are used because times and circumstances can change rapidly. When the business is going well, it is an important responsibility to ensure that it has effective relationships. When times are hard, the key partners need to come through for the organization.

Further, when it comes to relationships, the adage that you typically "reap what you sow" is appropriate. In this case, consistent sowing is best. Sow seeds of a good relationship with partners—with regular communication and fair dealings—and you will be able to reap the benefits when you need them most. Never abuse a position of strength; never keep relationships severely restricted to one person. Be fair with the relationship at whatever stage in the power cycle you find yourself. The balance of power will shift, and people will change.

It is the Treasurer's responsibility to ensure that good and appropriate relationships are maintained in a deliberate and thoughtful manner with other organizations, departments, or units within the firm. It is important that this business-to-business relationship be deeper than a one-to-one interpersonal relationship, and both sides must be able to relate to each other in a manner that outlasts any one person.

Scope of the Relationship Management Plan

Treasury is responsible for managing a number of important relationships for their organization. To properly manage important relationships requires a certain level of documentation. One key piece of this documentation is the relationship management plan. This relationship management plan must be formalized in writing and will cover all key relationships that the Treasurer is responsible for managing. This one relationship management plan will cover a range of external relationships including banks, other credit enablers, and service providers. Some organizations will ensure that their relationship management plans also contemplate rating agencies and financial advisers. Since there are already sufficient sources about managing financial advisers and rating agencies, the comments here focus on bank partners and vendors.

Key Components of a Relationship Management Plan

There are several key components to a relationship plan, which comprise certain steps or activities essential to the creation and communication of the plan that must be completed. Creating an effective relationship framework and relationship plan will take little time and can usually be executed in less than a single month. The rapidity with which this can be accomplished in no way diminishes its value. In examining some typical components of a plan, it is important to realize that some adjustments will be necessary to make it fit an organization's situation. These components include:

- **Purpose.** The purpose of the relationship plan needs to be stated clearly enough that nonfinance people should be able to grasp it. If the plan is focused solely on banks, the plan often has language that discusses the need to secure appropriate services and access to capital and liquidity to meet various organizational needs.
- **Objectives.** The objectives of the relationship plan often touch on a number of "purpose supporting" areas. For example, an organization that requires access to a sufficient level of capital may find that certain bank partners vary in their level of commitment from year to year, and this leads to some banks leaving the bank group. Other banks need to step in and take their place.

  The firm may want to formalize this situation and its need by indicating an objective such as: "To maintain an effective feeder system of credit and service providers to meet our liquidity and capital needs." Unsurprisingly, objectives will often vary from organization to organization.
- **Maintaining institutional memory.** Many organizations find that to maintain adequate institutional memory of relationships requires that someone act as a Treasury historian. This individual ensures that the organization records the various activities and positions of key relationships over time. This will provide useful guidance and support, when needed, to move a long-lived relationship that is no longer a fit for either or both parties.

  Alternatively, a relationship may have become more aligned over the recent past as either or both parties have changed. This may provide additional rationale for seeking to deepen particular relationships. Naturally, and over time, some relationships will increase in importance while others decrease.
- **Relationship categories and ranking descriptions.** Identifying the number of relationship levels that the firm has and defining the criteria used for assigning relationships to those categories establishes the process and builds in a level of consistency that is important for midmarket to larger multinationals. Even finance professionals have

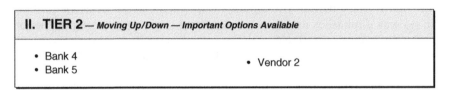

I. TIER 1 — *Partner/Critical/Unique*

- Bank 1
- Bank 2   • Vendor 1
- Bank 3

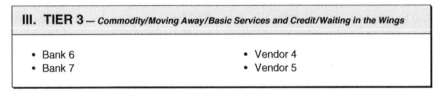

II. TIER 2 — *Moving Up/Down — Important Options Available*

- Bank 4
- Bank 5   • Vendor 2

III. TIER 3 — *Commodity/Moving Away/Basic Services and Credit/Waiting in the Wings*

- Bank 6   • Vendor 4
- Bank 7   • Vendor 5

EXHIBIT 4.1 Relationship Categories by Tiers

a tendency to remember the most recent slight or service issue a bit too strongly. Having a clear ranking process helps to keep the overall relationship in perspective.

Many organizations break up their bank and vendor relationships into three tiers or groups—although there is nothing magical about that number. The first tier often includes highly important relationships with a mix of significant credit and important operational services. The second tier may include those that currently provide important credit or operational services or have a strong potential and likelihood of doing so in the near future. This may indicate a tier-three firm that is moving up. It also may indicate a former tier-one relationship that is declining in importance.

Exhibit 4.1 shows a categorization by three tiers along with a simplified explanation of the category descriptions. Most firms will benefit from additional clarity on the category descriptions and may provide ranking details and rationale on individual banks and vendors.

Plan and Process for Accomplishing the Objectives

Exhibit 4.2 lists the relationship tiers on the left. In the subsequent columns, various positions or roles within the organization have their responsibilities, meeting frequencies, and perspectives outlined.

BANK TYPE	CFO	TREASURER	DIRECTOR OF TREASURY
TIER 1 **Relationship Review — Balanced Scorecard** **Relationship Management:** • *Highly Intentional* • *Very Deep* • *Very Broad*	• Meet annually as appropriate. • Brief meetings. • Use the relationship to ensure additional contacts at the bank for overall relationship.	• Total of 3–4 meetings annually. • One time at bank annually, if appropriate, for relationship depth. • Exposure to multiple senior officers.	• Total of four meetings annually. • Regular meetings with Treasury and other relevant business lines. • Exposure to senior officer(s). • Ensure that the Treasurer, other Treasury managers, and shared service center leaders are involved in providing balanced input from an operational and relationship level.
TIER 2 **Relationship Management:** • *Intentional* • *Frequent* • *Deep and Broad*	• Meet opportunistically and as appropriate.	• Total of 1–2 meetings annually. • One time at bank (12–18 months) for upwardly moving relationships. • Exposure with multiple senior officers.	• Total of two meetings annually. • Meetings as appropriate with Treasury and other relevant business lines. • Exposure to senior officer.
TIER 3 **Relationship Management:** • *Opportunistic*		• Meet opportunistically and as appropriate.	• Meet opportunistically and as appropriate.

EXHIBIT 4.2 Plan and Process for Accomplishing the Objectives—Relationship Tiers

Achieving Organizational Objectives through Effective Relationship Management

Exhibit 4.3 shows the major steps and primary order a company will use to manage its relationships in such a manner as to support its overall mission as a company. Additionally, this process diagram shows the context of relationship management objectives to Treasury's objectives above and individual activities and measurements below.

The organization's mission will drive the components of Treasury's mission. In order to fulfill Treasury's mission, there will be appropriate objectives established. The relationship management plan will necessarily flow from these objectives. Ultimately, various relationship objectives and activities will be identified and managed. Thus, all of the activities will be executed to support the relationship management plan, which supports the organization's mission. Exhibit 4.4 provides a sample method of tiering and the organization's relationships.

RELATIONSHIP-RANKING PROCESS Many organizations need multiple partners who provide services to ensure they have access to the appropriate amount of capital or because they need high-quality or high-touch service delivery. Ranking those partners is one part of the process necessary to optimize relationships.

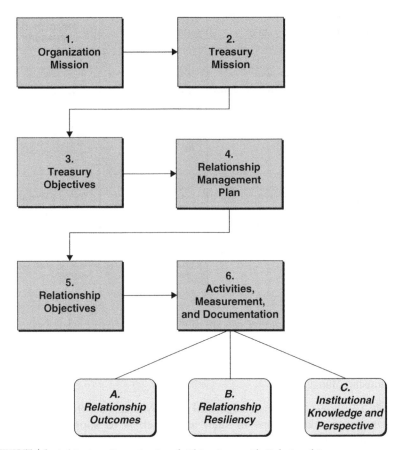

EXHIBIT 4.3 Achieving Organizational Objectives with Relationships

There are numerous ways to rank an organization's banks and other partners. When ranking banks, several key factors tend to come into view. The factors to consider and the weighting assigned them may vary based upon the firm's needs and the overall business cycle.

The following short list of three factors is provided as an example and is not intended to replace the annual surveys that show general shifts in relationship priorities over time.

1. The bank's ability to provide access to capital
2. The bank's ability to service your operational needs whether they are card-related, foreign exchange–driven, or cash-management oriented
3. The ability and consistency over time of providing new ideas and acting as a trusted adviser

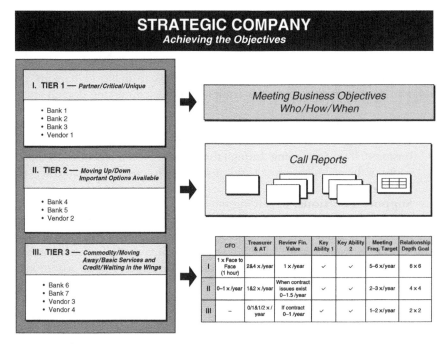

EXHIBIT 4.4 Tiering of Partnerships and Link to Activities that Create Institutionally Resilient Relationships

Most firms have a difficult time with ranking the second factor since their exposure to banks and vendors is naturally limited to a fairly small number of providers, and this restricts their ability to know and understand the market from an industry perspective. Getting external input on how well the existing and potential partners from your pool of bankers can service your operational needs can come from several sources, including surveys and knowledgeable consultants.

BANKER SELF-ASSESSMENT When seeking to align all of the stars in the firm's Treasury universe—credit, services, goods, and appropriate service providers—a useful tool is the bank self-assessment document. Using the bank as a source of information for ranking is often overlooked for the obvious reason of self-interest and bias. However, when executed properly, asking the banks to perform a self-ranking can provide excellent insight into what services the bank *desires to provide* and strong indications about the services they are *good at providing*.

The bank should certainly know what services it wants to provide. By making it document its ability to provide services that are leading and well-delivered, the bank will often need to reference third-party reviews, rankings, and awards to make its case. This information does not necessarily match up with your organization's needs, but it will give a good indication of where the bank spends its development and partnership funds, and it provides additional insight into how intensely the bank focuses on service quality and customer satisfaction.

The following list provides a few comments to make to bankers or vendors on their requirements for completing the self-ranking document:

- **Force rank the "desire to provide" section.** Do not accept a self-assessment or comments that indicate the bank wants all of your business. If you are going through this process, you likely need to share some of the services across vendors in order to ensure adequate access to liquidity.
- **Support assertions.** Regarding the bank's capability to provide a service at a high level and with rich and appropriate features, the bank needs to explain why it has made this ranking. Providing third-party support, such as quality rankings, market size, awards, and other information lends credibility to the general correctness of its assertions. Indeed, how the bank answers these questions gives additional insight into how well it knows its own strengths as well as areas for improvement.

By looking at your firm's process of awarding business and by helping your banker look more objectively at the services the bank offers, the overall relationship expectations should become more realistic. All of this information can then be synthesized with what you already know and with the data you have gathered to aid in your relationship management and service-allocation efforts.

Taken together, the self-ranking of *desire to provide* and *ability to provide* services provides an integrated view of each bank. Pulling all of this information together, analyzing it, and then synthesizing it with an organization's plan requires some work. However, when complete, an appropriate course of action can be created. In addition to determining a course of action, Treasury will want to share the reasons why it is pursuing the particular course of action with its relationship banks. The information gathered helps to consider both some facts and logic to provide this type of feedback to senior management.

Annual Banker's Meeting

Common among large organizations is the annual banker's meeting, an event that brings leadership of the organization and senior lenders from the bank group together. This meeting provides a highly efficient method of sharing business plans and results, and provides broader access into the company than would normally be possible if all these banks were contacted on a bilateral basis.

This event needs to be well planned. Planning will need to encompass logistics, messaging, and coaching. From a logistics standpoint, a professional forum for dialogue and intentional times of interaction are required—and unless your firm has full-time staff responsible for event planning, you should hire an outside planner/coordinator. The Treasurer and her staff have many other areas on which to focus their attention and energy.

Every organizational attendee will need to know four things to be ready for the annual banker's meeting:

1. What message or messages should be conveyed?
2. The rules of engagement should be clear, including what topics need to be referred to the designated communicator and additional banker-meeting protocol.
3. The relationship plan should be clear enough to understand how this plan ties to the messages that the organization intends to communicate.
4. A list of attendees from the banks with a simple biography of each and explanation of experience working with your organization.

Having a practice session for the presentation delivery and time for coaching those who are new to these types of meetings is in order. This preparation is well worth the effort. Remember, having this consolidated meeting is actually saving everyone many days.

Some astute organizations provide various forms of entertainment or reasonably unique experiences in efforts to help the bankers better remember the firm and its leaders.

Perspectives on Banker Relationships

The following are several behaviors that Treasurers should practice at the annual banker's meeting and at all times. These practices are appropriate for maintaining and fostering optimal relationships over years.

- **Don't abuse a current position of strength.** If you are working at an extremely well-known firm, many banks may want to have you as a customer or "name." Naturally, if you find yourself at this type of organization, there are benefits to negotiating deals and getting the best input. But do not abuse this power by unnecessarily browbeating the bankers. They are reasonably kind folk and should have the expectation of working with a reasonable partner. If they are so eager for your business that they are willing to provide services or execute a transaction at a loss or at breakeven, do you want to enter into a partnership that is that one-sided?

In situations where this appears to be the case, it is wise to think through the ramifications: Will you be dropped from the bank's roster if your position of strength suddenly changes? Does it make sense to provide you with a service at a loss, and what can happen to the quality level if that is the case?

While it may seem that the best negotiator in the world should browbeat from a position of strength, the need for good services, good advice, and ongoing relationship commitment and mutual value requires a more partnership-oriented approach.

- **High maintenance.** Some organizations are well aware that they are truly high maintenance. Others have convoluted processes so that vendors or potential vendors and partners must perform all manner of custom work and servicing to meet their needs. Knowing the needs and the level of care and feeding your organization requires is useful both for relationship management and for identifying process-improvement opportunities.

  Do the bankers joke about how difficult it is to handle your firm's work? Did the relationship manager have to twist his operational staff's arms to get them to do your work? Are exceptions the norm for your processes? Do you know whether you are requiring faster service or more intensive care than other organizations? To be sustainable, a higher level of care and servicing will need to be reflected in the pricing.

  Achieving optimal value does not always require the lowest price. Focusing solely on price, while attractive for the short term, will typically result in major changes later on when you may be in a position when you can least afford to make those changes. Banks do not mind tough clients who have a partner mentality, but they have become more proficient at exiting difficult and unprofitable clients.

- **Play fair.** Bankers will remember for years and years if someone deceives them. They tend to keep things at a business level and this is easier since they work with a number of firms at any point in time. Some corporates seem to remember real or perceived slights or denials of credit forever, whether it was warranted or not. Most of that memory is bound to the organic gray matter of just a few individuals. Rarely is the history recorded for others to see and make rationally based decisions on it.

  The problem with this memory is that it can change over time, and a person, and therefore the organization, can hold something against a bank partner to the detriment of both groups. For instance, if a bank is exiting a line of business because of its total level of exposure (perhaps to firms with asbestos claims), the Treasurer may be upset, but he should also understand the rational business reason. A bank that ends a firm's uncommitted credit line on a surprise basis with one day's notice is likely less professionally and relationally oriented than the banker who gives you three months' notice, which allows you time to make other arrangements in a more orderly fashion. Delivering bad news in an organized, rational, and professional manner merits far more relational grace than abrupt and disruptive changes in direction.

Rationale for Formally Documenting Relationships

This section covers the basis for formally memorializing the relationship with a relationship management plan and documenting individual bank/vendor meetings. Some additional relationship-oriented documents are discussed at various levels including the balanced scorecard and the relationship value document, as well as the request for proposal (RFP). The intent here is not to be exhaustive in the treatment of these topics but to provide the rationale for when and how they may be used. This portion of the chapter will raise some thought-provoking points intended to foster improved and more efficient relationships.

The Bank Documents Meetings with You

Banks issue call reports for each visit. This is a key metric for the relationship manager because she must make client visits, and those calls must be documented. Their documentation includes a number of things including what was told to them and by whom; what is going on at the firm; the firm's business and financial plans, promises made, or expectations shared; what follow-up items are necessary; and so on.

In the documents, personnel discussions are recorded, as well as key pieces of industry and business trends. These call reports are then shared with others at the bank. The bankers are being deliberate here. Relationship managers may change with the seasons, so it is necessary for the institutional knowledge of the relationship to continue and be shared broadly in order to gain insight into the dynamics of a relationship and the organization in order for the relationship to continue on an institutional level regardless of personnel involved.

Organizations Should Document Bank Meetings

Corporations rarely issue internal call reports. What did the banker say? What follow-up was promised? What are our responsibilities? What new service is being rolled out that might warrant a presentation to a division or a subsidiary?

Formally documenting bank meetings with call reports should be done for all banks that are categorized as being in the organization's top two tiers. Meetings with lower-tier-relationship banks should probably be documented, too, but at a less-detailed level. The documentation should be for all relationship banks and could include other key vendors. These key partners are those that would be in your top tiers and those that are deemed essential to your organization.

For those Treasurers who have never spent time on the bank side of the business, this concept at first may seem a bit foreign. However, the simple discipline of creating a basic call report is both instructive to the author and useful to the organization for many reasons. While it is easy to delay documenting the call, it is a best practice to immediately document the event while the memory is still fresh and your notes still make sense.

Balanced Scorecard

The discussion of the value of a balanced scorecard and whether and when it makes sense is a subject that is usually best covered on an individual basis. While a balanced scorecard can be selectively useful with certain firms and with select banks, it requires a substantial amount of work to manage the effort. Effective leaders in Treasury make sure that their staff is not creating a product and process of moderate value but at great cost.

Bank Value

A bank value report requires much less work to create and update. It is also always useful. This is the corporate equivalent to a profitability report that banks create. Knowing what services you bring to the bank and how profitable you are or are not to it is useful information on many fronts.

Since the mid-1990s, banks have become much better at assessing the value of their clients to the bank. They can usually look at a wide variety of their service offerings—Treasury, cards, pension, foreign exchange, and so on, along with credit activity—to assess whether it is committed, uncommitted, or capital-market driven. By looking at all the data together, the bank understands how much it is leveraging its balance sheet and what it is receiving in return for capital and the services provided.

Not all banks understand or see all the services that an individual company uses. It may be that the bank is delivering a service that the relationship manager receives no credit for, and thus the activity often will be overlooked. Sometimes the bank systems do not have all of an organization's business classified or linked properly so the relationship appears much different than reality.

This can be detrimental. An organization may look like a marginally profitable firm that uses a great deal of its balance sheet when, in fact, it has many operating services that are simply not reporting properly in the bank's account and profitability structure. Being misclassified can result in less attention, movement onto an inappropriate platform, or having a more junior or unseasoned relationship manager be your firm's point of interface. This may not be warranted, so it is necessary to understand how this can occur.

Preparing and maintaining a bank value report requires a few reasonably simple steps:

Step 1: Make an inventory of all major banks/service providers.

Step 2: Gather all credit, investment, and hedge data.

Step 3: Use the inventory of services and compile a list of services provided including volumes.

Step 4: Assign profitability to each component based on various averages and standards to arrive at an estimated profitability figure by bank.

The results can be surprising to an organization and its bank. This information should be used wisely and updated on an annual basis and whenever major changes occur. Also, review this data before each bank visit.

Communication: Accessible and Honest

Good communication requires regular and honest communication. This can be hard, for example, when an organization needs far more credit than its fee-based business will support. Clear stratification of its tiers and the trajectory of its partners is warranted here. Another breakthrough report declaring banks that offer the majority of credit have the lion's share of the fee-based wallet at those firms is not needed. Those studies are the Treasury equivalent of the weather rock: if the rock is wet, it is raining!

A bank partner may have a serious conversation indicating that it needs more profitability to hit its hurdle rates. If you absolutely cannot or will not give the bank more fee-based business, just say so.

Many firms have a lot more business that can be turned over to a bank partner. This work may be done by an outside vendor or by internal staff. There are often quite a few mundane tasks that banks are excellent at handling for firms. For instance, payment generation (check printing is a component) and invoice generation combined with an integrated lockbox can be provided by certain banks at an affordable and high quality level.

Additionally, your organization is probably already driving these processes from paper-based to electronic methods, and it makes sense to remove the mechanical part of the processes. Unless your business is printing or making payments, the burden of proof is on the organization to prove why it should be kept in-house. This proof would need to include both strategic and realistic financial aspects.

Some vendors provide a similar and, in some cases, a moderately superior service to traditional bank partners. Be brutally honest about how much better the service is with the vendor. Also, recognize that relationships bring different value. How much will that vendor lend you? If the capability differences are not crucial or earth-shattering, feed those who help your business operate or expand. Remember that the bank will put its balance sheet to work for your organization.

Request for Proposal

Requests for proposals (RFPs) will typically be delegated to someone within your group and not the Treasurer. Since there are entire books in print about RFPs and requests for information (RFIs), here are just a few of the key points to be mindful of when guiding staff as they consider or are in the process of executing an RFP process.

- **Don't be a time-waster.** Don't send the RFP as a favor to one of your banks. If it is not a good fit either from a capability or relationship standpoint, just do not do it—it is a waste of everyone's time. Even if the banker pleads, be strong. A few uncomfortable moments early are far better than abusing the time of your bank and your staff. At some point the bank will appreciate it—even though it pretends not to.
- **Don't be mean.** Copying four different RFPs and adding your own massive list of questions is just being mean. If the person responsible for the RFP cannot answer why a question was asked, this indicates a problem. The preparer should also be able to identify how each of the questions is important in their evaluation process and how it relates to basic requirements and critical needs.
- **Ask for what you want.** If you just need lower pricing, why not simply send a service/volume/price list out with some simple guidelines for finding that out? Most bankers will provide concessions on pricing when asked if they understand the reason and you maintain a solid relationship. Now, remember not to abuse the relationship just because you can.
- **Focus on the areas of distinction and your needs.** Moving toward an RFP process is a time for gathering information about the various

providers and understanding the major differences and the unique advantages one may bring over another. If you are clear about what your needs are and where this may be a challenge for some banks or providers, you can focus on those areas. This may include cut-off times, special processing that is a configuration for one provider and an exception process for another, and additional services that can improve the cash conversion process, among other differences. Knowing where to focus helps to make a reasonable decision quickly and in a defensible way.

Summary

Everyone manages some types of relationships. All great companies manage their relationships in a thoughtful and formal manner and ensure that the institutional knowledge of the relationship is maintained. Being accessible and honest is always the best policy. Remember, banks often lend money while vendors rarely do.

In order to ensure that your organization will be seen as important to those banks and vendors to which it wants to be important, you must act deliberately and thoughtfully. Times and situations can change rapidly. Having key partners who are knowledgeable about managing these relationships is especially invaluable during those times.

CHAPTER 5

Owning Cash and the Five *O*s of Treasury

Cash is King. And, risk management helps you realize that cash is King. Cash is your best insurance policy.

—Amy B. Kweskin, Treasurer, Washington University
in St. Louis

When contemplating the responsibilities of a Treasurer, different lists can be created by well-meaning and thoughtful people from different organizations. This difference in responsibilities is often quite acceptable. However, acceptable differences of opinion should not carry over to the view of how cash should be viewed and managed by the Treasurer. While a continuum of management will be described and applied to different activities with a suggested range, when we examine the treatment of cash, the answer is not a range. The answer is that the Treasurer must "own" cash. Owning cash means specific things to the Treasurer and to the organization.

Cash is King. The Treasurer is responsible for caring for and protecting the King. If something happens to the King, everyone looks first to the Treasurer. They may look to other parties, too, to place blame, but that happens later.

The Treasurer's view and perspective about cash is crucial. This chapter describes what it means to own cash as well as what it does not mean or

EXHIBIT 5.1 The Five Os of Treasury

require. The *Treasury continuum*, called the Five Os of Treasury, will be explained and described.

For purposes of this chapter, the definition used for *cash* will refer to the control of bank accounts and signers, cash in bank accounts, and short-term investments and short-term borrowings. This chapter does not use the accounting—generally accepted accounting principles (GAAP)—definition of cash, which includes bank cash and short-term investments.

The Os of Treasury

The "Five Os of Treasury" refers to the continuum of roles the Treasurer or Treasury may take with regard to various assets and liabilities. The diagram in Exhibit 5.1 is useful for showing what position or range of positions Treasury should take regarding the different aspects of an organization's finances.

In Exhibit 5.1 there are five perspectives that begin with the letter O. The lightly shaded items at the sides represent extremes. These are Oblivious and Oppressor. The more darkly shaded items in the center represent the core perspectives of Observer, Overseer, and Owner.

Maria D'Alessandro, while Senior Vice President of Wachovia Corp., created the initial concept of the three Os of Treasury cash. The three Os refer to the middle section of the broader diagram: observer, overseer, and owner status. This concept has been broadened to include the two additional categorizations (oblivious and oppressor) and has been applied to other Treasury concepts beyond cash and working capital. See Exhibit 5.2.

Centralized or Decentralized Treasury

The Treasurer is the owner of cash and liquidity. Liquidity is often viewed as including cash, short-term debt, short-term investments, and working capital components. While some differences of opinion exist as to the level

Five Os of Cash

Target Area			Cash		
Continuum	Oblivious	Observer	Overseer	Owner	Oppressor
Description/ Example	• I can see my international cash balances based on the G/L only at the end of the month, not in real time. • We don't really know where all of our accounts are, just the important one that we use a lot. • Departments pay for bank services and get what they want. They are responsible.	• Treasury forecasts cash, but no one really believes in forecasts anyway. • We see cash on some of our main operating accounts. • Please, may we use some of your cash to pay down some corporate debt?	• I set policy about account openings and closings. • We strongly encourage the use of good account and transaction controls and enforce that when possible. • There is shared responsibility for cash. We control some accounts, and the divisions control others.	• We have adequate visibility to and controls on our liquidity position in real time. • We can see every account. • Cash is a corporate asset, not a department or division asset.	• We don't have the cash available for this right now, it's invested, and I'm getting a good yield. • I'll tell you how fast we pay our vendors, not them. • Stop buying inventory; we need the cash. • If you made everyone pay COD, we could get rid of credit and collection staff.

EXHIBIT 5.2 The Five Os of Cash

49

Area	Target	Reason
Cash	Own	Any other position is ineffective and costs the organization money and adds excessive risk.
Debt	Own	The skills necessary to understand the markets and issue and manage debt are specialized and must be centralized. Systems used to track debt are Treasury-specific. Managing debt in a decentralized manner is not simply suboptimal; it is irresponsible.
Investments	Own	A case can be made that most Treasury groups should use an external party to manage the investment process. Non-Treasury areas do not have the expertise to manage the investment framework or process.
Working Capital	Oversee or Own	While Treasury does not control all of the working capital components directly (accounts receivable, inventory, and accounts payable), the level of influence and control must be very strong. Chapter 5 details the reasons why Treasury should be either an overseer or owner of working capital.
Hedging	Own	This perspective is somewhat controversial. Interest Rate (IR) and Foreign Exchange (FX) hedging is almost always owned and executed by Treasury. Commodity hedging is regularly distributed to an operating area. Controllers have a role in many organizations due to hedge accounting rules and the intersection with economics. However, the Treasurer should own the hedging process even as she works closely with the operating areas and the controller's department. No good can come of having another area own a subset of the hedges an organization takes on.

EXHIBIT 5.3 Target Treasury Areas

of responsibility along the continuum that the Treasurer should target with different areas, Exhibit 5.3 shows those areas that are most appropriate for any Treasurer to target. The exhibit shows these areas with some minimal discussion points as to why each target position is proper.

Exhibit 5.4 takes the various perspectives from Exhibit 5.3, which is shown in a grid and displays perspectives in pictorial form. This highlights where on the continuum Treasury should be with respect to each area of responsibility.

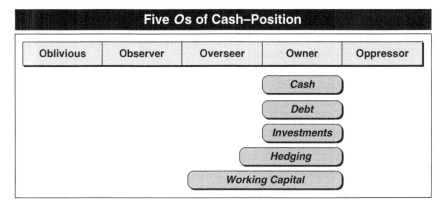

EXHIBIT 5.4 The Five Os of Cash—Position

The Five Os of Treasury places certain assets and liabilities clearly in the Owner category as shown in Exhibit 5.4. For Cash, Debt, Investments, and Hedges are some of the items that can be readily moved into Treasury as the Owner category. These are properly the domain of the Treasurer, for no organization can run effectively or properly if this is not the case. The following represents a sampling of questions that can help your organization determine if Treasury is acting as the owner in this category or if additional action is necessary. Treasury, where acting as the owner, will be able to answer these questions quickly and accurately.

Cash

- Which accounts are active?
- Who are the signers on each account?
- What is the cash balance (Treasury) by account, currency, country, as of yesterday?
- What is the bank-account policy?

Debt

- Can you provide a complete inventory of all debt instruments, including terms?
- Can you show compliance with your debt policy?
- How much room is there before you are out of compliance with any covenant?
- What amount of committed and uncommitted lines is available?

Investments

- Can you provide a complete inventory of all investments? By instrument class? By currency? By counterparty?
- Can you provide a report that shows compliance with your policy?

Hedges

- What are your interest rate, foreign exchange, and commodity hedges?
- What is your hedging policy?
- Can you show and explain your financial risk management framework?
- Does senior management understand your policy and financial risk management framework?
- Can you provide a report or reports that show if you are in compliance with your policy?

Overall Liquidity

- Can you provide a report that shows counterparty exposure in total? By category of asset?
- What does your cash forecast look like for the next month? Three months? Year?
- What confidence level do you have on your forecast data one month out?
- What will your balance sheet need to look like in two years to support your overall business plans?

Taking Ownership

When Treasury is acting as either an observer or overseer of cash, corrective action is necessary. To move to the proper role of owner may require activity in several areas to ensure that Treasury exerts proper ownership over this valuable asset called cash.

Policy

The financial-account policy must be supported by the overall framework employed to manage and protect cash. The specific policy for financial accounts will need to be authored, controlled, and updated by Treasury. Additionally, the policy for bank reconciliation may need to be updated and should be authored and issued by the Treasurer and include, by way of reference, the broad Controller's reconciliation policy.

The financial-account policy, referred to in some companies as the *bank-account policy*, will include the following components:

- **Account opening and closing authority.** This will include some people from the Treasury group. This responsibility also includes maintaining an accurate and up-to-date list of accounts and signers. Wise

Treasurers have their department perform self-audits of this information to discover accounts and ensure their directions were carried out. Every account represents a point of exposure.

- **Control of general ledger codes.** While the general ledger manager may open or establish a general ledger account, the Treasurer or his designee will determine which financial accounts have unique general ledger codes. This is almost always a one-for-one match. Each bank account must have a separate general ledger code for that cash account.

- **Signer authority.** The process and method of delegating account authority to various staff and officers of the firm must exist as designed by Treasury, which is delegated this authority from the board of directors or articles of incorporation.

- **Controls.** Various controls are established either as the result of a specific policy requirement or based on the professional judgment of the Treasurer. These controls include account level and transaction level controls. They may also include reconciliation and batch level controls as well.

- **Compliance reporting.** Most policies have a compliance reporting component, and the financial-account policy is not an exception. Reporting may include general statistics as well as an exception report (that is, accounts that should have an account level control on them but do not, and the reason for the exception and if and when this will be adjusted).

The bank-reconciliation policy is a tool used to control and guard cash. And, while bank reconciliation primarily performs the function in an after-the-fact manner, it remains important. The Treasury group must author the policy and work with Controllers to ensure it is appropriate for their organization. While the policy will contain a number of components, a few to highlight include:

- **Definition of *reconciled*.** To state that an account is reconciled means far too many different things to different people. This should not be the case. For an account to be reconciled, the following should be included in the checklist:
  - Adjusted book and adjusted bank figures equal.
  - Timing differences are identified as such and are not older than an acceptable age. This would normally be only items from the prior period.
  - Reconciling items will be identified as to when they will clear and will include the journal voucher number that will clear them. This should follow the timing period.

- No plug figures.
- Reconciliations are signed and dated by the preparer and the reviewer.
- **Timing of reconciliation.** Reconciliations must be completed within the defined time period. This period may vary based on the volume of activity and complexity of the process. The level of automation used can also decrease the time required to perform an adequate reconciliation.

Many organizations that have problems with reconciliation blame the reconciliation area and the reconcilers. It is true that the reconciliation area can contribute to the problem by not being well organized and not following up with areas to ensure the proper entries are made. However, it is important to note that reconciliation stands at the end of the financial process. If a process is poorly designed, it can become nearly impossible for reconciliation to resolve the issues. Accounting, Treasury, operating areas, and banks can all contribute to complicating the process. Treasury can often help to find the root cause—the real root cause—of the problem with reconciliations.

Treasury should design its banking processes and services to optimize Treasury, not accounting. Accounting concerns should not determine how a banking structure is established. However, they should not break a process or reasonable accounting controls in doing so.

Visibility

Chapter 17 is devoted to achieving visibility to the firm's cash and liquidity. The Treasurer ensures that Treasury has a clear view to the cash and near-cash items. Here is a brief summary of the goals of visibility related to owning cash:

- Clean bank account structure and concentration design mobilizing cash efficiently.
- Complete and current database of all financial accounts and signers.
- Daily view of all summary account balance information.
- Daily or weekly view of transaction detail on most accounts; more frequent views as necessary on select accounts.
- Complete inventory of debt and investments.
- Short-term cash forecast that identifies operating, financing, and capital flows (large one-time items included).
- Automated accounting.

Performance

The adage "what gets measured gets improved" is normally true with cash, too. Since cash is a corporate asset managed by Treasury, and Treasury is accountable for its proper use, the operating areas should not be charged for the direct use of cash. The ability to manage cash should not be within their control. However, having the performance metrics reflect various activities that impact cash is appropriate. Most of these activities will be reflected via the metrics used to manage working capital and should help drive proper and balanced behavior. Other behavior and activities will be reflected as they forecast significant items and accurately forecast regular operating flows.

Recording

Recording cash is not a topic to excite the normal Treasurer's mind. Yet properly recording cash in a manner that facilitates good cash control and Treasury practices must be done in a manner that supports generally accepted accounting principles. While many Treasurers do not enjoy accounting, it must be understood in order to properly manage cash. Chapter 6 discusses some recording concepts and practical applications in more depth.

Treasury groups that choose not to manage the cash recording process in a way that optimizes Treasury's responsibilities while meeting accounting needs have missed an important opportunity. As such, they will find their cash performance suffers.

Reconciliation

To understand in what manner the Treasurer will take ownership of reconciliation, some background information is in order. There are three general types of reconciliations that those in finance care about. There is an additional reconciliation that Treasury performs.

1. **General ledger reconciliation.** This reconciliation takes the general ledger accounts and reconciles them to the subledgers or to the supporting documentation. This ensures that the subledger detail matches the summary information on the control accounts on the general ledger. This provides assurance that the financial statements are in order and should help identify any problem in the control processes related to the subledgers. The Controller's department typically oversees this process.
2. **Bank reconciliation.** This process reconciles the bank statements with the general ledger cash accounts. This helps to ensure that the cash recorded in the general ledger is actually at the bank. Various departments may perform this activity, and both the Controller's and Treasurer's departments have responsibility for some oversight.

Ultimately the Treasurer is responsible for the control of cash. Bank reconciliation is merely one component of cash control.

3. **File control.** When files are passed between systems—whether between two corporate systems or a corporate system and an external system (such as a bank electronic funds transfer system)—there must be some type of reconciliation at the file level. This includes, at least, control totals for the value and for the volume of activity.

The responsibility for this type of control rests with the operating area in many instances. Any activity related to financial processes that intersect with the bank should follow some standard that is established with Treasury oversight and approval. Control will need to be managed going forward and may or may not include operational Treasury review. Information technology often establishes some standards as well for the control of files as a minimum requirement.

4. **Treasury reconciliation.** This step is better described in general finance terms as a Treasury proof or cash position validation. Treasury reconciliation is the daily process of establishing a cash position, and borrowing or investing usually includes a forecasting component. The following day Treasury sees how things actually turned out. When it finds a material difference from what was expected, there is normally a process whereby the individuals identify the cause or causes of the variance. This reconciliation, while often performed systematically, must occur on a daily basis and early in the morning.

This reconciliation is necessary since what was expected to happen yesterday may now happen today or tomorrow. This reconciliation should also identify items that settled yesterday that were unanticipated. The feedback from this reconciliation serves two purposes. First, Treasury will be aware of the cause of the difference and can determine a response in order to prevent another day of variances. Second, this information can be researched to determine if it is a one-time event or if there is a root cause that can be neutralized or managed. Treasury is responsible for this proof.

Protecting the Balance Sheet

Both the Controller and the Treasurer are in the protection business. They often work via different means to protect the assets of the firm. The Controller has a financial reporting and control responsibility. To fulfill that responsibility, the Controller must ensure that the internal control framework is able to detect a problem within an organization's processes related to financial reporting. The Controller's group ensures that the appropriate

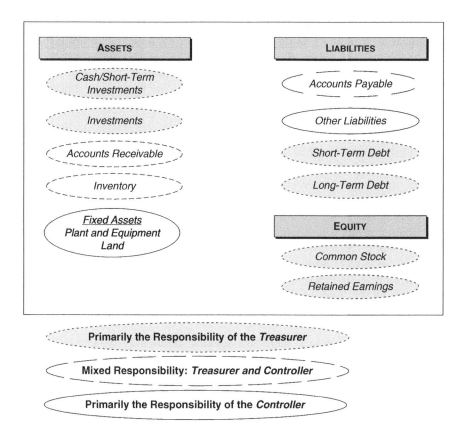

EXHIBIT 5.5 Responsibility for the Balance Sheet

control processes are established. Internal audit ensures that appropriate testing of those control processes is performed. Actual audits of a percentage of the assets and liabilities are also performed as a matter of course. Most of the controls that are referenced here are referred to as "detective controls."

The Treasurer, too, must protect and help manage certain key assets of the organization. The specific assets are typically those identified in Exhibit 5.5. These include cash, working capital components, and much of the right-hand side of the balance sheet. For several of these items, Treasury must ensure that appropriate preventative controls are in place with cash and certain liabilities such as borrowing. Some assets are used as collateral for securing less-expensive funding (for instance, accounts receivable securitization uses accounts receivable as the collateral basis for a loan).

If there is a problem with cash, investments, or debt, the head of the organization usually looks first to the Treasurer for an explanation. If there are problems with other assets and some liabilities, the question hits the Controller first. And while there are delineated responsibilities for the financial reporting and protection of cash, it is key to know how important it is that both groups work together to protect the organization's balance sheet.

Note that this section does not have the "income statement" in its title. Since some financial instruments, that is, derivative instruments or other securities that may be marked-to-market at their fair value each period, increase the interaction between the balance sheet and the income statement, both the Treasurer and Controller need to work closely together more often. Hedge accounting, for example, is significant in that the accounting treatment has a feedback loop on the purported "effectiveness" of a hedge, which can impact the overall economics of a transaction. Hedges are not all equal. Some are very effective in terms of accomplishing exactly what is intended, offsetting volatile cash flows of an exposure, for example. Others may be less effective at accomplishing the purpose for which they were taken on; that is, no "perfect hedge" for an underlying exposure exists.

In hedge accounting there are specific boundaries where a hedge crosses over from being effective to ineffective—outside a correlation range of 80 to 125 percent, for example. From an accounting perspective, a hedge that is deemed to be completely ineffective will require all of the ineffectiveness to flow directly to the income statement rather than being "parked" in the equity component of the balance sheet, leading to potential large swings or volatility in the income statement—whereas, the original intent of the hedge was to decrease volatility. However, for hedges that are deemed effective, the change in value of the hedge instrument is typically placed in a balance sheet account called *other comprehensive income* (OCI) and then released to the income statement in a more orderly manner (that is, when the underlying exposure is realized), thus achieving the expected offset. This allows the income statement to have less volatility. Recognizing that this example of hedge accounting is an oversimplification of a complex subject, the point to be made here is that this is an area where the Treasurer's actions (that is, hedging) can have significant impact on the income statement, and therefore requires the Treasurer and Controller to work closely together.

The Five Os of Treasury refers to a continuum of roles that Treasury can take with regard to Cash, Working Capital, and other core responsibilities. Exhibit 5.6 refers to the "Six Ohs of Treasury." The Six Ohs represent sample perspectives where those in Treasury may be caught mentally or organizationally unprepared.

Oh, ...

(1) *I need to understand accounting.*

(2) *I need to work hard at helping the business areas succeed.*

(3) *Communication is a process and not an event.*

(4) *To optimize working capital requires work and not simply publishing statistics.*

(5) *I was supposed to ensure that our relationships were managed for the organization and not be centered just on me.*

(6) *Even when we execute against our risk management framework perfectly, second guessers will arise and disparage the results, and state the decision that should have been made based upon perfect after-the-fact knowledge that was not available on a prospective basis. And, smart people who should know better will buy into that argument.*

Note: This list, to protect blood pressure levels, has been restricted to six items.

EXHIBIT 5.6 The Six *Ob*s of Treasury

Summary

Treasury must take clear and decisive ownership of cash for the organization. Oversight of cash is insufficient. Any response other than taking an ownership role is a waste of time and money, and exposes the organization to undue risks. Cash is a corporate asset owned by the Treasurer, who is chief steward of this critical item. The Treasurer determines how cash is kept, controlled, managed, and moved. While other areas may influence cash or handle this asset, they do so under the direct control of Treasury.

Owning cash requires setting clear policies with regard to cash and financial accounts. The framework for these policies and the policies themselves must be established and maintained by Treasury.

Being the owner of cash requires clear visibility to cash and all of the influences of cash. This requires appropriate management of bank relationships, structure, and accounts. For many organizations, technology will be required to help achieve this visibility.

To effectively manage cash requires the Treasurer and Treasury to understand accounting since they may need to influence recording practices to better control cash. Additionally, the Treasurer must ensure that proper reconciliation steps are performed and controls are established in order to fulfill the responsibility of being a good steward of this most valuable asset. Cash is King, and the Treasurer owns the King. If something happens to the King, the Treasurer is responsible.

Treasury needs to be run in a centralized manner. Centralizing Treasury does not mean that everyone works from the same location. Treasury is never optimized if it is run in a decentralized manner. Treasury centers are often quite effective and should be part of the central Treasury group.

CHAPTER 6

Cash Boot Camp for Treasurers

I can't be overdrawn, I still have checks.

—Anonymous

Chapter 5 discussed the priority for the Treasurer to act as the owner of cash. It further described what it means to own cash as opposed to simply being either an observer or overseer of that particular asset called cash. To fully own cash requires a certain level of visibility of cash and understanding of how various lenses can distort that view.

The following provides some details and examples of the different lenses that impact one's view of cash. Importantly, it further shows how to record and report on cash in a manner that complies with accounting principles while at the same time providing a better and more controlled process. Those who take advantage of this method of recording can better see cash in the balance sheet. Additionally, similar improvements are made to such items as accounts receivable and accounts payable. To get to the desired high-level value requires starting with some basics.

Cash

One of the most basic of all finance terms is *cash*. Instruction about cash begins well before the first official business course. In Accounting 101, all business majors learn the basic double-entry accounting method with an entry that uses cash. The purchase of equipment is shown as a debit

61

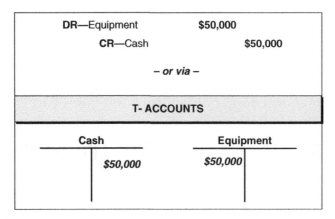

EXHIBIT 6.1 Buying Equipment with Cash

to "equipment," which increases the value of that asset category of plant and equipment. To pay for that equipment, cash was expended. Cash was decreased, and the value of the other asset increased by the same amount.

Thus, the credit entry is made to cash, which decreases the value of the asset called cash. See Exhibit 6.1 for both a view of the debit and credit along with a T-account mapping of this activity. Understanding that an asset exchange took place where cash was swapped for an asset is not just basic for finance people, it is also a fundamental concept of trade and business.

A Tale of Two Types of Cash

While cash is certainly cash, there are some different views of cash that need to be understood by the Treasurer, at least at a macro level. The two primary views are Generally Accepted Accounting Principles (GAAP) cash and "treasury cash." Many in Treasury refer to the second type of cash not as "treasury cash" but as "real cash." Use of that term is not particularly helpful in the discussion, as it tends to be seen as a bit presumptuous and can be a distraction for those who are learning the distinctions between these two types of cash.

GAAP Cash

GAAP is concerned about cash from a reporting standpoint. For all intents and purposes, it ignores the concept of float as it views that concept as an immaterial consideration. Accountants often view float as an interesting concept that Treasury should be concerned about. Further, they often believe that it is a concept that has no bearing from a financial reporting standpoint.

Float—the concept that it takes time to settle the financial transaction in your bank account—is deemed as irrelevant due to its limited duration. For example, the period of time from when a check is received and accounts receivable is reduced, to the time the check is deposited and funds are ultimately made available is viewed as imminent.

For an opposite-direction example, a disbursement is treated similarly. While a check may be issued or an Automated Clearing House (ACH) payment generated today, the concept is that cash is gone from your balance sheet at that time. And, even though the disbursement may not remove funds from the bank account for a few days, a week, or even longer, that is a banking consideration and is not truly important for financial reporting. This treatment makes sense from an accounting perspective since the moment you record the noncash side of the entry you must also record the impact to cash. Double-entry accounting is logical, and making this type of entry is in accord with that framework.

Treasury Cash

Treasury professionals use either the term "treasury cash" or "real cash" to distinguish their view of cash from the traditional accounting view. While this term can lead to fruitless discussions, the key conceptual difference highlights how each party views cash from their point of reference.

Treasury is concerned with liquidity management, which includes being a faithful steward of cash, investments, debt, and a few other asset and liability items. Part of being a good steward of those resources requires reducing borrowing costs and optimizing investment earnings in accord with certain key principles related to risk and return. On a gross or net basis, the amount of float for funds disbursed and received can be substantial. Float, in its various forms, must be considered when looking at liquidity needs.

Appropriately, the Treasurer takes advantage of cash management tools to optimize investment earnings. Leaving excess balances in a checking account to cover all of the checks that were issued is considered seriously outdated and highly inefficient. In some organizations, disbursement float can equal many tens of millions of dollars and more. And, while checks may be issued every day and others clear their bank account removing the funds, the intervening time can create a wonderful asset that can and should provide financial value to the organization.

Consider the organization that makes good use of that disbursement float and invests the tens of millions of dollars' worth of float or uses it to pay down debt more quickly. That firm fares far better than the organization that views cash in a rigid GAAP-only mentality. So far, there is no argument from the Controller. The Controller will readily admit that the Treasurer should use appropriate tools to manage cash. However, the Controller just does not want to change either the reporting method or recording process. The application of these different views can create suboptimal results.

Disbursement Example

Operationally, to disburse funds, a check is typically issued. Concurrently, accounting entries are made that support this activity. Fundamentally, there is a business need that gives rise to the overall process that creates this transaction. Necessarily, that transaction needs to be properly recorded in the books of the organization.

Let's take this concept and make it more specific. A businessperson makes the decision to buy a piece of equipment, perhaps with the additional advice of a lease-versus-purchase model created by finance, and then fills out some paperwork for the purchase. The item is received in good working order. Receiving an invoice and confirmation of receipt of that piece of equipment, accounts payable then creates that payment. (*Note: we are leaving off some steps and accounting to avoid the unnecessary noise as we seek to understand the concept in focus.*) An accounting entry is made when the check is issued to support the transaction. The check is mailed, and the funds come out of the account one week later.

Here is a look at what those entries are from a GAAP perspective.

Day 1. A check is issued to pay for an equipment purchase.

Balance sheet before the transaction

Cash	$1,000,000
Equipment	$400,000

The transaction is executed and the accounting entry is generated as follows:

Debit: Equipment	$100,000
Credit: Cash	$100,000

The T-Accounts in Exhibit 6.2 show the activity and balance. Here is the portion of the balance sheet after the transaction:

Cash	$900,000
Equipment	$500,000

Cash		Equipment	
$1,000,000		*$400,000*	
	$100,000	*100,000*	
$ 900,000		*$500,000*	

EXHIBIT 6.2 T-Account

Accounting is pleased. An asset has been received and is recorded as an increase to the equipment category. The cash asset used to pay for that equipment is reduced at the time of issuance. Whether the check is mailed out that day or the next is essentially a nonevent to the Controller from a financial recording and reporting perspective. The check is simply an out-standing check at the moment. That concept is useful for reconciling the bank statement activity.

If the organization had $1,000,000 on hand on the balance sheet and at the bank before this transaction, the bank would show $1,000,000 in the account for the intervening week and drop to $900,000 on day 8 as indicated earlier. Equipment would immediately increase by $100,000 to $500,000 in the balance sheet. Treasury would be able to invest $1,000,000 for a week since those funds were available from the bank. This is $100,000 more than the general ledger would show for cash since that account's balance dropped when the check was issued. Using this method of record-ing, Treasury cannot—in any real way—use the cash balance in the general ledger to make investment, borrowing, or forecasting decisions.

Day 8. The check clears the bank on the seventh day after issuance in this example.

Balance sheet before the transaction

Cash	$900,000
Equipment	$500,000
Debit:	No entry made
Credit:	No entry made

The balance sheet after the transaction is exactly the same since nothing is recorded for accounting purposes in this model. The clearing of checks has no meaning for reporting purposes. Notable is the fact that this activity shows up on the bank statement. And this timing difference impacts the reconciliation process because bank reconciliation takes general ledger cash and compares it to the bank statement activity. Note that the T-Accounts would remain the same as Exhibit 6.2 in this example.

No entry is made for this transaction that hit the bank. This process works for accounting. Looking at the general ledger, we see the cash balance that reflects GAAP cash. We have no indication of what disbursement float exists. We also have a more challenging time of reconciling the bank statement, since every transaction that hits the bank account will eventually roll through the reconciliation process.

Treasury may think that accounting is a bit odd for not recording an entry that hits the bank. Also, Treasury recognizes that this lack of an entry and the timing difference between balance sheet view of cash and the amount of cash at the bank creates issues that need to be overcome. Treasury is responsible for investing the $1,000,000 and will do so. If someone looks at the book of record for the cash asset, there is a difference since it appears from that source that the organization only has $900,000.

Treasury may be asked to explain why it had too much or too little cash or investments at a quarter-end or year-end period. The need to explain this difference often requires spending time identifying what made up the difference—and it can be difficult to reconcile the difference between cash that is usable and accounting cash. This difference can create extra work for both parties for formal bank reconciliation as well as other variance analysis activities.

Treasury may also want to use the general ledger to make short-term forecasts that will help with its liquidity planning and cash-positioning decisions. For cash, using the balance sheet to forecast becomes more difficult because of these different views of cash.

Exhibit 6.3 shows how cash is viewed through several different lenses. The *book* lens shows the value of cash from a GAAP (accounting) perspective on different days. Notice, in the bank section there are two types of reported balances.

The *ledger* balance is the accounting view, from the bank's perspective. It is the figure based on what hits the bank without regard to traditional float.

The *available* balance shows the amount of money that is liquid (available) and can be used to spend or invest, or be sent out. In other words, the check has cleared the system, and the bank allows those funds to be used. Any hold on the item is removed at this point.

Collection/Receivable Example

When funds are received, the asset called *accounts receivable* is reduced, and the specific customer account is relieved of its obligation. In this

DAY:	0	1	2	3	4	5	6	7	8	9	10
Bank — Ledger	$1M	$1M	$1M	$1M	$1M	$1M	$1M	$1M	$900K	$900K	$900K
Bank — Available	$1M	$1M	$1M	$1M	$1M	$1M	$1M	$1M	$900K	$900K	$900K
Company Books: GL — GAAP Cash	$1M	$900K	$900K	$900K	$900K	$900K	$900K	$900K	$900K	$900K	$900K

Assuming the organization keeps all cash uninvested in its bank account.

EXHIBIT 6.3 GAAP versus Bank Balance—Disbursement Example

example, assume that the payment was made via a check processed in an image lockbox. Float does not just exist with paper items. This process, too, involves business and operational activities that need to be supported by accounting entries, and the assets of the organization need to be managed effectively.

Here is a look at those events with the entries made from a GAAP perspective.

Day 1. A check is deposited in the lockbox with good funds being available on day 3.

Here is the balance sheet before the activity occurs (on day 0) as shown in Exhibit 6.4:

Cash	$1,000,000
Accounts Rec.	$700,000
Equipment	$400,000

The checks are received and processed by the lockbox. An entry is made by accounts receivable:

Debit:	Cash $125,000
Credit:	Accounts Receivable $125,000

The checks are received and processed by the lockbox. An entry is made (see Exhibit 6.5).

Exhibit 6.5 shows the T-Accounts for Cash, Accounts Receivable with Equipment thrown in for good measure.

Balance sheet after the transaction

Cash	$1,125,000
Accounts Rec.	$575,000
Equipment	$400,000

Cash		Accounts Receivable		Equipment	
$1,000,000		$700,000		$400,000	

EXHIBIT 6.4 T-Accounts Before the Posting of Accounts Receivable

Cash	A/R	Equipment
Day 0 — $1,000,000	**Day 0 — $700,000**	**Day 0 — $400,000**
125,000	**$125,000**	
Day 1 — $1,125,000	**Day 1 — $575,000**	**Day 1 — $400,000**

EXHIBIT 6.5 Accounts Receivable After Posting the Payment

Now the organization shows $1,125,000 of cash on the balance sheet. However, the $125,000 that was just received cannot be invested since the funds have not cleared.

The question posed to the Treasurer—"Why did you invest only $1,000,000 at month-end when we had $1,125,000?"—may seem a bit strange looking at this simplistic example, since it was easily explained. If the organization has stated that it wants to keep cash at a minimum at month-end or quarter-end, the $125,000 would show up on the balance sheet as cash. It was not cash that could be invested. It is cash according to GAAP. There is quite a bit of valuable staff time spent in corporations explaining this difference.

Accounting is fine with those entries, as it should be, since the entries meet the objectives of established accounting principles. And since the bank statement will show the deposit as part of the ledger balance, bank reconciliation seems pretty manageable. The available balance seems like some soothing background noise to be ignored.

Day 3. The funds become available.

The balance sheet before the transaction is the same as before:

Cash	$1,125,000
Accounts Rec.	$575,000
Equipment	$400,000

Is an entry made to the general ledger that reflects the availability of funds?

Debit:	No entry made
Credit:	No entry made

The balance sheet after the transaction is exactly the same, since nothing is recorded for accounting purposes in this model. The Treasurer is very interested in the fact that funds are now available to use. He perhaps secretly believes that the Controller views the availability of funds as something akin to fiction and puts on a great impersonation in the Controller's voice, saying "I can't be overdrawn—we have cash in the general ledger." In many organizations, the Controller wisely ignores impersonations and is focused on accurate reporting of the financial records of the firm.

Cash	$1,125,000
Accounts Rec.	$575,000
Equipment	$400,000

This looks familiar.

No entry is made for this event. There is no transaction that hits the bank account; the bank already recorded this activity and gave ledger credit on day 1. On day 3 it granted availability, but it does not report a separate transaction on the bank statement. This process works for accounting. The bank reported a distribution of float based on the total deposit. In this example, all $125,000 worth of the deposit had a two-day float.

Treasury recognizes that it may have some explaining to do since it looks as though it should be investing $1,125,000. However, Treasury can be responsible only for investing the $1,000,000 that can be invested. And, when the additional funds are available to invest on day 3, Treasury will be ready.

In examining Exhibit 6.6, notice days across the top with two sections in the rows: bank and book. By viewing the bank section first, we see the following:

Day 0 Ledger and available amounts match.

Day 1 The ledger and available amounts also match. The funds were deposited on this day (consistent with a normal calendar), but they were brought to the bank at 3 P.M., which in the banking world is now day 2. Sometimes it is simpler to recognize that bankers have created this alternative world rather than trying to figure everything out.

Day 2 The ledger balance increases to $1.125M. This is the bank's view from an accounting basis. Available cash remains at $1M, since the deposited check will not clear back to the bank for some time. Therefore, ledger or accounting credit was received. However, you have yet to receive availability for those funds.

Day 5 The available balance has increased to $1.125M, now matching the ledger balance. The funds cleared or were made available. These funds can now be used. The hold on the funds was lifted. Fortunately for our example, no other transactions hit the bank account—which can make it more difficult to understand what is going on here.

DAY:	0	1	2	3	4	5	6
Bank — Ledger	$1M	$1M	$1.125M	$1.125M	$1.125M	$1.125M	$1.125M
Bank — Available	$1M	$1M	$1M	$1M	$1M	$1.25M	$1.25M
Company Books: GL — GAAP Cash	$1M	$1.125M	$1.125M	$1.125M	$1.125M	$1.125M	$1.125M
Company Books: GL — A/R	$700K	$575K	$575K	$575K	$575K	$575K	$575K

The deposit hit the bank after that day's cut-off time of 3 P.M.

EXHIBIT 6.6 GAAP versus Bank Balance—Collection Example

Discussion

GAAP requirements for *reporting* cash do not, by themselves, make it resistant to more effective *recording* methods. GAAP requires cash to be reported in financial statements in a particular manner, and is certainly inflexible in its pronouncements. However, it is within the realm of acceptable accounting to be able to gracefully track float and separately track various liabilities for the benefit of Treasury.

Additionally, recording these transactions differently will provide an improvement to the accounting controls and processes. The changes employed will benefit and assist the Controller's function while supporting good treasury practices at the organization in the general ledger. The techniques and theories behind this are in use by many leading organizations. Using current technology enables this to be a win-win situation and is worthy of a separate and detailed discussion.

Technology Enables Appropriate Cash Recording and Reporting

Recording cash in the general ledger (GL) in a way that is useful to the Treasurer and complies with accounting principles is crucial in several ways.

For the Treasurer, having this information in the GL allows for easy access to history, since the GL is the book of record and is accessible for a long period of time.

For the Controller, since the entries are now largely generated in an automated manner, the added information that can be seen in the general ledger will lead to easier bank reconciliations and improved control with regard to a number of balance sheet accounts, as each stage in the financial process will be reflected financially. It is straightforward and simple work to make the financial reporting interrogate and combine the proper balance sheet accounts to properly report cash according to GAAP.

Current technology provides Treasurers and Controllers the ability to meet both reporting and cash management objectives gracefully. Automated recording allows this type of segregation duties to exist. The better segregation of duties occurs because:

1. Treasury records all cash and can do so in an automated manner.
2. Operating areas record their subledger directly.
3. Bank reconciliation is simplified as all bank transactions are specifically recorded and matched quickly.
4. Subledger reconciliation is far simpler. On a daily and automated basis, Treasury will create entries to cash and cash clearing for each particular area or department. That department will have specific responsibility to remove those items from the cash-clearing account. Any item that is not cleared quickly from the cash-clearing account will be obvious from its age.
5. It supports an efficient design for the bank system for Treasury purposes.
6. It supports the accounting needs and meets them and actually strengthens them through a clear segregation of duties.

Typical cash reporting to meet GAAP requirements often results in the situation where the books do not reflect bank activity even closely. For example, an outstanding check liability is sometimes not captured separately in the books of the organization. In addition, because there are entries made only at certain times and only with GAAP in mind, it often becomes much harder to reconcile differences within areas and between units, and the segregation of duties and functions oftentimes suffers.

In collection activity, checks are received in-house. A check might be received in a lockbox. Let's look at what those entries are from a GAAP perspective.

The check is received in-house.

Debit:	Cash $35,000
Credit:	Accounts Receivable $35,000

EXHIBIT 6.7 GAAP Perspective

The receivable is reduced as shown in Exhibit 6.7.

Several solutions exist to address these different views of cash that will allow Treasury and anyone using the financial statements to be able to see the impact of cash that is still in the clearing process. At the point of check issue, the debit can be made to expense and instead of a credit to cash, there will be a credit to cash clearing. See Exhibit 6.8.

A. Debit: Expense	$770	
Credit: Cash Clearing	$770	

The entry above is made by the accounts payable area. As the checks are cleared, instead of not making an entry, Treasury would automatically make the following entry:

B. Debit: Cash Clearing	$550	
Credit: Cash	$550	

This would be recorded by the Treasury area based off of the electronic data feed from the bank of paid items. This entry would be reflected in the T-Accounts in Exhibit 6.9.

Reporting GAAP cash allows you to combine both cash and cash-clearing accounts to report GAAP cash. It also allows you to see the distinctions between outstanding checks—what is going to clear, where you

Expense	Cash Clearing	Cash
A. + 770	+ 770 A.	

EXHIBIT 6.8 Cash Clearing (1)

Expense		Cash Clearing—Disbursements		Cash	
A. + 770			+ 770 A.		550 B.
		B. – 550			
			220		

EXHIBIT 6.9 Cash Clearing (2)

will need actual funds from a Treasury perspective and yet maintain the ability to report the GAAP cash—and will provide a good segregation of duties because only Treasury is entering cash.

Cash clearing provides the controlling mechanism for the accounts payable area in this case, so there is a clear segregation of duties. The bank reconciliation becomes easy, cash-clearing accounts are resolved on a daily basis, and items should not be sitting in a cash-clearing account for more than a few days.

The cash-clearing account for outstanding check liabilities should match the balance of outstanding checks that the firm has. Simply put, any outstanding check liability represents items from the accounting perspective that are already cashed, but addresses these as separate items.

Cash Implications

Cash from a Treasury and accounting perspective can vary quite radically. Cash in the context of generally accepted accounting principles (GAAP) has a particular connotation.

Many a Treasury group has had to reconcile the differences between GAAP cash and what is actually at the bank. And this is not just talking about deposits in transit or simply timing issues. This exercise typically reminds Treasury staff of the phrase "I can't be out of cash, I still have checks." Just because an organization has GAAP cash does not mean those funds can be invested or used to pay bills.

Astute companies avoid this situation by meeting the reporting requirements for GAAP and providing for the distinction between funds that are available for use and those funds that are not available by recording those initial entries against a cash-clearing account. For example, when a deposit is prepared in house, the entry is made to debit cash clearing and credit accounts receivable. When the deposit is reported by the bank on its previous day reporting system, an automated entry will be made by Treasury.

This entry will reduce cash clearing and increase cash by debiting cash and crediting cash clearing. To report cash for GAAP purposes they will combine the cash and cash-clearing accounts. This allows companies to have a clearer view into the various cash components directly in the general ledger.

Summary

Understanding the different needs and perspectives of cash is of great value to the Treasurer and to Treasury. Such an understanding provides a good background to further understand the necessary framework for optimizing the use of cash and the financial statements without creating a war between the Controller and the Treasurer.

The benefits of understanding the framework for optimal cash recording allow the thoughtful and Strategic Treasurer to explain how to better record transactions in order to align the records for Treasury needs while maintaining integrity for GAAP reporting. Technology to automate this process is broadly available and serves many other useful functions for the Strategic Treasurer. There are three key concepts to remember:

1. Cash means different things to Treasurers and Controllers.
2. Treasury needs can be addressed in a manner fully compliant with GAAP reporting.
3. Treasury's need for cash recording provides for better controls and improved information in the financial records of the organization.

CHAPTER 7

Owning Working Capital

Working capital is not just ratios and balances on paper. It exists out in the operations of the company. By going out to the local divisions and watching how the receivables, payables and other areas function, you will truly understand the working capital of your business, how it works and how it can be optimized.

—Arthur P. Lorenz, Treasurer & Director of Financial Planning & Analysis, HunterDouglas

The Treasurer is often the rightful owner of working capital and must, therefore, manage it appropriately. To accomplish this goal, there are some new methods and techniques that are gaining traction with Treasurers. The value of optimizing most organizations' working capital is well recognized. And every well-run organization manages working capital in a thoughtful and active manner.

The following will identify and distinguish two common definitions of *working capital* and their differing purposes. The two methods will be explained. Appropriate and different uses will be discussed, and the impact of distinctions between liquidity measures and historical working capital–related items will be highlighted. Several considerations will be explored along the lines of projecting working capital usage and, finally, several areas of recommendations will be presented to assist those who are charged with managing working capital.

Two Definitions of Working Capital

The term *working capital* refers to a formula. Since there are two primary definitions of working capital—accounting and treasury—it is instructive to know which one is being referred to in order to understand the context.

Working Capital: Accounting Definition (Traditional)

The first definition may be referred to as the "accounting definition of working capital." This definition is also known by many to be the traditional formula for working capital. The definition, shown as a formula, is:

Working Capital = Current Assets − Current Liabilities

Or shortened : WC = CA − CL

This method of calculating working capital is useful and simple to calculate. Anyone with access to the balance sheet can calculate the organization's accounting working capital. This measurement is still quite common. Some lenders continue to use this as one important measure of an organization's ability to meet current obligations.

Please note, however, that this formula is inadequate if one wishes to determine the value of converting accounts receivable (A/R) items (a current asset) to cash (also a current asset). This formula would not reflect that change because the formula was not designed with that purpose in mind. It is not designed to help an organization manage its key working capital categories. It remains a useful formula that serves its intended purpose. But it is not the only formula an organization needs.

Working Capital: Treasury Definition (Alternative)

The second definition is the "Treasury definition of working capital." This definition is more widely known as either the adjusted or alternative formula for working capital. This formula is used by those who are charged with optimizing and improving working capital in their organizations. The definition, shown as a formula, is:

Adjusted Working Capital = Accounts Receivable + Inventory −

Accounts Payable

Or shortened : adjusted WC = A/R + Inv − A/P

This measurement consolidates the cash conversion cycle balance sheet components. This formula is typically used by those who are responsible for improving the total organizational costs of working capital. When using this formula, it is easy to see the change achieved by more rapidly converting receivables to cash.

This obvious benefit would reduce working capital (referred to as *adjusted working capital* in this section to distinguish it from the traditional measure). Throughout this book, the term *working capital*, when used by itself, refers to the Treasury or alternative definition, and not the accounting or historical usage of that term.

Having more working capital in the first model indicates, within ranges, that the organization has a greater ability to meet short-term financial demands and would be in a better financial position. Thus, when using the term *working capital* and considering it from the accounting or traditional standpoint, it is typically more desirable to have more of this type of working capital than less of it. However, having more working capital is often not considered beneficial when examining it from the perspective of the Treasury definition. It may, in fact, represent a problem.

Simply collecting accounts receivable more slowly or actively building a firm's inventory levels up will increase the level of working capital. When an organization is seeking to improve working capital, it often intends to reduce the level of working capital to an optimal level. The goal of working capital optimization indicates that the optimal or best level of working capital is not at the lowest level possible.

For example, stopping sales on credit may do amazing things to help drive down accounts receivable numbers and reduce working capital. However, this will have some unintended consequences that are even more amazing and frightening. Eliminating credit will turn sales away to competitors, which will in turn harm profitability. This unpleasant and very negative financial result is what can happen when the focus is narrowly on decreasing working capital and not optimizing it appropriately.

Similarly, an excessive reduction in inventory may delight those who focus solely on the balance sheet. But the tradeoff of lost sales will not be a prudent exchange. And a company's suppliers may decide to halt shipments if it unilaterally decides to increase its days payable outstanding (DPO) by an additional 30 days.

One way to distinguish the two definitions of working capital is by asking the question of whether it is preferable to have more working capital or less. For those considering the accounting or traditional method, the typical answer is "more." For those looking at working capital optimization and using the Treasury or alternative method, the response will generally be "less." To properly answer this leading question would require a response that addresses the need to optimize working capital.

Two Different Measurements for Working Capital

Working toward the optimal equilibrium between the balance sheet (working capital) and income statement (sales and margins) is of critical importance. Accordingly, optimizing working capital rather than simply seeking to increase or decrease it is far more fitting. The metrics used within organizations can sometimes inadvertently create more challenges in maintaining this equilibrium.

The reason for two different measures for working capital components are driven by two different purposes. It is incorrect to argue which one is better, since they both serve different purposes. Knowing the purpose can give one the ability to apply the proper formula and interpret both the data and the results. Again, working capital management focuses on three key elements:

1. Accounts receivable
2. Inventory
3. Accounts payable

When seeking to optimize working capital, measurements and trends are needed in each area to properly focus attention on proper behaviors and to elicit positive change in order to accomplish the goals. In addition to the detailed look at each of these three components, the Treasurer must have an understanding of the total cost of working capital and its impact on the organization. One set of measurements is extremely useful for the individual components. The other is appropriate for looking at working capital broadly.

The Traditional Method

The traditional measurements for working capital components are known as days sales outstanding (for A/R), days inventory (for inventory), and days payable (for accounts payable (A/P). Exhibit 7.1 shows the formulas for the traditional method in the top section.

In this exhibit, we see the formulas showing inventory, accounts receivable, and accounts payable in the numerator and either sales or cost of goods sold (CGS) in the denominator. Some methods of calculating those numbers are based off of an average between two balance sheet reporting periods. (*Note: This book is not intended to provide all of the various formulas and reasoning behind each one.*)

For two of the three formulas—days inventory (DI) and days payable (DP)—use CGS for the denominator. This is certainly appropriate when looking at inventory and payables as the values align and will provide a reasonable approximation of how many days. Since this formula is intended to show how much inventory is available in terms of days, either CGS or sales must be used as the denominator, and CGS is appropriate for the reasons discussed; the explanation is fairly straightforward to those who have

---

Uses CGS and Sales to Reflect Related Items

Traditional—*Uses Cost of Goods Sold (CGS) and Sales appropriately to reflect the most closely related items.*

- Days Inventory: **Inventory/CGS** ×365
- Days Receivable: **Accounts Receivable/Sales** ×365
- Days Payable: **Accounts Payable/CGS** ×365
  Utilize formula to identify issues in specific working capital area.
  Note: Different denominators make cross-comparison inappropriate.

Alternative—*Uses Sales to reflect a common basis for the total cost.*
- Days Inventory: **Inventory/Sales** ×365
- Days Receivable: **Accounts Receivable/Sales** ×365
- Days Payable: **Accounts Payable/Sales** ×365

Cash Conversion Cycle:
- Days Inventory + Days Receivable – Days Payable
  Used to understand the overall impact and cost of working capital.

EXHIBIT 7.1 Metrics for Working Capital and Liquidity

an accounting or finance background. Those readers with an accounting or finance background may wish to jump ahead to the next section.

Using CGS as the denominator for these calculations (DI and DP), the result is a number of days. Since inventory and payables are most closely related to the cost used to acquire inventory (and therefore what the firm will also need to disperse), using CGS will provide a good reflection on the number of days of inventory (or payables) on a macro basis. This is true whether the profit margin is 50 percent or 10 percent. Thus, the basic mathematical ability to compare, for example, DPO between two different firms is possible. Other differences between firms and the level of financial statement details remain and create other challenges.

In Exhibit 7.2, the summation showed question marks. While some calculate this number, it has no useful financial value when discussing days. The three question marks in the illustration indicate that the total of the three traditional metrics is not an appropriate number. This is due to the fact that the calculations are based on different denominators when using the traditional metrics.

The calculation of days sales outstanding (DSO) uses accounts receivable in the numerator and divides that by sales. Since accounts receivable is largely created by sales, using sales in the denominator will cause the result to approximately reflect how many days' worth of average sales are still receivable. This would be true regardless of the margin the firm has on its

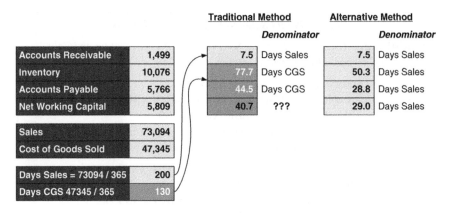

Alternative method uses sales as a common denominator and allows
the total of the three categories to be compatible.

EXHIBIT 7.2 Comparison of Formulas

products. As noted earlier, the actual formula for calculating DSO includes
multiple numbers to create an average. Exhibit 7.3 provides a comparison
of the formulas showing differences between two individual components
and the total.

The traditional method for calculating DSO, DI, and DPO is useful for
various purposes including:

- **Monitoring and management of specific areas of the cash conversion cycle (CCC).** These measures provide useful information for

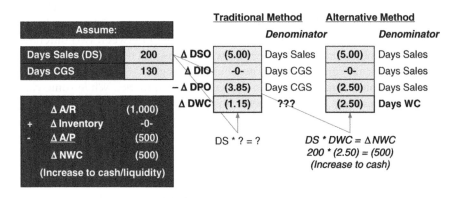

Days Sales (DS) * Δ Days Working Capital (Δ DWC) =
Change in Net Working Capital (NWC)

EXHIBIT 7.3 Continuation of Comparison of Formulas from Exhibit 7.2

a particular area of the cash conversion cycle and act as a baseline for determining the current performance as well as performance changes over time. They allow the organization to easily compare performance between different departments or divisions. They also allow the organization to make external comparisons on a more consistent basis. And while there are many caveats to making those comparisons, the ability to make careful and deliberate comparisons can be therapeutic to an organization seeking to improve working capital use.

- **Simple to calculate and understand.** Both the traditional and alternative measures are based on data that is provided in the financial statements of the organization. This makes it easy to pull historical information and run the working capital formulas without requiring some special reporting or research. From a forecasting perspective, it is relatively easy to convert from days to a financial amount by making assumptions. Increasing inventory or sales will likely have a direct and proportional impact on the amount of working capital needed. It is, therefore, a simple calculation to determine the level of change in working capital required, based on the particular area examined.

The traditional measurements are generally very useful for companies to make comparisons against themselves over time. And traditional metrics provide a basis for careful and thoughtful comparisons with competitors. Additionally, they provide for a relatively consistent measure that allows for comparison with other industries that is at least proportional, even if many other differences and nuances exist.

The Alternative Method

The alternative measure is useful for examining the total cost of working capital for all three components. The traditional method uses two different denominators to calculate the three measures. The result of these calculations comes in the unit of measure referred to as "days."

The challenge of the traditional measure comes when comparisons between the different components are made and as the organization explores different options to manage working capital. A day may equal a day from a time perspective. But a day does not translate to the same amount of working capital for all three measures.

An improvement of a day with DSO, for example, results in a corresponding amount of financial benefit with the unit of measure being dollars or the local currency. The difficulty arises when the discussion starts comparing a change in days for DPO or inventory with DSO. The difficulty arises since these are not intended to be combined. They use different denominators. Combining this information will result in confusion.

This confusion has been evident in various professional presentations and from analyst groups where days and values are combined without first ensuring clarity of numbers or value between the different categories. Taking the value of A/R, adding inventory and subtracting A/P, provides the total amount of working capital used with currency as the unit of measure. This results in a dollar figure.

Taking the days of A/R, adding inventory and subtracting A/P, provides some sense of the amount of time it takes for all three pieces of a firm's cash conversion cycle to complete their cycles, which has some specific uses. However, it does not provide the financial valuation for the alternatives. In other words, one might arrive at the same number of days in the working capital conversion cycle by making a change that is helpful but will not show up in the formula.

The alternative method uses sales for the denominator in all three instances. This will appear to reduce DSO and DI versus the traditional method. Since the three measures have the same unit of measure, one day has the same financial value no matter which component is being explored. The alternative method is not the best formula to use when examining only DSO or DI.

Since the basic working capital formula is based off of the dollar value, using the simple formula for working capital (A/R + Inv − A/P) will not vary whether looking at the traditional or alternative method.

The alternative method has become widely accepted through various means. The annual working capital survey published by *CFO* magazine since 1997 has served as a major catalyst to popularize this method of calculation.

Working Capital Impact on Organizational Value

Changes in working capital usage typically influence the value of the organization. This influence can either be negative or positive. Henry Waszkowski, former head of the Wachovia Treasury & Financial Consulting group, highlighted the logical domino effect of a significant increase in working capital.

Exhibit 7.4 shows the progression of an increase in working capital causing a draw on cash. This naturally results in greater borrowing or a decrease in the level of investment. This increases interest expense based on a larger amount borrowed. Additionally, outside certain ranges, this may also result in a higher rate being charged for borrowing these funds. Because of the higher interest expense, the organization's income will be lowered. This leads to a deterioration of some key financial ratios, which may ultimately lead to a lower perceived financial rating.

This lower perceived rating brings about a lower financial valuation, resulting in a reduced market capitalization level. Thus, the link between

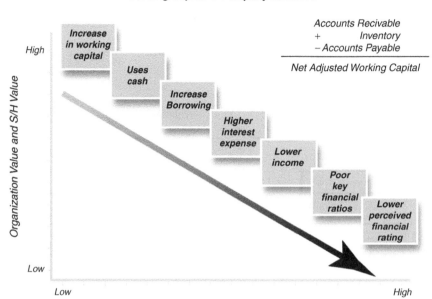

EXHIBIT 7.4 Optimizing Working Capital and Competing Goals

working capital usage and shareholder value (S/H Value) was made. The reverse would begin with less working capital, which frees up cash. Ultimately a higher perceived financial rating and increased market capitalization could be realized.

The correlation is well understood and accepted. Working capital has an influence on the valuation of a firm.

When corporate goals are established, there is usually clarity and agreement as to what they are and signify at an organizational level. Then, as these goals are translated into department responsibilities and metrics are established to help achieve those goals, certain competing activities may emerge.

This is a typical result of the negative aspect of organizational structures. The efficiency of an organization organized by department often leads to a narrow or *silo* focus. The result is less focus or understanding of the impact their actions will have up or down the financial processes from where these activities originated. These activities, created by intelligent and well-intentioned people, are meant to support the overall goals. The result is typically quite different. It is generally the result of optimizing part of the process, which inevitably suboptimizes the whole.

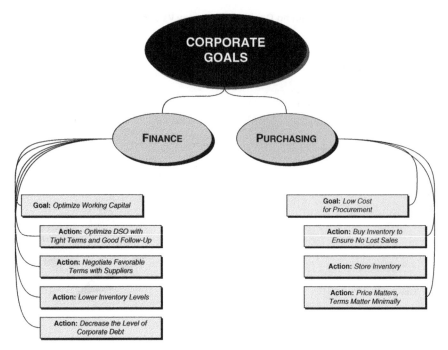

EXHIBIT 7.5 Differing Departmental Goals

Exhibit 7.5 shows how finance and purchasing have created different goals that seem to support the overall organization. However, as they have translated their goals into more narrow actions, they may be unintentionally fighting against one another. For example, the head of purchasing may be supporting the overall financial performance goal in her mind by decreasing CGS, by making huge purchases of inventory to gain a large discount. The unintended consequence of the extra financial cost of inventory is never fully recognized or understood by the head of purchasing.

Alternatively, Treasury may promote activities and actions designed to support a lower level of balance sheet concentration into working capital components by issuing an edict to reduce inventory to a specific level. If enacted, this can negatively impact both sales and CGS to a far greater level than the balance sheet benefits derived.

Solutions and goals should not be designed in a vacuum. This is especially true for those organizations that seek to *optimize* working capital. It is crucial that many in the organization are mindful of how competing goals can be established as they seek to optimize working capital. Indeed, those who plan and work on making improvements in working capital find that setting the proper expectations is also highly important.

The fact that different measures are used for working capital and liquidity can create confusion and can raise improper expectations. Effective communication about which measure is being used can help reduce the danger of confusion by ensuring expectations and understandings are consistent and appropriate.

Competing goals arise between departments, as illustrated earlier. Competing demands can also be viewed at the financial statement level. A sole focus on working capital usually means that the balance sheet holds a dominant position in the mind of that department, while another department may be focused on the income statement almost to the complete exclusion of the balance sheet perspective of the business. Exhibit 7.6 shows one example of the connectedness of these different viewpoints.

Differences Between Liquidity and Historical Working Capital Measures

It is generally well understood that setting realistic expectations is a prudent course of action. This is certainly true with regard to working capital management. However, Treasurers face a challenge due to some key differences between liquidity measurements and working capital calculations. It is imperative that Treasurers set proper expectations, using both perspectives, and make certain to explain the difference to their management as they start their various working capital initiatives.

Some significant and positive changes that improve the level of liquidity for the organization show little or no impact on working capital measures. The primary reason for these differences stems from the timing disconnect of the accounting and of funds availability.

For example, a company seeks to improve working capital and overall process efficiency by moving more customer receipts to an electronic process. Currently, the organization has payments sent to their office location for funds application and then has the checks brought to the bank for deposit. In this situation, A/R is reduced on the day of receipt. The funds may become available funds that can be used by the organization about the third or fourth business day after receipt based on deposit and clearing float.

Working with key customers to make their payments electronically may result in no change in A/R. The A/R balance is the General Ledger (G/L) figure used in the calculation of DSO. Therefore, this process improvement may result in no change in the reported working capital metric. Notably, the firm may have use of funds three or four days sooner. This is significant, and this benefit may have been used to justify the effort of moving customers to electronic payment methods. The topic of cash and some of these differences is covered in more detail in Chapters 5 and 6.

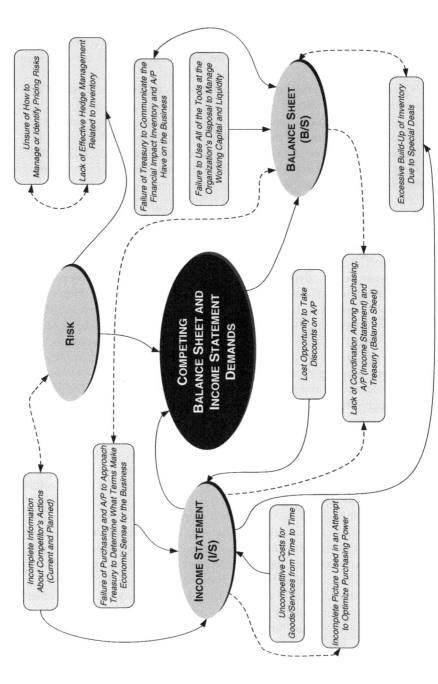

EXHIBIT 7.6 Optimizing Requires Balancing Competing Demands

In this example, at the outset of the work to support this electronic receipts initiative, the Treasurer would identify the expected magnitude of the liquidity improvement. Concurrently, the Treasurer would note that the working capital measure may show little or no effect of this financial improvement. As the work of this initiative progresses and finally concludes, the Treasurer needs to report on both the achieved liquidity benefit and the reported working capital measurement improvement.

Projecting Working Capital Usage and Variations

In making projections of future working capital usage from a capital-planning perspective a common technique is to model the current process and use sales as an input into the equation. As organizations look to better optimize their working capital usage, they seek not merely to forecast, but to impact their working capital usage and then project what those changes will mean to the balance sheet.

Projections will often include the following considerations:

- **Self-comparison.** When did each process (accounts payable, accounts receivable, inventory) achieve their best numerical performance? What did those best-year performances look like from a business perspective? Was anyone abusing the system at the time? What amount of working capital would be reasonable today in each area without any changes? What if all three areas had their best year last year (the lowest DSO, DI, and highest DPO)? How much working capital would have been freed up?
- **Opportunities and impact.** How are things changing in your business? What opportunities exist in each area of the financial process? What countries and regions are you expanding in? What is going on in the business mix that will or could change your results? Much ink has been spilled over the impact of globalization already. These are a few areas that can influence Treasury's forecast and projections for working capital usage.

Differences abound. For example, one may find a 50- to 60-day difference in DSO between the United States and Italy or between other regions and countries. Using this example, if sales in Italy grow disproportionately faster, this will create a greater demand on working capital. The total company-wide DSO may increase, which appears to be negative. This may be in spite of significant progress being made but is covered up by a shift of business percentage across regions.

Creating a usable model that weights growth and changes by either percentage or value is highly useful. Outlining the assumptions and exposing them to others provides critical feedback while educating others on what these changes mean to the financial statements and to the business.

Steps Needed to Optimize Working Capital

Treasurers and organizations that seek to better manage working capital take several critical steps to achieve their goals. As the overseer or owner of working capital, the Treasurer will need to lead these activities and form a working capital council.

The first step, even before forming the working capital council, involves gathering initial working capital measurements for a number of periods and analyzing the data and the specifics of the organization's situation and recent history.

Optimizing working capital in an organization requires intelligent participation by a number of people representing different areas of the organization. In order to achieve such educated involvement the Treasurer or chief financial officer will form and chair a working capital council. In order to be most effective, the name of the council as well as its organizational structure may vary based on the company's culture.

Forming a Working Capital Council

The working capital council is an organization made up of multiple disciplines and is chaired by the Treasurer. The goals are to drive behavior to have an effective working capital council that provides guidance and insight, and drives the proper activities as well as the right thinking in the organization, which are to educate, report, and evangelize the necessary activities and the value to the organization. They are able to speak in the vernacular. They will be able to translate working capital terms into business language in a way that people will be able to understand and act on them and see the correlation between their actions and total financial performance.

The working capital council will bring in and engage key players as leaders. The participants will come from sales, credit, inventory, purchasing, payables—even Treasury and Controllers will be part of this group. The group will establish metrics and work on eliminating some of the competing key performance indicators (KPI) issues that come up where one KPI is waging war against another or is impairing the other.

The following outline shows a few characteristics and starting suggestions to form a working capital council.

- **Establish council mission and objectives.** While the leadership group will refine both the mission and objectives, the Treasurer should create a draft of both. Among some sample mission and general council objectives:
  - **Mission.** To ensure that the organization optimizes the use of working capital (AR, AP, inventory) in concert with other business objectives and needs.
  - **Objectives.**
    - Educate personnel on the impact and influence of working capital on profit and business operations.
    - Identify issues and trends and become proactive in the management of working capital.
    - Encourage and incentivize proper behavior.
    - Optimize the balance sheet and income statement tradeoffs.
    - Perform this work in concert with broader liquidity planning.
- **Establish the leadership group.** The Treasurer or senior appointee chairs the leadership council. Senior members have significant control or influence over sales, inventory, or other pieces of the cash conversion cycle.
- **Preliminary analysis.** Analyze the company's performance against its historical performance in recent years and against well-understood peers to arrive at some preliminary projections. These projections will include secular changes as well as changes brought about by intentional activity and focus on working capital optimization.
- **Create initial education plan.** Show the links between effective working capital management and achieving the overall goals of the organization. Explain how current processes and measurements tie in to the broader organization goals and measurements. Discuss the challenge of balancing the income statement drivers with the balance sheet considerations. Translate this information into the language and ideas that the rest of the organization can readily understand and apply.
- **Create the initial metric(s).** These metrics will be reported and ensure that this measurement is part of the compensation plan.
- **Form process teams from the order-to-collect or procure-to-pay business processes.** Provide some specific accountabilities and target dates to report back to the working capital council. Involving the owners of the financial process enhances credibility throughout the organization. Importantly, it increases the overall level of understanding of the impact of various activities on working capital and how that drives overall financial performance.

Working Capital Council Team's Responsibilities

The council leadership teams have authority and responsibility to educate and improve working capital by:

- Analyzing and improving the processes under that team's purview.
- Creating and delivering ongoing education as to the impact of working capital management on the organization, its process, and the individual functional areas.
- Reporting the results and initiatives of the group to the departments and areas that are part of its sphere of influence.
- Determining detailed metrics and measurements that can be created and reported automatically; the link between improvements and compensation will be substantial, clearly identified, and tracked.
- Optimizing working capital by educating, reporting, and driving proper behaviors throughout the organization.

Summary

The Treasurer and Treasury need to be active in moving from observer to overseer and, ultimately, to owner of working capital. This takes time and requires achieving success along the way. It requires understanding, education, and the support of others. It provides a key opportunity to help individual units help the organization meet its goals and achieve its objectives.

Engaging in such activities will stretch many a Treasurer and almost all Treasury staffs to become effective owners of working capital. It requires much communication and influence and will be outside the comfort zone for many. Those who remember working capital management is a process and not an event provide far greater value to their organizations than those who hold a more narrow view.

Understanding the different meanings and measurements of working capital is just the initial step in optimizing working capital. Working capital must be neither minimized nor maximized. But rather, it must be optimized. This optimization must balance working capital targets with income statement drivers and the overall needs of the organization.

No matter how financially strong an organization is at present, it cannot be considered excellent if it fails to be intentional and effective in how it manages and optimizes its use of working capital. All well-run organizations manage working capital in a thoughtful manner. Understanding the different metrics and business changes is important. Getting all of the right people pulling in the same direction requires commitment, perseverance, and communication—a job that is perfectly suited for the Strategic Treasurer!

CHAPTER 8

Differences Between a Process View and a Silo View

Optimizing part of the process suboptimizes the whole.

—Anonymous

D iscussions about processes may cause a soporific feeling that will not dissipate, no matter how much caffeine is consumed. To the Treasurer, process discussions often seem to be very uninteresting and operational in nature. As a Treasurer, there is a need to be strategic and rise above the level of operations. However true that may be in theory, there are some key points that a Treasurer should understand about the value of understanding the financial processes. The dialogue will be kept at a high level. There will not be discussion about process mapping theory or how to create effective swim lane charts.

The Process Perspective Is Vital

It is impossible for a Treasury department to be strategic and effective if it does not take deliberate steps to understand the financial processes of the organization. Since the Treasury group seeks to be a valuable business partner that will act as a positive agent of change, it must know how the financial process works in order to make improvements. The Treasurer and

Treasury must understand how their activities and work should support the overall objectives of the organization.

To support the overall objectives requires knowing what is being supported including the financial processes that touch Treasury at some point. To be improved or optimized, every financial process must be examined and redesigned in the context of the overall process of where they reside.

Optimize the Entire Process

Exhibit 8.1 shows the order-to-pay and order-to-collect processes. There are multiple departments involved with each section. Each department has an impact on the process efficiency. And since these financial processes are part of the cash conversion cycle, each department can impact working capital and liquidity in a negative or positive manner. Treasury is greatly concerned about working capital management and liquidity. If Treasury takes a narrow view of its responsibilities and looks only at the actions within its immediate and direct control, the results will be negative. Working capital will suboptimize and cost the organization greatly. Processes and services from external services will not address the core needs as appropriately and effectively as necessary.

The Treasurer must ensure that Treasury is helping the organization succeed. Taking the process view into consideration for process efficiency efforts for improving working capital will directly support the mission of the organization. Accomplishing those things is required for the Strategic Treasurer. Conversely, focusing narrowly on only a department's part of the process puts the organization and the Treasurer in an inefficient and operational mode.

Tunnel (Silo) Vision

While Henry Ford's specialization brought a new level of efficiency into the workforce, such a process can easily foster a type of tunnel vision in many people. As staff focus solely on their area of expertise and responsibility, it is natural to develop an insular view about their activities.

Having tunnel vision can create unintended consequences. Competing key performance indicators (KPIs) are a common result. The metrics used to drive the cash application group to greater speed in posting items can have the unintended consequence of creating larger problems downstream. As more items are assigned incorrectly some of the unintended consequences include angering the client, creating larger delays in payments and receipts, and more time spent talking to customers about misapplication and credit issues than necessary. This ultimately creates more work for other members of the credit and sales group.

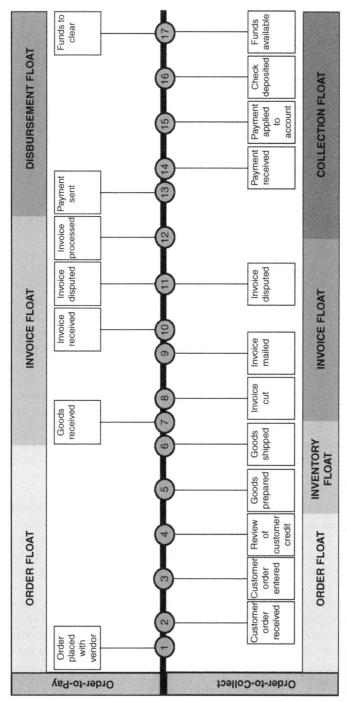

EXHIBIT 8.1 The Interconnected Steps of the Cash Conversion Cycle

Understanding the Entire Process

In tracking and mapping the entire process, it is easier to realize why people upstream perform functions in a certain way. This may allow them to better adapt their work to make it easier on the downstream recipient. Alternatively, they can show or demonstrate the tremendously difficult situation they are placed in by what someone, perhaps unwittingly, is doing upstream. In this way, they can now communicate effectively or offer suggestions on how this could be done better.

Beyond simply assessing the process together, seeing what others are doing is useful. The occasional exchange of roles or staff for a few days or weeks gives a certain perspective that was heretofore impossible to achieve. This exchange of staff can have similar results as the marriages between kingdoms had in the past. More peaceful coexistence and cooperation would be possible, and outright wars would be unlikely.

The handoff between runners is usually the point where a relay race is won or lost. By examining the process from department silo to department silo, the Treasury staff will clearly observe all manner of awkward and inefficient handoffs. Seeing control logs that serve only to point the blame in the event of a problem initially seems logical, then excessive and, finally, absurd. These controls are often bolted-on activities that neither foster teamwork nor truly make the process less error prone. Control logs serve a primary function of pointing blame away from the log owner.

Departments are interconnected by the various financial processes that they participate in. By taking a process view, Treasury steps out of its comfort zone and is better for it. To understand a business process correctly requires the internal Treasury consultant to look at separate activities and controls as a single process. She must synthesize different disciplines to ensure that all who are involved understand it and make proper changes to improve the process.

The process involves accounting and other controls that should work together in a balanced manner for the effort to be optimized. Treasury will typically begin to understand what must happen by looking at the account structure and how transactions will flow through the bank accounts. While an appropriate starting point, it cannot be the end point.

You must understand each step of the process and the corresponding accounting entries and controls. This will help ensure that the subledger and bank reconciliation activities can be performed properly. Some of the biggest problems in processes stem from forcing or taking a limited view of the activities and excluding those upstream or downstream.

Symptoms of a Silo View

In an effort to eradicate the myopic silo view within an organization, it is helpful to identify the symptoms of that view. These symptoms become more apparent through several channels. Certain phrases that are used may either indicate a complete disregard for a process view or perhaps reflect a bias for action for its own sake rather than correct action. In addition to phrases, some warning signs may point back to a rampant silo view or perhaps an immature process perspective.

Indicative Phrases

There are a number of common phrases that indicate with a reasonable degree of probability that people are not considering the process or that they may be looking only at one department upstream or downstream from their own department—but no further. The following phrases may trigger a mental warning siren that a process problem could occur without intervention:

- "Why should we involve bank reconciliation? This project doesn't impact them."
- "We'll need to get the ___ department's input, but we'll do that after we make some more key decisions. Besides, they would just slow things down."
- "We have a tight deadline. We can circle back with the other departments after we get things worked out. Besides, Controllers have an extra 40 days to fix their process from a reporting standpoint, and we have to get this thing up in a hurry. Since we have more time to address their needs, we'll take care of those later."
- "They are responsible for controlling the work in their own area. We need to focus on controlling what is in our group."

Warning Signs

While words can alert one to a possible issue, there are other signs that can indicate a silo view prevailed during the design phase of a project:

- The certified public accountants (CPAs) are in charge of the bank reconciliation process since it is so complicated.
- Month-end close is slow and/or regularly delayed.
- It is common to blame problems on other departments. There is little or no agreement about what the root cause of the problem is or how it can be prevented.

- Blame about problems tends to be surprisingly general in nature. No one seems to own the process. The ball is dropped during handoffs between departments.
- Control logs are created to document handoffs. The primary purpose of these control logs is to point blame away from one's department. The control logs are not used to improve a process.
- Subledgers or extensive supporting documentation is spreadsheet based, and multiple, separate reconciliations are necessary to control the activities or to complete the reconciliation work.

Reviewing an audit report and documentation is often useful for many purposes, including seeing where process breakdowns occur between functional departments. External audits (particularly SAS 70 reports) are particularly useful. They can provide additional insight into the mindset of the managers and may detail whether they operate with the process view or are simply focusing on their individual department's responsibilities.

The following statement, taken from an actual SAS 70 report, shows the difference between a process and silo view, indicating each functional area optimizing its own process steps in isolation and identifying risks and implementing controls based on an insular or silo view. When looking at overall efficiency and risks, it is appropriate to look at the entire process. Looking narrowly, one will miss bigger risks and bigger opportunities. The organization that only looks within an area for efficiency or risks will only be able to, at best, suboptimize the whole. This is a common problem. From an SAS 70 report in the risk-management section:

This process requires management to identify significant risks in their areas of responsibility and to implement appropriate measures to address those risks.

Name withheld, Page 7 of 59

This and other paragraphs describing process improvements in isolation are depicted as appropriate, and the firm receives a nice letter for its SAS 70 report that it will then share with its clients. No mention of the failure to look at risks, controls, and efficiency opportunities across and between departments and processes. This, unfortunately, comes from one of the auditing firms that specializes in enterprise risk management and internal controls, and prides itself on being mindful of optimizing the entire process.

Sadly, the type of situation where the focus is exclusively on a particular silo is common. The Strategic Treasurer will work to ensure that his staff's view is one intended to optimize the entire process.

Why the Silo View Must Be Fought

There are many factors that lead people and organizations to view activities through a department or silo lens. This can stem from the organizational pre-occupation and experience within a single silo. Supervisors and managers are usually selected from the ranks of those who perform well at certain tasks within a silo. They typically achieve success with dedicated and narrow focus and will normally continue this trajectory unless something else drives them to a more sustainable and strategic course.

The second law of thermodynamics—that things tend toward disorder—has an impact in organizational efficiency and control. Over time, the broad reasons for a well-designed process will be forgotten, adjustments will be made in isolation, and what was efficient will become less so. The movement is toward decay and inefficiency. Since it is easier for managers to make improvements within their sphere of control, there is a more rapid rate of decay than the second law would indicate.

When an organization focuses on functional responsibilities and seeks to optimize its own part of the process, the overall process becomes sub-optimized. Sometimes this suboptimization becomes humorous, that is, if the example is found in another organization. As mentioned earlier, competing KPIs are an example of a negative result of an insular department focus.

Many financial processes have limited staff and must ensure that appropriate segregation of duties exists. By taking a process view, Treasury and other departments can design better overall controls along the entire process and not just within each department. Additional opportunities to employ effective segregation of duties exist through the use of outside service providers.

Fighting the Silo Mentality with the Process

When fighting against a silo mentality and the negative ramifications of that mindset, it is wise to remember some key points:

- Handoffs are natural in business processes. Handoffs should be smoother than is often the case.
- Handoffs are often where the greatest risks reside. This is where the baton can most easily hit the ground.
- Controls usually are bolted on at the handoff point. These bolted-on controls act like barnacles on a ship. They add weight and cost and decrease efficiency.

- Controls should be part of the process. They need to be baked into the process and not bolted on. Controls should help the organization to accomplish its objectives.
- All new initiatives must consider these facts.
- Processes need to be reviewed regularly.

Summary

Henry Ford is both credited and blamed for the same thing. He is credited with promoting specialization and standardization, resulting in efficient production. Then, Ford is also blamed by some for creating a functional myopia or silo view of work activities. No matter who is to be blamed or credited, Treasurers must understand the importance and implication of having a process view.

Viewing an entire process has enormous implications for risk management, working capital, and liquidity management, controls, and efficiency.

To be an effective and Strategic Treasurer, individuals must understand financial processes. To understand the processes requires an open mind and time to review them. By understanding the financial processes, Treasurers will be able to better act as strategic business partners and establish more appropriate controls and metrics, and they will have far greater success in making changes that help the balance sheet and income statement of their organizations.

CHAPTER 9

Financial Risk Management: Part One

Considering Risk Through the Eye of the Beholder

David W. Stowe

CFA, Director, Strategic Treasurer

Risk management is evaluated and achieved through the simple process of thinking, planning and doing.

—Martin Duncan[1]

R isk is a critical part of the operations and investments of a business. Without risk, returns would be minimal or the barriers to competition low. Although it rarely goes unnoticed, risk may often be either unaddressed, or more typically, poorly addressed or superficially managed.

Why do so many large and apparently sophisticated companies get it wrong? Mostly, this is due to the fact that too little time is spent upfront developing the company's risk management framework, including thoroughly understanding its risk exposures, and, more importantly, deriving clear and measurable objectives to address them. This is a dynamic and ongoing process, which often does not get its due attention.

Often, companies are too quick to jump into hedging without the necessary upfront and ongoing work regarding the risk management process. This leads to ineffective hedging, or a misperception of ineffective hedging, because what one is trying to accomplish in the first place is not fully understood. This obviously makes it difficult to know whether the Treasurer is doing an effective job of managing risk. The goal of this chapter is to provide a general introduction to risk and risk management. While the Treasurer's focus is typically on financial risks, such risks are a subset of more encompassing enterprise risks. As such, the following discussion also touches on the interplay of risks within the enterprise and the potential role for the Treasurer in enterprise risk management (ERM). This chapter should provide a basic understanding of why organizations hedge and what is involved in establishing a risk management framework.

After reading this chapter and Chapter 10, the reader should have a better understanding of what is meant by risk, choices regarding it, the value in managing it, and what is involved in setting up a risk management process. This should help you ask better questions and provide the board of directors with better answers. Or, just as important when dealing with the board, if the Treasurer does not have the answer, she can confidently say, "I don't know the answer, but I do have an action plan."

There are no simple recipes for risk management. It is not a cut-and-dry process; not only is it difficult to accurately quantify risk exposures, but, just as important, it is difficult to fully define or stick to the objectives for the risk management process. In the end, it is often these two critical areas, defining both the exposure and the risk management objectives, that get the lesser attention.

More focus is typically placed on when to execute the hedge. That is, when will I get the best price? Keep in mind it is a dynamic process, potentially based on trial and error, and one needs to be willing to adapt and approve as needed. This can be accomplished only with a clear understanding of one's goals against established performance metrics that provide relevant and value-added feedback.

Finally, an effective risk management process cannot be carried out without the support and buy-in of the board and executive management, for they serve as the proxy for communicating the stakeholders' risk appetite. In order to get their support, it is up to the Treasurer to demonstrate the value in risk management and to have a solid framework for carrying it out (that is, the controls, economics, and accounting aspects that are critical to a complete model).

Risk

Risk typically connotes a negative impact, such as "the exposure to the chance of injury or loss; a hazard or dangerous chance."[2] In finance terms, however, it may be viewed more objectively as the variance in possible outcomes, or the "exposure to uncertainty."[3]

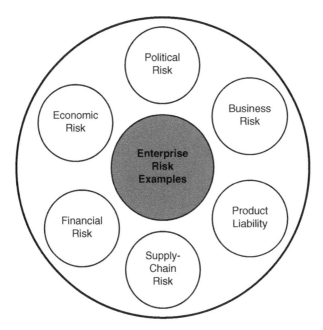

EXHIBIT 9.1 Enterprise Risk Examples

It is understood that we assume risk every day simply by being in business. Hopefully, however, we are taking on calculated risk by choice. That is, the risk is identified, or at least anticipated, as it is often difficult to quantify with a high degree of certainty and to estimate whether the potential benefits of assuming such risk outweigh the potential cost. A robust cost-benefit analysis notwithstanding, even our so-called calculations are still impacted by the unknown. It is often difficult to precisely define risk, or exposure, so it may get only tertiary attention or misplaced attention if the focus is on the wrong risks. The critical question to ask, therefore, is: Are you prepared for the unknown?

As shown in Exhibit 9.1, business managers face a wide variety of risks. So, it is critical that the Treasurer understand what is entailed in identifying and managing the risks the business faces. What is within your role as a Treasurer, and where do you play a role in the risks beyond the typical Treasurer's domain?

Visualizing Risk

Neither is the author a statistician, nor is this a statistics-based book, so, we will stick to the simple basics here; interested readers can find many other books that do a superb job of discussing this area in more detail.[4]

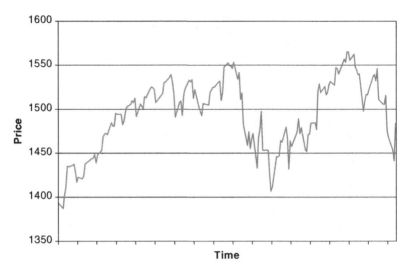

EXHIBIT 9.2 Historical Time Series

HISTORICAL TIME SERIES The adage "a picture is worth a thousand words" is at least doubled when trying to demonstrate to the board, stakeholders, and so on the risks the company is exposed to. While risk is defined and/or measured in many ways, one critical metric is volatility or the variance in returns or price levels, for example.

If there is no volatility, then is there risk? That is really a loaded question because there is always risk—we don't know what we don't know, and that in itself is a risk. Nevertheless, to keep it simple here, the more volatility or variance in the prices, rates, and so on that the business is exposed to, then, logically, the more risk it faces. And there is no better way to *see* volatility than by a simple time-series plot as shown in Exhibit 9.2.

It is simple, but limited. Yet it is one tool in your chest, which not only helps to make the point, visually, but also helps to see from history a potential worst-case scenario, rank possible outcomes by their frequency of occurrence, or, more important, see levels, or thresholds, that would have caused the company financial pain. Keep in mind, however, that history may be of little help in predicting the future; "for the times they are a-changin."[5]

Risk Impact

Volatility is a key concern, but what is the impact of such volatility? If you consume gasoline, then you are exposed to the volatility in oil prices, but is it a risk? To better phrase that: Is it a risk that you need to be concerned with? What is the impact of this volatility? What if the only gas I consume is to fuel my scooter to drive to work? This particular gas consumption would not appear to have much of an impact on my overall cash flow. Therefore, it is the two variables taken together, volatility and cash impact, that determine my risk level.

Note: others may insert *probability of occurrence* in the place of *volatility*. This issue is not being debated here. Since the probability of something occurring—gas prices going to $10/barrel, for example—is unknown, this author prefers to use volatility to demonstrate, not necessarily predict, the impact of risk exposure. This helps when communicating to the board, as one might not want to stand behind one's own probability prediction.

STRESS TEST/SCENARIO ANALYSIS One tool to demonstrate, or view, the potential impact of risk is to employ a simple scenario analysis. That is, view the impact to cash expense, for example, amid various price scenarios for the underlying exposure (see Exhibit 9.3). This can help determine thresholds at which the expense can hit critical levels, or stress points; hence the term *stress test*. In the end, the likelihood of these *thresholds* occurring may be unknown, but based on the potential volatility of the exposure, you know they are possible. And, more important, based on the scenario analysis, it is known that the impact to cash can be severe. Therefore the Treasurer can determine the *action thresholds*, points at which he needs a plan to get out, or put a hedge in place. This is step one, or maybe one of many, in establishing a *hedge objective*.

As with any tool, use of scenario analysis is not without its caveats. It is up to the Treasurer to bring in possible scenarios, either from past

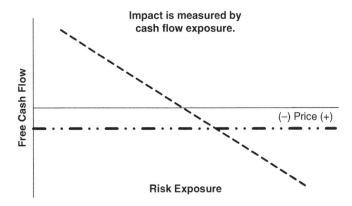

EXHIBIT 9.3 Scenario Analysis

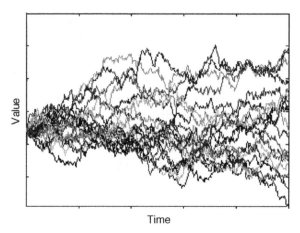

Time

EXHIBIT 9.4 Monte Carlo Simulation

experience (remember the risk of using historical data), or from imagination. In the end, who knows what's going to happen?

SIMULATION MODELS Additionally, there are more advanced, model-based techniques, such as Monte Carlo simulation, that help demonstrate many possible scenarios (see Exhibit 9.4), and the *expected scenario (probability weighted scenario)*. Essentially, this model employs a base case, volatility, a random number generator, and an assumed probability distribution to derive an expected value for the exposure, that is, a future state. Again, this is a way to *visualize* the risk and see the possible paths that the exposure can take. Moreover, once the hedge position is added to the model, a better view of the net position is apparent, as well as a view of how well or poorly the position is protected. These models can be very effective, and are widely employed in both the financial and nonfinancial corporate worlds. Nevertheless, they are only additional tools, which may lead to more effective risk management, but not necessarily to more certain answers. They are not without their limitations.

For example, some of the more widely employed uses of a simulation-based model in risk management within the nonfinancial corporation include a value at risk model (VAR), cash flow at risk model (CFAR), and earnings at risk model (EAR), to name a few.

In general, the value at risk model may be commonly used to derive the expected change in the market value of a portfolio of assets, liabilities, or a combination over a given time period, which is typically very short, at a predetermined confidence level. For example, the VAR model may indicate with 95 percent confidence that the market-value loss on the firm's investment portfolio will not exceed $100 million over a one-day period. This value would help the firm set a threshold at which time it may need either to liquidate assets, to avoid further losses, or ensure that it has the cash and/or credit liquidity to withstand such level of losses.

The cash flow at risk model could provide an estimated level of exposure for a particular cash flow; that is, an expected forecast or deviation from the budget amount in either a hedged or unhedged environment, or both. For example, one might use the model to determine how much the company's cash interest expense may deviate from its forecast or budgeted cash expense over a given time period at a desired confidence level. For instance, the CFAR model may indicate with 95 percent confidence that the cash impact of the company's variable interest expense will not exceed the budgeted amount by more than $10 million over a six-month period.

Now, what does the Treasurer do with this information? The limitations of this model notwithstanding, you may determine that $10 million is an acceptable level of cash risk for the company to assume, based on its risk appetite and liquidity reserves, and do nothing more. Alternatively, you may use the model to determine what impact a hedge at various levels would have on the $10 million of expected risk and use the findings to determine an acceptable hedge ratio.

Finally, an earnings at risk calculation is similar to the CFAR in concept except that the EAR's focus is on book earnings as opposed to a cash flow, per se. The choice as to which one to use may depend on what the Treasurer is trying to protect: earnings or cash flow.

The above models should serve as additional effective tools in the box for corporate risk managers as they try to bring some level of objectivity to the hedging decision (that is, by running them pre- and post-various hedging levels). This is more formally referred to as *inherent risk*, the risk you are exposed to before hedging, and *residual risk*, the risk remaining once your hedge position is included.[6] Keep in mind, however, that these are just models and are not without their own limitations and risk in their use.

The limitations of these models are driven by the assumptions that have to be made, including, for example, the volatility parameter and a probability distribution. The problem is that these parameters are unknown and can be estimated only from historical data. Moreover, consider the timeframes, that is, one day for a VAR calculation, and the confidence level (that is, 95 percent). Increasing either or both of these parameters increases the potential error in the model's reliability. These limitations do not make the models worthless—they still aid in visualizing risk—but they do make them limited in usefulness. So, use caution, and employ them with other tools and thoughtful decision making.

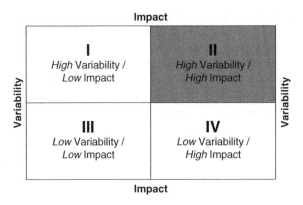

EXHIBIT 9.5 Risk Map

Risk Ranking

Now that the critical components in defining the risk are understood—*variability and impact* (or *probability and impact*)—how does one organize to determine which risks to focus on? Focusing on them all is sure to be less efficient. So, which risks matter most? Again, that is a question of risk appetite.

Regardless, however, of which risks one selects to focus on, the way to begin is with some sort of categorization to help prioritize. One such technique is to place the risks in quadrants categorized by their *variability* and *impact* axes. For example, high variability, that is, gas prices, and low impact, that is, filling up the scooter, would fall into quadrant I in this example (see Exhibit 9.5). In contrast, the highly variable gas prices for a trucking company would likely fall into quadrant II: high cash impact.

Although simplistic, whether these are financial risks or other risks within an enterprise, this type of categorization helps senior management and the board visualize what risks they may need to pay attention to.

Like all of the tools mentioned so far, this is not without its limitations; and more important, not without its own risk in using it. Again, it is simple; there are many more details behind each exposed risk that need to be sought out. Moreover, as others have been quick to bring to light, this type of risk map may ignore the most important risks,[7] that is, the low probability of occurrence, but high impact risk. The event could happen, although its probability of occurrence is projected to be low; anything can happen. It is a matter of being prepared for the event if it happens—having a contingency plan.

The risks in this case, the *unknown or unexpected risks*, would fall into quadrant IV. The premise here is that senior management and the board are probably already keenly aware of the exposures in quadrant II, but may not know of the potential impact of the ones in quadrant IV. It is the Strategic Treasurer's job to make them aware, and the board's and other players' responsibility to let the Treasurer know how much these risks matter, based on the firm's risk preference.

To illustrate this point further, consider the VAR and/or cash-flow-at-risk model discussed previously. What happened to the 5 percent lack of confidence issue? That is, if the model indicated a potential loss threshold with 95 percent confidence, then what should you do with the 5 percent lack of confidence, or prediction error? In the example used to illustrate VAR, the model was 95 percent confident that the portfolio's market value loss would not exceed $100 million over a one-day period, which means there is at least a 5 percent chance that it would exceed $100 million. Depending on the firm's risk preference and/or liquidity situation, that large of a loss may be too much for the company to tolerate. That is quadrant IV. Don't ignore it.

Summary

This chapter was basically a high-level overview of risk. We reviewed simple methods to visualize risk, including a historical time series, as well as the impact of risk on cash flows. Tools such as stress tests or scenario analysis, as well as more sophisticated simulation-based models such as cash flow at risk (CFAR) and value at risk (VAR), can provide additional objectivity to aid in decisions regarding risk management, but these tools are not without their own risks and limitations. In the end, nothing takes the place of careful and thoughtful analysis. A critical step within a risk management process is to first understand your exposures (risk) and, as important, understand your "pain points" or risk thresholds, levels at which you need to protect yourself against any further volatility in cash flow. In the end, it is difficult to predict if or when an event could occur. Moreover, it could be that low-probability/high-impact risk from quadrant IV (risk map), which may not typically be on your radar screen, can have the most severe impact. Therefore, it pays to be prepared.

Now that you better understand your risks, the following chapter will delve further into understanding the components of an effective risk management framework to help you address them.

Notes

1. Duncan Martin, *Managing Risk in Extreme Environments* (London: Kogan Page Ltd., 2007).
2. Random House, Inc. Unabridged (v 1.1). Definition of *risk*, at http://dictionary .reference.com/browse/risk.

3. Glyn A. Holton, "Subjective Value-At-Risk," *Financial Engineering News*, No. 1 (August 1997).
4. Nassim Nicholas Taleb, *Fooled by Randomness: The Hidden Role of Chance in Life and in the Markets* (New York: Texere, 2004).
5. Bob Dylan, "The Times They Are A-Changin," 1964.
6. The Committee of Sponsoring Organizations of the Treadway Commission, *Enterprise Risk Management—Integrated Framework*, Vol. 1: Executive Summary Framework, September 2004, available at www.coso.org/documents/COSO_ERM_ExecutiveSummary.pdf.
7. Ali Samad-Khan, "Why COSO Is Flawed," *Operational Risk* (January 2005).

CHAPTER 10

Financial Risk Management: Part Two

Altering the Risk a Company Faces to Match the Risk It Desires

David W. Stowe

CFA, Director, Strategic Treasurer

Risk management alters the risk a company faces to match the risks it desires.

—Greg Krissek[1]

No matter which tool or tools are employed in identifying risk, whether the risk is acceptable or not is dependent upon management's risk preference. That is, how much risk is management willing to accept in pursuit of the business strategy?

Risk is in the eye of the beholder. It is a relative, rather than an absolute, term. One Treasurer's acceptance of an exposure to a particular level of volatility and impact is likely different than another's. The commodity speculator, for example, likely has a much different view of risk than does the retirement portfolio manager.

In determining how best to deal with the risk an organization faces, the Treasurer needs first to understand the risk appetite of the firm and its stakeholders (see Exhibit 10.1). To address this issue, begin by answering the following questions:

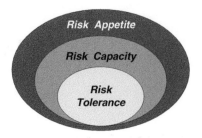

EXHIBIT 10.1 Risk Appetite

- How much risk do we have?
- How much can we endure?
- How much do we want to keep?

A firm's risk appetite, or risk philosophy, may be a high-level view of how much risk its stakeholders—equity investors, creditors, employees, and so on—are willing to assume in pursuit of the business's returns, but it may be constrained by a tighter level of the firm's *risk capacity*.

The risk capacity of a firm is basically how much risk it can endure before a potential financial crisis such as going bankrupt (a liquidity or credit capacity constraint), tripping debt covenants, or violating potential regulatory capital levels or cash flow volatility restrictions.

Once a firm's risk capacity is outlined, then it is critical to establish *risk tolerance* levels or quantified thresholds at which hedge levels may be set and/or other action steps taken. These thresholds, individually and on aggregate, provide the basis for the firm's critical risk management objectives. They can be defined by earnings, cash flow, or other financial measures.

Risk Management Choices

An organization has three basic choices with respect to dealing with risk:[2] accept it, avoid it, or manage it, the latter of which may entail altering and/or hedging the risk (see Exhibit 10.2).

Accept

Depending on management's tolerance for risk, it may choose to absorb the volatility through earnings, assuming that the upside may eventually outweigh the downside. That is, the risk exposure is within the stakeholders' accepted risk appetite. Consider a wildcatter, or oil prospector, who does not

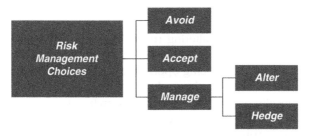

EXHIBIT 10.2 Risk Management Choices

hedge his oil price risk in the financial markets, but speculates on the price of oil going up. He accepts the inherent risk of prices going down. The reason he is in the business to begin with is that his appetite for risk is high.

Management's risk preference notwithstanding, absorbing such risk may not always be feasible or even tolerable by stakeholders, given the potential volatility and its impact. Absorbing risk may put earnings on a potential roller coaster ride: the good ones may be exhilarating, while the bad ones can make a stomach turn!

Avoid

If all other attempts to deal with risk fail, in that it cannot be brought within the entity's risk appetite—via laying it off in the financial markets or by other means—then a change in business strategy to avoid the risk may be warranted. Such a choice may involve a decision to get out of the product line, the geographic market, or the business entirely. In the end, it is a cost-benefit, or risk-reward, decision.

Manage

If the risk is unacceptable and the only way to avoid it is to get out of business, then the risk needs to be managed to bring the *residual risk,* the risk remaining once it has been managed or addressed, within the firm's risk appetite. Managing risk does not necessarily mean one has to jump into hedging it with derivatives. As with most things in business, it comes down to a cost-benefit decision regarding the best method to manage the risk, which may include:

1. A change in operating strategy to alter or transfer the risk
2. Hedging the risk utilizing offsetting financial or physical-delivery contracts

Alter the Risk

The best place to begin in altering risk exposure is within the company's operations. That is, can the exposure be reduced, for example, by reducing consumption through enhancing operational efficiencies? Or can the physical procurement strategy be changed to control volatility (produce the raw material organically or procure it cheaper elsewhere)?

On the other hand, is it possible to transfer the risk, to push the volatility back down the supply chain or pass the risk on to customers through price changes? The ability to alter an organization's risk, either by passing it on to customers or by pressuring vendors to absorb it, if applicable, depends on the market environment at the time.

In a highly competitive price environment in which a firm may have little control over setting prices, passing cost variability through to customers—in the form of price increases or a surcharge—may not be practicable. On the other hand, pressuring a vendor to absorb risk only transfers its cost. It is still a component cost that has to be managed. As such, one must consider who is better equipped or experienced to manage the risk at the optimal cost.

Hedge the Risk

If all efforts to alter or reduce the risk to an acceptable level within the firm's risk appetite either fail, are exhausted, or are cost prohibitive relative to the potential benefits, then the alternative may be to manage it through a hedging program or the purchase of insurance. The goal is the mitigation of risk, by bringing it within your organization's risk tolerance, not necessarily eliminating the risk completely.

The process of mitigating the risk is to acquire an offsetting exposure. This may be, for example, either a derivative instrument such as an option, future, or swap; a fixed purchase or sales contract for physical delivery; or an offsetting asset or liability in order to limit the uncertain impact to fair value or cash flow.

Possible Reasons for Hedging

Reduce Volatility

Hedging is used to reduce the volatility in the firm's cash flow, earnings, and/or fair value of investments. The goal is to reduce the variance in possible outcomes. The question may arise: Why reduce the volatility in, for example, cash flow? The primary reasons for hedging are to:

1. Avoid financial distress.
2. Allow better predictability that enables management to plan.

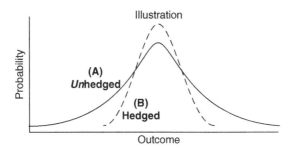

EXHIBIT 10.3 Hedging: Probability/Outcome

An effective hedging program narrows the distribution of probable outcomes (volatility) and, therefore, lowers the probability of financial distress and/or extraneous financial risks impacting results, all else being equal (see Exhibit 10.3).

Avoid Financial Distress

Financial distress may be a short-term liquidity crunch that impedes an entity's ability to satisfy its cash requirements; or it may be as severe as bankruptcy (worse-case threshold). Recall the premise of _gamblers ruin_, where one may be right in the long term, have an advantage even, but due to limited capital be out of money in the short-term due to adverse events.

Risk is a part of doing business, but it should not knock a firm out of business. It is not just the occurrence of financial distress, but the _potential_ for financial distress that has an impact. The more an entity's cash flows are subject to potential volatility, the more likely an entity is to face some sort of financial stress, requiring it to hold larger cash reserves or pay for expensive lines of credit, both of which are a drag on returns.

To visualize and/or measure the impact of cash flow volatility and determine the thresholds for financial pain, a simple scenario analysis tool for unhedged cash flow (discussed in Chapter 9 in the section on Stress Test/Scenario Analysis) can be employed as in Exhibit 10.4.

Provide Predictability

Consistent with the objective of avoiding financial distress is the benefit of allowing management to plan. A firm's expected cash flows, or its future value, is dependent on management's decisions and actions. As such, management needs the ability to plan without the uncertainty associated with events outside its control, especially events or risks that can be mitigated. Hedging not only potentially creates a more controlled environment

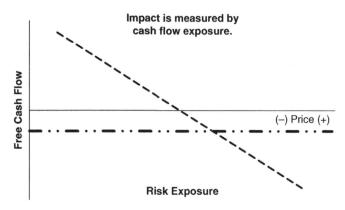

EXHIBIT 10.4 Stress Test/Scenario Analysis

in which management can execute its plan and measure its results; but it also makes management more accountable for such results without the outside influence of financial risks. "It can and has been argued that this ability to transfer risk (and hence reduce or even remove certain kinds of the risks of doing business) has freed companies to pursue what they do best, and increased world prosperity based on business activities."[3]

Value in Risk Management

Now that the primary benefits, or value drivers, of risk management have been explained, a next step is to determine the value of risk management for a particular firm. Why is this important? Any effective program within a business needs the understanding and buy-in of senior management and the board of directors. Risk management is no exception.

To lead senior management to provide the resources and feedback that the Treasurer requires to execute an effective risk management program, he needs to demonstrate the relevant areas in which risk management adds value.

Finance Theory

Recall from basic corporate finance courses that a firm's value is derived as the present value of its future cash flows,[4] and those cash flows are generally a result of management's investment decisions and actions. So, if risk management can impact management's decisions and actions, then it should impact a firm's value. But what does corporate finance theory indicate? Modigliani and Miller (M&M) proposed that "value is produced by cash flows of real assets."[5] That would mean that purely financial transactions, that is, hedging and/or capital structure decisions, are irrelevant. They do not affect operating cash flows (the size of the pie) but merely lead to a resizing of the pieces of the pie.

Alternatively, Sharpe's Capital Asset Pricing Model (CAPM)[6,7] indicates that investors are not compensated for holding *diversifiable risks*, those that can be offset by holding another, uncorrelated asset, for example. As such, hedging does not impact an entity's risk premium, which is derived as the correlation of a firm's returns with those of the market for all assets, otherwise known as *systematic risk*.

Moreover, the theory that a firm's equity should be valued as an option on the firm's assets[8] further points to the fact that, consistent with option pricing theory, volatility is a good thing. The higher the volatility, then the higher the option's value, all else being equal.

Theory versus Reality

So if, as the academic references seem to indicate, there is little to no real value in hedging, why then do so many apparently sophisticated banks and corporations hedge their risk? Theory is a basis for thought and decision making. Further, it is based on the long run; and, as Keynes said, "in the long run we are all dead." That may be true, but, recalling gamblers' ruin, in the short run we could be out of business if we cannot meet our financial obligations. Finally, as is well known by now, theory excludes key factors of reality, including taxes, the cost of bankruptcy, and the fact that access to capital is not continuous, for example.

There are other issues to consider that theory may overlook. One such issue is the fact that a firm's equity holders are not its only concerned *stakeholders*. Essentially, there are others—creditors, employees, senior officers, and current and prospective members of its board of directors—who all have a stake in the firm and an interest in its continued existence, but not necessarily a means, or the flexibility, to diversify. Further, not only is it recognized that management likely possesses asymmetric information regarding the firm and its risk exposures, but as a group, management should be more informed and better equipped to manage the risks more efficiently.

Volatility and Impact

Ultimately, an effective risk management program should enhance a firm's value. While the perceived internal value depends on management's risk preference, or level of risk aversion, the value to external stakeholders is

EXHIBIT 10.5 Value of Risk Management

driven by both the level of volatility and its potential impact to cash flow, which results in an impact on other key, valued-added areas, including:

- Capital structure
- Liquidity reserves/access to capital
- Investment decisions/risk of underinvestment

Shouldn't there be value in being able to act when others cannot (for instance, because they are in a cash flow bind due to their financial risk volatility)? Moreover, shouldn't there be value in being able to take on business opportunities that others choose not to pursue because they are not equipped or knowledgeable enough to handle the risks?

Value in risk management is proportional to the risks an organization faces, as illustrated in Exhibit 10.5.

Capital Structure

While it is typically debated whether or how hedging affects a company's cost of capital, or its risk premium, it is generally accepted that hedging provides flexibility with respect to a company's capital structure, all else being equal. The basic premise is that as the volatility of cash earnings is reduced through hedging, then the more stable the cash flows, which should increase the available debt capacity—a potentially cheaper source of capital after taxes.

Further, it has become increasingly apparent to the various debt rating agencies, such as Moody's Investors Services and Standard & Poor's, that effective risk management can impact a firm's cash flow volatility. As such, the rating agencies have begun incorporating various risk management metrics within their ratings evaluations, which ultimately impact a firm's cost of capital.

Liquidity Reserves

Liquidity reserves are the cash, or cash-like balances, including bank lines of credit, that companies maintain for working capital needs, capital expenditure requirements, and other investment purposes. The size of such reserves is influenced, in part, by the volatility in the company's cash flow as well as management's tolerance for such fluctuation. The more risk-adverse management is, the more likely they are to hold higher cash balances, all else being equal. Large cash balances can be a drag on asset returns, and most importantly, may not be available for reinvestment.

By managing volatility, and, therefore, creating a more predictable cash flow stream, companies can free up expensive liquidity capital held in reserve. This potentially impacts a firm's value if it affects a firm's investment decisions, that is, capital is more optimally deployed toward growth opportunities.

Finally, access to capital is more predictable and in the company's control if cash flow volatility due to financial risks is contained. This puts the firm in the driver's seat as to when to access the capital markets, versus being forced into them to shore up reserves amid financially stressful times. This not only protects the cost of capital to shareholders, but also mitigates the potential dilution of capital returns to them.

Investment Decisions

In and of itself, hedging may benefit the debt holders through reduced cash flow risk. That is not to say equity holders get no benefit. They do, however, it is generally less direct and is derived in part from management's ability to execute its plan with confidence and continue with its investment decisions.

Aside from the impact to earnings from the cost of capital, either by holding too much or paying too high a price for it, as discussed earlier, financial stress has an impact on either or both the choices for new investment opportunities and/or the ability to carry them out and stick with them. That is, cash flow volatility impacts the risk of underinvestment[9] which is the risk that, due to other concerns, the firm cannot carry out certain new investment opportunities, which impacts potential future cash flows and thus a firm's value.

What to Hedge?

Once the Strategic Treasurer has convinced her board and senior management of the need to hedge and the value in hedging, what specifically does she hedge? By now, the reader might know this depends on the firm's risk appetite as well as the Treasurer's risk management objectives. What is it that you are trying to protect? What risks can bite you and cause financial distress or limit other investment opportunities?

Generally, the focus of risk management is on cash flow. It is more direct and easier to target than book earnings which may be influenced by other accounting tricks. On the other hand, reported earnings influence the perception of future cash flow, which can impact a firm's valuation. Keep this in mind for considering the accounting impact of hedging, as it does not always affect cash and earnings equally (to be discussed later).

Further, there may be reason to hedge other non–cash flow risk such as the net investment in a foreign subsidiary, if the foreign currency valuation adjustment of such is large enough to impact certain equity covenants on the consolidated financial position, for example. In short, there are myriad reasons pointing to what to hedge. Each situation is unique to the individual making the determination.

Financial Risk Management Process

Financial risk management goes well beyond simply purchasing an offsetting derivative security. The process is complex, requiring at a minimum a keen understanding of one's exposure(s), as well as knowledge of the valuation of derivative securities and applicable accounting regulations per Financial Accounting Standard No. 133[10] (FAS 133) or International Accounting Standard No. 39[11] (IAS 39).

Moreover, a company must ensure that it has proper internal controls in place to protect itself, including appropriate limits as well as checks and balances. That is, the company needs to be able to *prevent blow-ups* as well as ensure that it is carrying out the risk management activities to meet the objectives set forth.

Finally, the accounting issues associated with risk management must be thoroughly understood, so as not to add to the firm's potential for earnings volatility and/or miss opportunities to protect economic risks because of fear of accounting risks. Unfortunately, the Treasurer's role does not end with execution of the hedge; accounting for hedging activity is a necessary evil to understand.

A good risk management framework consists primarily of three interacting parts, and is supported by equal strength within each area. The three are economics, controls, and accounting (see Exhibit 10.6).

Economics

The economics of hedging defines the value in risk management (see Exhibit 10.7). It begins with a thorough understanding of the company's exposures

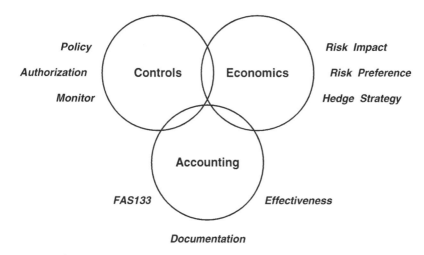

EXHIBIT 10.6 Risk Management Framework

and their impact and follows through to the impact of the hedging activity in offsetting the risks—as defined by the popular adage, *to manage it, you must be able to measure it.*

As part of the economic analysis a company must:

- Identify risk and its potential for occurrence.
- Determine impact of risk.

EXHIBIT 10.7 Economics of Risk Management

- Determine corporate risk management philosophy/risk appetite.
- Develop risk management strategy/objective, that is, risk tolerance levels.
- Execute strategy.
- Monitor/evaluate performance.
- Adapt/revise as needed.
- Communicate to impacted parties.

Controls

Controls ensure that the objectives of risk management activities are being met and are providing oversight and guidelines for the hedging activity.[12] Controls represent the nuts and bolts of the process, reflecting the *who, what, when,* and *how.* In simple terms, this process details who has the authority to do what over a specified time period and how it will be monitored and reported.

Ultimately, the Treasurer wants to answer the question: *Do the right people have the right tools, and do management and the board have the right information in a timely manner to make decisions?*

There are two basic categories of controls.[13] *Preventive controls,* as the name indicates, are there to head off an adverse action; stop it before it happens. The second category, *detective controls,* are there to ensure that anything that may happen gets caught. Examples of controls within these categories may include:

- Management oversight
- Delegation of authority
- Policy and procedures
- Reporting
- Monitoring/benchmarking

Remember the *derivative blow-ups* of the 1990s of such brand-name companies as Kidder Peabody & Co., Procter & Gamble Co., Gibson Greetings Inc., and Barings Bank, to name a few? These financial *mishaps* basically came down to a lack of sufficient or poorly implemented controls that were put in place to prevent or catch manipulation, rogue speculation, and so on of a group or individual employees, which in some cases led to the total demise of the institution.

These examples gave derivatives a bad name—at one time leading investment guru Warren Buffett pronounced that "derivatives were weapons of mass destruction." The question that continues to be asked is: *Could this happen again today?* The answer is, and will continue to be, yes, unless you think you have rid the world of all the *bad apples* and eliminated the incentives, not all of which would necessarily involve fraud or theft that led someone or a group to put a firm into a potentially highly speculative position, for example, that leads to its eventual collapse when things *blow up*, à la Société Générale.[14] Ultimately, even the best controls may be overridden by management or weakened by collusion.

Accounting

The last main area of focus within the financial risk management process involves accounting for the hedging activity under the requirements of either FAS 133 or IAS 39. The primary requirements here relate to:

- Hedge designation at inception
- Accounting documentation
- Valuation of hedge instrument and hedged item
- Effectiveness assessment of hedge relationship
- Financial statement impact of hedge relationship
- System requirements (that is, for accounting and/or valuation)

As mentioned, the Treasurer's role does not necessarily end with the hedge execution. Accounting for hedging activity is best carried out through a partnership between the Treasurer and the controller's groups. Understanding the accounting impact may help avoid such a situation: that is, it may avoid the potential for earnings volatility, due to either *ineffectiveness in the hedge relationship (not a perfect offset between either the hedge instrument and hedged item's cash flows or fair values)* or the failure to receive hedge accounting. Moreover, a good understanding can aid in making an educated decision during the time when it is a choice of *accounting risk* (the risk of earnings volatility due to lack of favorable hedge accounting treatment) versus *economic risk* (the volatility of cash flow or market value due to an unhedged exposure).

It is eye-opening to note the number of large companies—and the expected sophistication of such companies as indicated by their size and history—that have had such publicly disclosed issues and impact to their financial statements with respect to risk management–related activity.

An article in the May 2006 issue of *CFO* magazine exposed over 55 companies with well-known names and with capitalization of over $100 million each for having to restate prior financial statements for misapplication of the rules for hedge accounting.[15] This indicates that the potential for problems and public disclosure related to hedging activity and the accounting for such go beyond simple blatant fraud and may simply fall to a misunderstanding of the rules, or more important, an incomplete risk management process.

Treasurer's Role

In general, the Treasurer is typically charged with overseeing the financial risks faced by the company as outlined in the following sections.

Liquidity Risk

Basically, this is risk to the firm's cash reserves and/or the access to capital. Already discussed was the risk an unhedged exposure can have on potential cash volatility, leading to a potential drawdown of cash reserves or an inopportune need to access the financial markets or tap the firm's credit facilities. There are other risks to cash balances that the Treasurer needs to be concerned with.

Consider, for example, the meltdown of the auction-rate securities (ARS) investment market in late 2007–early 2008. This once-perceived-safe vehicle for short-term cash investments ended up catching companies by surprise when the auction process failed and broker-dealers were too cash-strapped amid other financial problems associated with the mortgage market meltdown, for instance, to back up their deals and buy the ARSs back at par.

The perceived safety net in these instruments was always an *implied* guarantee as opposed to an absolute backdrop. This resulted in trapped cash, significant loss of asset values, and the dismissal of several senior financial officers who were caught unaware. The evolving result has been a renewed focus on a firm's *cash* investment strategy. Moreover, many have come to question whether a typical nonfinancial corporation was a suitable investment manager in the first place.

Credit Risk

The Treasurer's concern here is not just with his own company's risk of a credit rating change, but also with customers, counterparties (affecting their ability to pay), and even suppliers (impacting their ability to perform or deliver).

Foreign Currency Exposure

In general, foreign currency exposure encompasses the impact on cash flows from sales, purchases, and/or investments due to the potential volatility of foreign exchange rates.

Interest Rate Risk

Logically, there is a risk to interest expense due to floating rate debt exposure. This notwithstanding, there are other areas impacted that may not always be on the radar screen, at least not soon enough. For one thing, there is the risk to interest expense from the future need to refinance maturing debt or rate exposure, as previously discussed, from the need to access the capital markets at suboptimum times due to unexpected financing needs. This latter risk is not limited only to debt capital since stock prices are affected by interest rates as well.

Commodity/Energy Prices

The *direct* exposures are typically at the forefront of management's attention, including the cost of raw materials, which can be impacted by potentially volatile commodity prices. Additionally, there is the direct consumption of energy, either fuel or electricity, in processing and/or transportation costs, for instance.

However, most managers are typically less aware, or more likely less sure, of the extent of the risk to manage the *indirect* exposure to commodity and/or energy prices. Consider the fuel surcharge on shipping costs incurred through a third-party shipper or copper components in the computer circuit boards purchased from a third party. These are still risks to be managed, as they affect a company's costs.

Which gets the more favorable hedge accounting treatment, *direct* or *indirect?* It is often the management of direct costs that gets afforded favorable hedge accounting. So, unfortunately, indirect costs may go unmanaged or simply endured. Accounting should not necessarily be a reason for an economic decision such as *not* hedging.

Enterprise Risk

A discussion of enterprise risk management (ERM) can be a book in itself—and is certainly covered in many published works. The popularity of the concept has continued to gain momentum in recent years in the nonfinancial corporate world, at least from a curiosity level of interest, considering not only the woes of the financial firms, but also the concern by the credit rating agencies in applying it to the nonfinancial sector.

While the list comprising a typical Treasurer's risk domain would seem comprehensive enough, it often does not, nor should it necessarily, end there. The nature of Treasurers' roles—their typical analytical strengths, experience with risk management, as well as their habit of thinking about risk and return in general—makes them candidates to lead an enterprise's risk management focus.

An ERM focus is an approach in which all risks of a company are managed from a portfolio standpoint, considering the interaction among risks within an organization as a whole.[16] Even the risks that typically fall within

Treasury (as mentioned earlier) may often be managed under individual or silo views, encompassing potentially different strategies, objectives, and, of most concern, risk appetites because they may be managed by different individuals. Whether the Treasurer leads this initiative or not, she will likely play an integral role.

Black Swans

Black Swan[17] is a new buzzword for financial soothsayers for characterizing any significant event. The term *Black Swan* was coined to refer to a significant, unexpected event that happens but could not be planned for. Consider 9/11 as a Black Swan event. A Black Swan event is one that typically wipes out the firm or puts it in grave danger financially. Consider the mortgage market meltdown in the United States which began in the summer of 2007 and the victims it took down with it, including such notable names as Bear Stearns Cos. and Countrywide Financial Corp.

In these cases, where were their risk models? Did they fail, or did they get overridden? Only history will tell for sure, but applying what was stated earlier in Chapter 9 about models, namely simulation-based models such as Value at Risk (VAR) models, it is apparent, given their limitations, that all risks cannot be foreseen. Recall that the basic VAR model may indicate with 95 percent confidence that the loss would not exceed X-dollars over a one-day period. With its limitation, the fact that the model is primarily derived from historical data notwithstanding (how did they come up with the probability distribution?), what about the 5 percent (100 percent confidence less 95 percent predicted confidence) that the model cannot predict? This would characterize the potential for a Black Swan, or catastrophic event.

So, what can be done about the unknown risk? As Nassim Nicholas Taleb, author of *The Black Swan: The Impact of the Highly Improbable*, indicates, one should have an action plan—"a stop-loss." There may well have been an action plan for Bear Stearns and others who suffered a similar demise during this time, but it may have been subverted, ignored, and/or overridden by management, potentially in pursuit of higher returns. Models cannot do anything to correct that—even good controls can do only so much.

When Do We Hedge?

What works, as Taleb brings to light, is that we really do not know what is going to happen. "You don't know the probabilities in finance...you never know the probabilities outside of a casino...." While this may give the Treasurer comfort in saying "I don't know," it does not relieve him of his responsibility to manage the risks, which may be nothing more than a contingency plan, but at least that leaves one somewhat prepared.

Knowledge of the limitations of history and probabilities also helps provide ammunition for a response to senior management when they ask what exchange rates or interest rates are going to do next year. Your response is, "They will be volatile." It is the volatility you are trying to protect against; that is your hedge objective, not necessarily trying to buy or sell at the best price. You do not know what prices are going to do. Decide on what levels, if they happen, would cause your firm pain (that is, your risk tolerance thresholds) and recommend them as potential hedge levels. Leave the forecasting up to the TV economists.

No Cheers for Hedges; It's the Objective That Matters

It is apparent that Treasurers and other risk managers live in an asymmetric world. With respect to hedging, there is often little appreciation if the hedge position nets a gain, mitigating the potential loss on an exposure, such as commodity prices for raw materials. As a Strategic Treasurer, you are just doing your job; no cheers from the executive grandstands coming your way. But consider the opposite scenario where a hedge position, per se, loses money. The response from above can often be negative—"you failed"; money was spent—either real or an opportunity cost—that did not apparently have to be spent, ex-post, because prices did not rise.

How do you respond? You need to think back to why you were hedging in the first place. What were you trying to accomplish? Did you achieve it? Ultimately, the goal is to ensure the focus is on the right question of whether you achieved the hedge objective that was set out in the beginning—to protect cash flow volatility, and/or protect budget expense targets, for example.

Help management and the board understand why a profitable hedge portfolio, per se, is actually a bad thing if you are not 100 percent hedged. It is the net exposure, which is the cost of the underlying exposure less the gain/(loss) on the hedge portfolio, that matters.

In this situation, clear objectives from the outset and effective communication are the Treasurer's best allies. The boss may not be waiting with pom-poms next quarter—cheering for your hedges to lose—but you will have succeeded in changing the focus to the real issues.

Summary

The takeaway from this general view of risk and risk management is that hedging is much more than the ability to trade derivative securities. The process is complex and requires the right personnel with knowledge of derivatives, hedge accounting, strategy, and controls. Most important, financial risk management requires at the forefront a complete understanding of the risks the company is exposed to, and, just as important, management's risk preference. A complete risk management process cannot stand on its own without the strength of each leg. Think of risk management in terms of a complete framework of economics, controls, and accounting:

- Develop a robust risk management framework.
- Identify your exposures; understand your risks.
- Understand risk appetite, capacity, and tolerance.
- Determine alternatives for dealing with risks.
- Outline hedging objectives.
- Communicate objectives and strategy to senior management and/or board.
- Demonstrate the value of hedging.
- Focus on the portfolio of risks.
- Partner with your accounting group.
- Be prepared for a Black Swan—have an action plan!
- Measure performance.
- Communicate.
- Adapt and revise as needed.
- Avoid the pitfalls of others (see Exhibit 10.8).

It appears that companies need to be burned once or twice before they begin to believe in the value of hedging. Don't let others' Potential Reasons for Not Hedging (Exhibit 10.9) provide you with any excuses not to get started right away.

- Paralysis by analysis
- Suboptimal controls
- Management by committee
- Lack of expertise
- Too focused on price/market timing
- Poor communication of objectives/performance
- Head in the sand
- Overly restrictive hedge policy
- Inadequate systems for valuation and accounting
- Poor forecasts of risk exposures
- Number-1 pitfall: Not managing risks—inaction!

EXHIBIT 10.8 Risk Management Pitfalls to Avoid

10. Our risk management commtttee (RMC) hasn't decided on a strategy; or we haven't formed our RMC.
9. Wall Street doesn't give us credit for hedging.
8. Hedging loses money/can't beat the market.
7. Risk is a cost of doing business.
6. Earnings volatility due to hedging (*ineffectiveness*).
5. Don't know how to hedge.
4. Derivatives = speculation.
3. In the long run, it doesn't matter.
2. One word: FAS133.
1. "We're still looking at that."

EXHIBIT 10.9 Top Potential Reasons for *Not* Hedging

Notes

1. Greg Krissek, "Effective Risk Management Programs for Fuel Ethanol Plants Charting an Unpredictable Future," American Coalition for Ethanol, 2006 Annual Meeting, August 9, 2006.
2. Robert Cooper, "Guide to Risk Management," *The Treasurer's Handbook 2005* (London: The Association of Corporate Treasurers, 2005), pp. 161–167.
3. Philip Potter, "Formulas and Numerics: Stochastic on the Street," *Financial Engineering News*, No. 50 (July/Aug. 2006).
4. Richard A. Brealey and Stewart C. Myers, *Principles of Corporate Finance*. Fourth Edition (New York: McGraw-Hill, 1991), pp. 397, 922–923, 165.
5. Ibid.
6. Ibid.
7. Don Adams, "Why Corporations Should Hedge," *ASX Perspective*, 4th Quarter, 1999, pp. 29–32. Available at: www.mafc.mq.edu.au/other_publications.htm.
8. Brealey and Stewart, *Principles of Corporate Finance*.
9. Adams, "Why Corporations Should Hedge," pp. 29–32.
10. Financial Accounting Standards Board, "Accounting for Derivative Instruments and Hedging Activities," FASB Statement No. 133, incorporating FASB Statements No. 138, February 10, 2004.
11. International Accounting Standards Board, "IAS 39, Financial Instruments: Recognition and Measurement."
12. Committee of Sponsoring Organizations of the Treadway Commission, *Enterprise Risk Management—Integrated Framework*, Vol. 1, *Executive Summary Framework* (September 2004).
13. Committee of Sponsoring Organizations of the Treadway Commission, *Internal Control—Integrated Framework* (July 1994).
14. Nilly Essaides, "A Treasury 'Rogue' Trader à la SocGen & MF Global?" *International Treasurer* (March 2008).

15. Linda Corman, "Lost in the Maze: Problems with Hedge Accounting Caused a Wave of Restatements in 2005; Are FASB's Rules Too Hard to Follow, or Are Companies Simply Too Lax?" CFO.com, May 8, 2006.

16. Committee of Sponsoring Organizations of the Treadway Commission. *Enterprise Risk Management—Integrated Framework*, Vol. 1, *Executive Summary Framework* (September 2004).

17. Nassim Nicholas Taleb, *The Black Swan* (New York: Random House. 2007).

CHAPTER 11

Losses and Fraud: What Can Keep Treasurers Awake at Night

Treasury is the easiest place to make money and the easiest place to make your company fail.

—Timothy Hart, Senior Vice President and Treasurer,
First National Bank of Nebraska

It is interesting to watch dogs sleeping, appearing to be dreaming. Seeing their legs and heads moving in different directions makes one wonder if they are replaying the events of the day that went wrong. The squirrel that got away is perhaps a great torment to them. Or the cat that outsmarted them in some devious way is causing them to relive the event to see if they could create an alternative ending.

Now, this is not to compare Treasurers to dogs. However, Treasurers too, may have fitful sleep born of disconcerting events and decisions of their day. This may be for good reason: since there are few other areas in any organization that can take down a company as fast or as completely as Treasury, there are some actions that cannot simply be undone or corrected.

For Treasurers, some errors or failings mean that the organization would be imperiled by a devastating loss or incapacitating event. Timothy Hart, Senior Vice President and Treasurer of First National Bank of Nebraska, stated it correctly: "Treasury is the easiest place to make money and the easiest place to make your company fail."

Hart's statement is true for almost every organization. If that were the entirety of the situation, it could certainly cause some sleepless nights for Treasurers as well as the top executive officers. However, that fact is not the only one that must be contemplated.

Consider next the situation of Treasury departments in a large number of firms. First, organizations often have thinly staffed Treasury departments that are usually pressed for time. Second, the level of technology tools for which Treasury is allowed funding is grossly inadequate. Third, the funding provided for access to other resources and expertise on a project or ongoing basis is parsimonious at best. Fourth, much of senior management, including a large number of chief financial officers have little or an inaccurate understanding of the role or value of Treasury and Treasurers. The CFO may have grown up through sales, marketing, operations, or financial reporting. Those functions rarely lead to a good understanding of the role and responsibilities of the Treasurer. At best, the CFO's focus may have been on the income statement, not the balance sheet.

Couple the preceding about the level of risk inherent in a typical Treasury department with the lack of resources and funding. It is an unhealthy mix that should give Treasurers and boards of directors reason to pause and assess the situation.

As readers examine the contents of this book, it is clear that much of the material relates to risks that must be identified and handled. Two chapters focus on financial risk management (Chapters 9 and 10) and two others are devoted to the identification of liquidity and related risks and what a Treasurer must do to protect the organization (Chapters 16 and 17). And throughout many of the other chapters, financial risk management plays a significant part.

This focus on risk management is intentional, even though the stated focus of this book is about partnering for growth. This is intentional since the Treasurer's list of responsibilities includes protecting the organization's assets and ensuring adequate liquidity. This responsibility is crucial. Without it, there might not be an organization to grow or protect.

Thus, this chapter is intended to help the Treasurer gain perspective on the proper mindset of his role. Therefore, the chapter will cover:

- **Loss** by exploring some situations of great loss of assets and liquidity.
- **Fraud** by detailing enough examples of fraud to cause the reader sufficient concern to be careful.
- **Guidance** to help prevent some of these game-over events from happening in your organization.

Situations of Loss

Exhibits 11.1, 11.2, 11.3, 11.4, and 11.5 show examples of loss of assets or liquidity that have all been broadcast and/or covered in national or international news in various forms and with an interesting amount of detail. Of course, no Treasurer is interested in wearing that bright orange jumpsuit or doing the perpetrator walk due to committing fraud or stealing funds or assets from others. It is also true that most Treasurers work to keep their organization's name—as well as their own—out of any negative news.

Entity/Business Type	Bank
Situation	**Rogue trading:** 1995—Nick Leeson and Barings Bank. A 28-year-old derivatives trader based in Singapore, Leeson brought down 233-year-old Barings by betting Japanese stocks would rise. He hid his losses—$1.4 billion—for a while, but eventually served more than three years in jail. "It takes some pretty spectacular behavior to get busted in this country for a white-collar crime. But the business world has had a lot of overachievers willing to give it a shot." "Schemers and Scams: A Brief History of Bad Business," *Fortune*, March 18, 2002.
Result	**Insolvency.** Barings Bank, founded in 1762, was sold for one pound, in March 1995, to ING Group, a Dutch bank, which assumed all its liabilities.
Caution/Lesson	**Lack of controls.** One of many examples of lack of controls, — policies, authority, and/or accountability, which included, besides Barings, such notable cases as Gibson Greetings Inc., Procter & Gamble Co., Bankers Trust, Kidder Peabody & Co., Orange County, Calif., and Metallgesellschaft AG. The common themes among many of these cases included: • An aggressive attitude toward risk • Incentives for taking risk • Poor oversight and communication • Inadequate segregation of duties • Ignored policies • Fraud • Manual processes ripe for manipulation • Lack of knowledge and experience

EXHIBIT 11.1 Barings Bank—Trading

Entity/Business Type	Government/Municipality/County
Situation	Invested in Lehman Brothers Holdings Inc. immediately before the investment bank filed for bankruptcy protection. "Lehman Brothers' bankruptcy resulted in an estimated $150 million hit to the county's $2.6 billion investment pool, impacting cities, school districts and special districts that contributed to the fund. Investors relied on their representations that the company was adequately capitalized, which we now know were false. County Treasurer Lee Buffington said Lehman Brothers gave little indication that it was on the brink of bankruptcy. Next week, county supervisors will discuss changes to the county investment policy and will question Buffington at a public board meeting about decisions he made leading up to the Lehman Brothers bankruptcy." *San Mateo County to Sue Lehman executives,* www.insidebayarea.com, Oct. 29, 2008. Lehman filed for bankruptcy on Sep. 15, 2008
Result	Approximately $150 million loss; lawsuit against Lehman.
Caution/Lesson	**Know your counterparties.** In turbulent times, reviewing counterparty risk cannot be minimized. **Leverage other resources.** There was much dialogue in the market about Lehman and this type of activity. Maintain a network of peers to talk to about these types of things—most especially during turbulent times. **Consider whether firm has the tools/expertise to make these decisions.** Many Treasury departments are not adequately staffed to do the necessary credit analysis within their investment-management activities.

EXHIBIT 11.2 San Mateo County—Counterparty

Not everyone has been able to avoid that type of situation, however, so here are some stories to learn from. Please note that learning from others' mistakes requires understanding the principles of the individual situation and what type of controls and activities would have prevented the end result. It can be an error to focus on a particular case so narrowly that one cannot visualize the application of those principles to other situations.

Entity/Business Type	Energy company—ethanol producer
Situation	Apparently, VeraSun Energy Corp. was hedging its corn purchases/inventory by selling them forward in the futures market, but as prices rose, the firm terminated its *short* positions and instead began buying corn in the futures market. Additionally, VeraSun appeared to have been speculating on further price increases in corn by entering into "accumulator" contracts that required the firm to buy more corn if the price dropped (similar to being short put options on corn). The price of corn dropped significantly, leaving the company with substantial obligations to buy corn at above-market prices, potentially even more volume than was needed for ethanol production. This severely impacted the firm's margins and liquidity, given the declining price of ethanol amid the collapse in oil prices and other substitutes.
	"We historically have employed short financial positions to hedge our physical purchases of corn. In July 2008, after corn prices had risen from approximately $6.00 per bushel at the end of May 2008 to almost $8.00 per bushel . . ., we chose to exit our short financial positions in corn. . . .
	"In addition, based on market forecasts that corn prices would continue to rise, we entered into a number of 'accumulator' contracts relative to corn requirements for the third and fourth quarters that, in each case, allowed us to purchase a specified volume of corn at prices below then-prevailing market rates, but also required us to purchase that same volume of corn (in addition to the initial purchase) at one or more lower prices per bushel should market prices decline to or below those lower levels over the duration of the contract. Shortly thereafter, corn prices commenced a sharp decline from almost $8.00 per bushel to a low of under $5.00 per bushel in mid-Aug. 2008.
	"As a result, we were required under the accumulator contracts to purchase additional amounts of corn at prices that proved to be higher than prevailing market prices. As a result of these various hedge positions, as well as the difficult operating environment, we expect to record average corn prices of between $6.75 and $7.00 per bushel during the third quarter of 2008. As of Aug. 29, 2008, the prevailing price of ethanol in the New York Harbor. . . averaged between $2.35 and $2.45 per gallon.

EXHIBIT 11.3 VeraSun Energy—"Hedging" Loss

	"Should we price the remainder of our ethanol sales at these levels, we would expect our average ethanol selling price for the third quarter of 2008 to be between $2.45 and $2.55 per gallon." VeraSun Energy Corporation, 8-K, September 16, 2008. "The company clearly panicked, went long corn during the upswing, and now is riding on an undetermined loss on commodity trading and corn inventories." "VeraSun Energy: Buyout Candidate, If Obama Wins," http://seekingalpha.com/, September 24, 2008.
Result	Bankruptcy—filed Chapter 11 on Oct. 31, 2008; CFO fired.
Caution/Lesson	**Lacked a clear hedge objective.** When is a hedge not a hedge, but speculation? **Mismatched assets/liabilities.** Were they effectively floating on one side of the trade, that is, selling of ethanol, but fixing the other side of the trade, that is, locking in corn prices?

EXHIBIT 11.3 (Continued)

Entity/Business Type	Airline—various
Situation	Inaction/inability to act/hedge. **Issue One—Deteriorating Credit:** Severe deterioration in credit standing and liquidity among airlines in the early part of 2000 and the following decade led to the inability to obtain long-term hedging contracts in the over-the-counter market as counterparties refused to take on added credit exposure to airlines, leaving airlines with limited hedging alternatives; that is, counterparties were reluctant to lock in fixed price contracts such as oil swaps given the potential credit risk. Even the use of call options/caps was curtailed given the cash requirements/costs to enter such contracts. **Issue Two—Lack of Action:** The drastic rise in crude oil prices from below $20/barrel (bbl) prior to 2000 prices to a peak of just under $150/bbl by the summer of 2008 left airlines, and many other fuel consumers, reluctant to hedge, or lock in oil prices at higher levels

EXHIBIT 11.4 Airlines—Credit/Hedging

	given the severe profit margin impact this could have if prices declined. This led to inaction and *chasing the market higher* as companies were unsure as to when to hedge, leaving many unhedged.
Result	Potential cash flow volatility due to fuel price fluctuations went un-/underprotected, resulting in severe margin impact/cash drain/lack of cash flow predictability. Many U.S. airlines filed for bankruptcy protection.
Caution/Lesson	**Maintain a position of strength.** Ensure and nurture good relationships at all times. Even with good relationships, if the firm becomes financially impaired, it has fewer options available. It may need to hedge but be unable to since no others want the firm as a counterparty. What is your contingency plan for this type of situation? **Establish clear hedge objectives.** Identify what you are trying to accomplish with the hedging program; that is, limit cash flow volatility or capture the *best* price. Otherwise it may leave the organization chasing the market looking for hedging *opportunities*, but never acting.

EXHIBIT 11.4 (Continued)

Amount (*USD Equivalent*)	Year	Firm/Description	Issue
$4B+	1999	**Parmalat**—Italian-based dairy conglomerate.	$4 billion overstatement of cash and falsified audit validation of funds related to the firm's Bank of America account.
$1B+	2009	**Satyam**—Indian-based IT outsourcing firm.	Falsified financials over several years. Listed 53,000 employees. Used fictitious employees to siphon funds. Overstated assets, understated liabilities. Created fictitious cash balance of over $1 billion USD equivalent.

EXHIBIT 11.5 Major Fraudulent Cash Overstatements

Fraud

This section will explore several areas where situations of fraud have occurred at various organizations. These describe a type of problem and why it is a problem. Since these are being described in a publicly available document, discussing the specific methods that criminals use to commit fraud is unwise; thus, the descriptions will be generalized.

When examining areas where fraud is perpetrated, it is useful to discuss these items within the Treasury group or other areas of the firm to assess what the organization's particular exposure might be. And many firms will benefit by having such a discussion with their bankers and consultants—in order to provide tools and other methods for protecting the organization.

Check Forgery

Multiple employee expense reimbursement checks were stolen from a company located on the West Coast. These checks were washed (the payee being changed) or forged (an additional payee listed). Instances of valid checks being stolen and altered are far more common than should be possible. While altering checks may be rather simple, acquiring valid checks should be more difficult. The reason checks were stolen from inside the organization was due to lax controls in just a few key areas. Once checks were printed and signed, they were left out in the open in several locations of the firm, awaiting a control process of review and signature. It is interesting that the part of the process meant to add controls provided an avenue for fraud. The fraud worked like this: the inside person sent checks to an accomplice in a particular area in the southern United States. That accomplice cashed the checks at different locations from a mix of banks, stores, and check-cashing facilities. The account had positive pay, but since the amount was not being adjusted, the positive pay service did not identify this type of forgery.

Controls Possible

- Convert employee reimbursements to electronic and handle through the payroll process.
- Segregate functions and enforce control of checks throughout the organization.
- Outsource check printing to the firm's bank (this enforces a clean segregation of duties and places control of checks with the bank).
- Use check stock security features.
- Use payee-match positive pay, which should identify any changes, deletions, and additions.

Payroll Fraud

The firm found several fictitious employees on the books when a payroll report was delivered to the Treasurer by mistake. In addition to employees who never worked at the firm, another common occurrence is paying terminated employees for an extra few pay cycles. The terminated employee is not the one receiving the funds. The sensitivity of employee pay data keeps the distribution of this information down to a minimum, and not all organizations establish adequate controls around total pay, employees, additions, and deletions.

Controls Possible

- Segregation of duties: use the report that shows changes to Employee Master Records (additions, changes, and deletions) and have that reviewed by an independent person and have a dual authorization required online.
- Ensure supervisors and managers track total employees and all employee movement.
- Use simple biometrics on the time-keeping systems.

Accounts Payable—Vendor Master

This is one of the most well-known areas that is ripe for fraud. And surprisingly, many organizations remain lax in their controls anyway. Often, the false vendor master record can be established quite easily and no segregation of duties is required. Examples of how this is accomplished include using a simple e-mail or setup form to establish the vendor (without validating that the information is correct or from the authorized requestor); the accounts payable (AP) clerk enters the vendor into the system himself. Next, the criminal or his outsourced invoice writer creates an invoice to the firm and has it approved or appear to be approved. The payments are then made to the false vendor (which may be a real company).

Controls Possible

- Segregation of duties: use the report that shows changes to vendor master records (additions, changes, and deletions) and have that reviewed by an independent person and have a dual authorization required online.
- Ensure inactive AP vendor master records have their status changed once they are inactive for 13 months.
- Perform a systematic audit of vendor master records reviewing approximately one-twelfth of the total each month. Confirm terms, physical address, electronic bank address, and so on.

Bank Account Problems

Problems related to bank accounts represent a veritable treasure trove for perpetrators of fraud. Here are some real issues or situations. Each bank account represents a point of exposure and cost. The exposure must be managed and the cost optimized.

- **Unknown accounts.** Many firms have rather poor processes in place for managing their bank accounts. Numerous organizations do not even have a complete list of their bank accounts. This creates the embarrassing and unfortunate situation of existing accounts being discovered by Treasury. This raises a significant control concern. These accounts are not connected to the concentration system and are, therefore, not viewed regularly, if at all. These accounts may not even be set up on the general ledger.

  Dangers of Treasury not knowing all of their accounts include trapped cash, exposed accounts, and long periods of time where fraud would not even be detected. One organization was having a difficult year financially and was surprised to find an account with an ever-increasing balance that had funds flow into the account but no method of concentrating those funds.

- **Lack of account and transaction-control framework.** While positive payment was used on most disbursement accounts, other debits hit various bank accounts that did not have those protections. Some checks were converted to electronic transactions in spite of a prohibition by the Automated Clearing House (ACH) rules and then cleared against the bank account. Unauthorized ACH debits were also cleared against this account. Failure of the Treasurer, Controller, and others to understand what was happening in their accounts coupled with the lack of appropriate account and transaction controls represent an exposure that must be resolved.

- **Nonliving and nonactive signers.** Whether due to mergers or the general failure to keep track of changes in signers, this area represents significant risks and inconvenience for organizations. Examples abound of having signers who have passed on to other firms—or even to the next life. The signer list must be well maintained and updated as soon as an active signer leaves.

  Fraud can occur quite simply. Inconvenient situations can arise, particularly in takeovers, when all of the active signers leave a firm so that no active signers exist. One firm had to send a small group of people to several locations in other countries to secure access to accounts and systems that had been lost. Phones calls and letters would not suffice. This was not a good use of time and could have been prevented with proper planning.

Controls Possible
- Create and manage the bank-account policy.
- Establish and maintain the account structure and concentration system.
- Identify accounts that do not comply with account-control policy.
- Bank account audit: check the general ledger, bank systems, bank reconciliation area, and the bank itself.
- Use software or a service that is designed to help manage bank accounts (for those with eight or more banks and 100 or more financial accounts).
- Use payroll adjustments to determine when signers have left the organization.

Decentralized Debt Issuance

For purposes of sensitivity, the following situation is described in general terms to avoid identifying the actual entity. The organization was decentralized for some Treasury activities arising from historical and political reasons. Treasury is not a function that lends itself to decentralization, in general. Investments and debt management are two areas that are best managed in a centralized and professionally run group. This organization had more than five areas that issued debt for their separate areas and departments. The risks were tremendous. Hiring and continued staffing for this level of skill set is expensive, and replicating it multiple times was highly ineffective. This situation added risks as everyone was quite junior in understanding debt issuance, and few could gain an adequate level of expertise. In such situations, errors can be made quite simply. In this case, errors were made that cost the organization a medium-sized sum of money and a double portion of humble pie.

Controls Possible
- Centralize core Treasury activities by policy and framework.
- Ensure Treasury is responsive to the needs of the organization.
- Staff Treasury with competent staff that can either execute on the various tasks directly or oversee and manage another party who does this work.

Reconciliation Surprise

Treasury owns cash and is certainly concerned about accurate bank reconciliations since it helps ensure control of the company's cash. A clear and appropriate definition of reconciliation is necessary at every organization. An organization east of the Mississippi River had identified various reconciling items but was not able to clear them in a timely manner. It also reconciled more than seven bank accounts together to make the process easier. It maintained a list of these items.

Since the net of this list was reasonably small, everyone felt comfortable that it was simply a matter of being behind on the reconciliation. However, after an assessment of the situation at a detail level, it was discovered that there were several instances of fraud and situations where money was owed to the organization. In the case of fraud, funds lost exceeded $200,000. Recovery for the funds that were owed over eight months became incredibly difficult and less than 65 percent of the money was recovered.

Controls Possible

- Establish a clear reconciliation policy and definition with accountability.
- Have one bank account to one general-ledger account.
- Reconcile accounts separately.
- Reconcile on a timely basis.
- When someone says there is a reconciliation problem, it almost always means that there is a design problem.

Preventing Fraud and Game-Over Events

There are many fine books and reference materials on establishing and optimizing an internal-control framework, and much is written about particular instances of loss and fraud. The intellectually curious Treasurer will read these materials and ensure that she employs wise controls and safeguards to prevent her organization from falling into the same trap. Strategic Treasurers will also discuss these materials internally and externally, in efforts to make sure to prevent their organization from falling into similar traps and snares.

Here are a few categories of activities and perspectives that Treasurers will employ to help prevent significant losses and fraud from happening to the organization they are charged with protecting. The following should be viewed as a starting point and not as an exhaustive list.

- **Design and regularly review.**
  - Risk management framework and related policies; review them every year and whenever significant market disruption occurs.
  - Plan banking structures and treasury information in such a way as to support visibility to the firm's liquidity.
  - Account and transaction controls for all accounts in concert with the firm's banking structure.
- **Observe and monitor.**
  - Standard reports for cash flow, variances, compliance with policies, and covenants on a systematic basis.

- Generating reports that allow the group to focus in on specific exceptions is an excellent use of resources (the management-by-exception reporting method allows Treasury staff to hone in on areas that are either approaching a danger zone or have become an exception to a process or control).
- Transactional activity with abnormal setups, direction, activity, or volume changes.
- **Assess treasury and treasury processes.**
  - Perform an internal assessment of controls; ensure that adequate segregation of duties exists; note any shortcomings and determine if there are long- or short-term fixes needed; fix the problems as priority items.
- **Talk to others.**
  - Maintain regular discussions with others in Treasury and finance about internal and external events.
  - Execute a relationship management plan and tap bankers for information and insight.
  - Use other external experts on treasury topics and issues.
- **Trust but verify.**
  - Credit checks, criminal background checks, and drug testing are or should be mandatory for anyone working in Treasury.
  - For ongoing credit checks, consult the human resources department about how to have this done on an annual basis.
  - Segregation of duties is a requirement, and while a challenge in small Treasury departments, it must be enforced.
- **Question authority and authorize questions.**
  - Ensure that the right questions are being asked and answered by everyone in Treasury:
    - What is important?
    - Who knows what to ask?
    - What can go wrong?
    - How can a loss or problem be managed?
    - What resources do we need?

Summary

Due to their role and responsibilities, Treasurers are in a position where they can bankrupt or ruin their organization faster than or as fast as any other department. This is not an issue of pride, but a point of caution. Adding to this situation, Treasury departments tend to be very thinly staffed. This, by default, increases the risk to the area of loss and exposure to fraud.

To decrease the likelihood of damage and to minimize the level of harm a company or organization may face, resources should be used. These resources are both internal and external. Internal resources come from various areas, and access is usually easy to manage. External resources include bankers, consultants, and other experts, as well as peers from other organizations. The resources need to be used regularly and not held in reserve for a time of utmost need.

Fraud and losses require the effective use of an internal control framework with particular attention to the design of a firm's banking system, monitoring, and visibility, assessing the internal and external situations. To accomplish this requires intellectual curiosity that manifests itself in purposeful communication. For the Treasurer, the downside of not being alert and thoughtful is all too frequently terminal. A Treasury equivalent of the "undo" button does not exist.

CHAPTER 12

Communication: Mars and Venus

Minimizing Communication Conflict Between Treasurers and Controllers

> *"When I use a word,"* Humpty Dumpty said, *in rather a scornful tone,*
> *"it means just what I choose it to mean—neither more nor less."*
> *"The question,"* said Alice, *"is whether you can make words mean so*
> *many different things."*
>
> —Lewis Carroll, *Through the Looking Glass*, Chapter 7

Treasurers and controllers are close work relatives and use much of the same terminology. Yet they often fail to clearly communicate with each other. This reduces the ability of both to optimize the organization's performance level. The Strategic Treasurer will understand the causes of these differences and communicate effectively with his finance siblings.

The language differences between Treasurers and Controllers are significant because each approaches finance and business from a varied trajectory. Having different responsibilities creates a different focus and perspective. It is similar to having two eye-witnesses to an automobile accident. Each witness may have been standing at a different angle, and each will report some events very differently from the other. Often, the situation occurring between the Treasurer and the Controller is similar. The Strategic Treasurer will understand that contemplating both perspectives can be of great worth to the organization.

Sometimes, the discussions and debates between the Treasurer and Controller are an either/or or a conflict between these two groups. This does not need to be so, and understanding the language will go a long way. These either/or situations may be viewed by each as: "*Either* we have good accounting controls *or* we have an efficient Treasury system." "*Either* we use the banking system to do our accounting *or* we have a clean Treasury structure." However, these are not true tradeoffs as they are not mutually exclusive options.

Some of the general differences are well noted by Joya DeFoor, Treasurer of the City of Los Angeles, who observes, "A Treasurer has to look forward and prepare for the future. But, they have to do more than that. As a finance professional, a Treasurer, you need to forge ahead into new territories. A Controller records and there are a myriad of rules on how to record, when to record and why to record. A comparable set of rules doesn't exist to that extent in the Treasury world. There are best practices but then those are very fluid and more varied organization by organization." These different operating rules create different perspectives between these two important positions.

One of the big challenges for any business person, and particularly finance-oriented folks, is communicating in a way that is easily understood by someone from marketing, production, or the distribution side of the business. When we say things like, *EBITDA, ROI, NPV,* this is more than a problem of just using acronyms that have no meaning to those outside of finance—every business has acronyms. This is a great shorthand for communicating within a particular discipline.

When we are communicating beyond our particular group or beyond Treasury, in this case, we need to make sure that we do so in a clear and understandable manner, and in a way that colleagues will understand to ensure that they can take the proper actions and steps to reach the goal all are seeking.

An example of converting terminology into a local and understandable language was offered by Rebecca Flick, VP and Treasurer for The Home Depot Inc. Flick had discussed how her department communicates particular needs and activities in the business that might be related to working capital, improving sales, or reducing expenses. They try to convert things to simple and easy-to-understand terms, she said. Thus, instead of saying, "We need to increase sales or revenue," they provide an example of putting items at the check-out that were easy for customers to pick up and add to their list—things that they needed, instead of making another trip—but also in a way to increase the sales.

If every single customer going through a Home Depot store were to add an additional $1 item to his or her cart, Home Depot would increase sales by $1 billion! While a $1 sale seems minute, the amount of revenue that can be driven by just having every person pick up one more item was a very easy concept for all the employees to grasp—from store manager to someone who is schooled in finance.

Whether the finance professional is discussing cash, controls, forecasting, working capital, or a variety of other topics, it is always useful to make sure that both parties mean the same thing when using the same word. To achieve more effective communication, the effective Treasurer will understand what guides the other person's thinking. This objective is often met by understanding the responsibilities of the other party and this professional background. By making this effort, the conversation can become much less frustrating and far more productive.

Given the importance of understanding the other person's perspective, some additional guidelines include knowing the business drivers as well as the terms that are commonly used. Knowing the business drivers and measurements provides a clear window into what the other party is measured on and will pay the most attention to. There is a lot of noise in today's workplace, and getting your message across can be quite a challenge without the added complication of having the other party tune your message out because it seems irrelevant. There is a "Far Side" cartoon by Gary Larson that shows a person talking to a dog. It shows what the person is saying and what the dog is hearing. The person is communicating a great deal and interspersing the message with the dog's name. The dog simply hears "_blah, blah, blah_" and its name. A few examples of the differing use of finance language prove instructive in reinforcing the concept that perspective and responsibility shape understanding. By remaining cognizant of these differences, it becomes far easier to be an effective communicator.

Cash

One of the most basic of all finance terms is _cash_. Instruction about cash begins well before the first official business course. In Accounting 101, all business majors learn the basic double-entry accounting method with an entry that uses cash. The purchase of equipment is shown as a debit to "equipment," which increases the value of that asset category of plant and equipment. To pay for the equipment, cash was expended, and cash decreased. Thus, the credit entry is made to cash, which decreases the value of the asset called "cash." Understanding that an asset exchange took place where cash was swapped for an asset is not just basic for finance people, it is also a fundamental concept of trade and business.

While cash is certainly cash, there are some different views of cash that need to be understood—at least at a macro level—in order to communicate effectively within finance. The two primary views can be called _generally accepted accounting principles (GAAP)_ cash and _Treasury_ cash.

GAAP is concerned about cash from a reporting standpoint. For all intents and purposes, it ignores the concept of _float_, and views it as an immaterial consideration. Float, the concept that it takes time to settle the financial transaction in a bank account, is deemed irrelevant due to the time-frame of float. For example, the period of time when a check is received and Accounts Receivable (AR) is relieved to the time the check is deposited and funds are ultimately made available is viewed as imminent.

The opposite example, a *disbursement*, is treated in a similar manner. While a check may be issued or an automated clearing house (ACH) payment generated today, the concept is that cash is gone from the balance sheet. And, even though the disbursement may not remove funds from the bank account for a few days or even a week or more, that is simply a banking nuance and is not relevant from a financial reporting standpoint.

Treasury professionals often use the term *real cash* to describe their view of cash. While this term can often lead to fruitless discussions, the key concept is that there is a distinction between how each party views cash.

Treasury is concerned with liquidity management, which includes being a faithful steward of cash, investments, debt, and a few other asset and liability items. Part of being a good steward of the company's resources is to reduce borrowing costs and optimize investment earnings in accordance with some key principles related to risk and return. In aggregate, the amount of funds disbursed and received can be quite substantial. The Treasurer takes advantage of cash management tools to optimize her investment earnings. Leaving excess balances in a checking account to cover all of the checks that were issued is considered outdated and inefficient. In some organizations, disbursement float can equal many tens of millions of dollars and more. And, while checks may be issued every day and others clear their bank account removing funds, the intervening time creates a sizable asset that can yield a return.

Consider the organization that makes good use of that disbursement float and invests the tens of millions of dollars' worth of float, or uses it to pay down debt more quickly. That organization fares much better than the organization that allows its banking system to be dictated by an accounting framework that is geared to support financial reporting. So far, there is no argument in concept from the Controller. The controller will readily admit that the Treasurer should use appropriate tools to manage cash. However, when the discussion moves to the details, the argument can change.

Because GAAP ignores float, a company can be in a situation where it has almost no cash from an accounting standpoint, and yet have many millions that could be invested. The reverse could also be true. A firm could have substantial GAAP cash, but lack usable funds and thus run into a liquidity crisis.

The language difference can show up with disputes over the proper way to fund disbursement accounts, or in a Treasury group, spending days explaining the difference between GAAP cash and Treasury cash.

There are some common obstacles that are raised that must be addressed in order to use optimized Treasury practices. Many Controllers have initially raised GAAP as a reason to restrict any changes to how cash is recorded. Any suggestions that would include tracking cash differently are met with the ultimate accounting response that "GAAP will not allow for that." However, GAAP requirements for reporting cash do not, by themselves, make it resistant to different or more effective recording methods. GAAP requires cash to be reported in financial statements in a particular manner and is certainly inflexible in its pronouncements. However, it is not merely within the realm of acceptable accounting to be able to gracefully track float and separately track various liabilities for the benefit of treasury; it is usually considered a leading practice. In fact, an improvement to the accounting controls and processes can be employed that will benefit and assist the controller's function while supporting good Treasury practices in the general ledger. The techniques and theories behind this are in use by many top organizations with modern Treasury staffs. The use of current technology allows this win-win situation and is worthy of a separate and detailed discussion (see Chapter 6).

The benefits of understanding the framework for optimal cash recording will allow the thoughtful Treasurer to explain how to better record transactions in order to align the records for Treasury needs while maintaining integrity for GAAP reporting.

Forecasting

Forecasting is another contentious word in finance. Corporate planning and a controller's forecast are almost always a forecast of profit and loss. The forecast is a projection of the income statement. While this forecast will occasionally include some components of the balance sheet, this is usually not much more sophisticated than backing into the balance sheet components. The purpose of this forecast is for longer-range planning and it is typically deemed to be useful over a period of time that falls in line with the income statement's time perspective. This type of forecast properly done is often quite useful for business planning and determining what resources and attention will be given to different areas of the organization. Also, this type of forecast is an important part of ensuring the proper stewardship of the organization's assets.

The forecast by treasury often begins with the mantra that "cash is king." It is focused on select parts of the balance sheet and activities that impact cash most directly. Areas of focus include cash, investments and debt, capital expenditures, and so on. These and other categories are given top priority due to their direct impact on liquidity. The focus is on liquidity and ensuring that the organization can meet its obligations.

Meeting obligations requires having access to the proper assets or lines of credit and not simply having made accounting profit while having a cash flow issue. Many a profitable enterprise has gone bankrupt or suffered financial harm because they could not meet their short-term obligations. This type of forecast is essential for ensuring the short-term effective operation of the business.

Financial Plan Forecast

The financial plan forecast can also be both interesting and useful for the Treasurer. Granted, it needs to be handled carefully. Many Treasurers recognize that to rely solely on that document to do their cash and liquidity planning would be far too risky for their organization and their career. It is, in many firms, either a hope or in some cases a type of fiction. And while optimistic projections and aggressive goals can be useful and have a place in the life of the organization, they should not be treated as a fact before they occur.

Documenting the variance to plan or budget is an essential exercise. However, the variance analysis and explanation documents tend to be done over time, with some fiction being created along the way. If the top line growth is a little slower, explanations often abound ranging from general economic trends or simple delay of some sales. The numbers are often promised to be accurate in aggregate by the time one gets to the end of the period being scrutinized. Many forecasts represent little more than a hope and have minimal bearing on the business, income, or cash flow. Even when these numbers are set, they far too often resemble a hope rather than a realistic plan. Hope is not a plan. Entering numbers in a spreadsheet to produce the forecast will not make that plan's assumptions realistic or even attainable. The Treasurer needs to plan for liquidity cautiously since the financial health of the firm depends upon it.

Despite no or low growth over the past several years, the new plan will often indicate that income will grow without any real change, other than emphatic statements indicating how hard the division will work to achieve it. The level of adjustments necessary by month or quarter may seem quite minor for the Controller. However, these shifts can be quite dramatic for the Treasurer and require rapid, and sometimes costly, reactions. The magnitude of a change can be far more dramatic from a balance sheet perspective than from the income statement. The difference in scale is an easy concept to grasp. Yet once the Treasurer has experienced it in reality, she develops a strong appreciation for it in practice.

The capital budget may be set any number of months before the planned disbursement. If the timing is shifted from the plan, and it often is, the difference in magnitude of the impact becomes apparent. Shifting a $60 million capital expenditure (with a life of five years) up two months, from August to June, will impact the income statement that year by only $2 million. The impact on cash usage during June will be $60 million and will also require an adjustment in the August forecast. This type of shift may seem minimal to the Controller or a line person, who may not have appreciation for the fire drill that Treasury is suffering by having to adjust to this late-breaking liquidity news. In some organizations, the entire capital budgeting process seems designed to create wanton destruction to some of the best Treasury forecasts.

The Treasurer needs to have a realistic perspective on what will happen. This may need to be based on nonplan data or analysis. In many organizations, the Treasurer's group simply uses the financial plan as one input. They have been trained to recognize its shortcomings and not to rely on it in crafting their own forecast.

Cash Forecast and Analysis

Treasury is concerned with liquidity management and with optimizing the capital structure of the organization. Regarding liquidity management, the Treasurer must have several useful components: an accurate forecast for the very short term, by document, for the simple calculation of contention between the planning area of finance and Treasury. This arises from the same root cause of the other contentious items. The need for and use of forecasts can be quite varied.

From a forecast perspective, Treasury is often looking at a short-term cash forecast based on trying to determine what its liquidity needs are, whereas the financial planning and forecast from a Controller's area is often income statement oriented. The main thrust of this type of forecast is to determine where the organization will be based on a profit/loss perspective. The balance sheet is not in view with this forecast. Focusing on the balance sheet tends to sit squarely in the domain of the Treasurer. Conversely, the income statement focus for forecasting typically resides with the Controller.

A forecast that is based on averages or month-end activity is a forecast that will not be of much use during the various business and payment cycles that nearly all organizations experience. An organization that makes a huge push on collecting receivables at month end will look pretty good at that point in time. Just because the balance sheet is a financial statement that shows where things stand at a point in time, does not help to see what is needed on a day-by-day basis. Treasury is responsible for ensuring liquidity on every day of the month and year. And Treasury knows that its peak cash need may be 10 days before month end, requiring a good forecast.

Treasurers perform different types of analysis and calculations from many others in the organization. This can make some people uncomfortable with the different approaches. Tom King, Treasurer of Progressive Insurance, comments on the nature of these differences: "Treasurers are forward looking and perform a lot of ad hoc reports and one-off-analysis. Their numbers are typically approximations and schedules don't cross foot because they are providing a positional number. The Treasurer is concerned about future investments. Their responsibility is to frame the idea of the project and of the concept, taking in the high level considerations of tax, legal and various projections."

Working Capital

Working capital management in great companies is primarily driven and should be driven by the Treasurer. This is focused almost exclusively on accounts receivable, inventory, and accounts payable and the interplay of those items with each other or with cash (that is, increasing inventory to foster better sales uses cash by increasing net adjusted working capital). The Treasurer is trying to optimize working capital, oftentimes trying to free up working capital to pay down debt or return it to the shareholders. Sometimes optimizing will mean using more cash to, for example, extend terms on AR to increase sales among profitable segments.

The scope and definition of *working capital* can create some initial confusion. This is rarely a contentious issue, but can waste time if the Treasurer and Controller do not understand the differences.

From an accounting basis, working capital is a simple and traditional formula taken from several components of the balance sheet. It is current assets minus current liabilities. This is easy to calculate, since it comes from the financial statements of the firm and is thus always available. It is a useful formula to quickly determine if the organization has the ability to meet its short-term liabilities from its short-term assets. Bankers have traditionally used this calculation as one means of determining whether the target firm was worthy of receiving access to capital. This formula is sometimes referred to as the "traditional working capital calculation."

Working capital optimization is most frequently used by Treasurers, but many Controllers are familiar with the approach also. Organizations managing working capital use a calculation that includes some select balance sheet components, all of which are a subset of the accounting definition. This formula is accounts receivable plus inventory minus accounts payable. This formula is quite useful for the Treasurer and the CFO to see how much of the organization's liquid assets are tied up in the cash conversion cycle. It is also useful for determining the cost to the organization of the working capital used. This formula is more and more frequently referred to as the "alternative working capital calculation."

Those who work on optimizing working capital employ the alternative method over the traditional method for logical reasons, not the least of which is what purpose they were created to serve. For those looking to convert accounts receivable to cash, the traditional formula is an inappropriate measure. The traditional measure would see the exchange as nothing more than movement from one current asset account to another. There would be no change and, effectively, no difference between the two current assets. The traditional working capital measure is not meant to track or measure progress of an effort to optimize the amount of capital employed in the cash conversion cycle.

The alternative method is a useful starting point. Collecting accounts receivable more quickly (within parameters) is typically considered one excellent way of freeing up capital. This action will reduce the total working capital (AR + IN − AP) and turn it over to the organization to invest, pay down debt, or return it to the owners.

The other challenge of the term *working capital* stems from some other measurements that are commonly made based on the financial statements. Financial statements are excellent sources for calculations, since they must be created and preserved over time. This makes them a consistent source. Calculations made off of manually captured statistics create problems of consistency and accuracy. Statistics fall behind. People stop capturing them. Business priorities happen, and this work can be delayed.

Ultimately, it is hard to track trends over the years when there are multiple gaps of data. This issue needs to be considered with using the balance sheet for working capital usage, or if it is based on the difference between accounting measures and liquidity measures. The following two examples will illustrate the issue; Chapter 7 explores its implications and various solutions.

Example 1. If an organization moves from a traditional lockbox to an image lockbox, it receives funds on the exact same day, with the same availability. However, with the use of images delivered via the Internet, it is now able to post to accounts receivable (AR) one day earlier (versus the physical delivery method of a traditional lockbox). This is both useful and helpful. However, it will also show a decrease of one day of days sales outstanding (DSO), and appear to provide a financial benefit when viewed through the financial statements. *Funds will not be available for investment any sooner, despite appearances of faster collection as viewed through the financial statements, which are based on GAAP reporting.*

Example 2. An organization moves to a process of electronically collecting or receiving funds. The accounting occurs on the same day, as in the past. Funds are available sooner, but the financial statement remains the same. Thus, the working capital formula seems to show no difference. *A real improvement in the timing of when good funds were received was achieved. However, this improvement will not show up in the financial statement or the working capital formula.*

In both examples, setting proper and realistic expectations is in order. It would be wise to point out the accounting impact of one day with no attendant liquidity benefit. The second example would show the smart Treasury professional pointing out the very real liquidity benefit while telegraphing the absence of that impact in accounting records.

Controls

The Controller is often focused on *detective* controls. Are the financial systems and processes and reporting processes set up in such a manner that they can detect and identify where errors happened, where fraud occurred, or if there were accounting improprieties? The emphasis is on detective controls.

Operating areas that touch the financial supply chain may focus on segregation of duties and trying to prevent errors earlier in a process. They often rely on the Controller's processes to detect problems after they occur. In such situations, a prudent businessperson ensures that he has segregation of duties and a clear audit trail coupled with a good accounting and control framework.

In many organizations, Treasury is in a unique position with respect to controls. Due to the nature and types of transactions that Treasurers initiate and control, they must establish robust preventative controls. Sending an erroneous wire transfer—which is an irrevocable transfer—could immediately create a severe liquidity situation in a company. This situation is one that clearly must be prevented, and clear segregation and preventative controls must be in place in the Treasury area. Finding out a month later of the loss of substantial funds that have left the company by a great reconciliation process is not acceptable in the Treasury realm.

Treasury must stop these from happening due to the size and finality of many of their transactions. There are numerous examples of wire transfers and execution of trades that have ranged from blackened eyes to the demise of a corporation.

Losses can be severe in an operating area such as accounts payable and payroll, but they tend to be much smaller in scale and size. Additionally, some of the settlement mechanisms for these areas may have other rights of return, stop payment, and fraud identification processes that provide an additional window of time to correct the issue. This varies by payment type and by country.

When the Treasurer thinks about controls within Treasury, she must think about *preventative* controls. And while both Controller and Treasurer have different focuses, each should understand the importance of both types of controls and support the range of preventative and detective controls.

Importantly, most auditors come from an accounting background and mindset. Far too frequently, both internal and external auditors are not up to the task of auditing Treasury effectively. The auditing firms typically place new audit staff on Treasury, provide them with the inadequate prior-year workpapers, and send them off alone into Treasury—with the resultant performance one might expect. Knowing this weakness of the audit process on Treasury, it is absolutely imperative that Treasurers regularly ensure that their controls are completely adequate to prevent substantial loss. Given that most Treasury departments are thinly staffed, this can represent a challenge. But it is never an excuse.

Summary

It is not surprising that since Treasurers and Controllers have different focuses and different purposes for what they do, their perspectives will also differ. Given that they use the same language of finance, and even identical words to mean different things, it is a ripe environment for miscommunication. This shows up in how they treat cash and liquidity, what forecasting means to them, how they would record entries, how to influence working capital uses, and what controls need to be in place. To ultimately benefit the organization—which they both serve—it is imperative that these differences be understood by both parties as they seek to communicate effectively with each other.

CHAPTER 13

Building and Developing the Treasury Team

*Great Treasurers bring in the best people because "A" players want to be
with "A" players so they can learn from them. When hiring, they make
sure they bring in somebody who will be a catalyst for the rest of the
team."*

—Linda Cascardo, Senior Vice President,
Wholesale Sales Executive, Wells Fargo

M ost Treasury organizations are thinly staffed, and this requires a greater
emphasis on how the Treasurer puts the group together and how he
develops the people within that team. No matter what level Treasury is
staffed at, it has the responsibility to fulfill its mission without fail. Given the
fact that Treasury must secure adequate liquidity and manage a wide variety
of risks, forming the typically small team to accomplish this effort is a top
objective.

There is much that can be said about putting a team together, developing that team, and then optimizing its performance. Chapter 2 introduces
some concepts surrounding the first two items. This current chapter provides some additional dialogue on those sections along with some additional
descriptions of success in addressing those needs. Some ground is covered
a second time in a slightly different manner and is included for those who
may have skipped that chapter since they have been in the Treasurer's chair
for a number of years.

After those sections, the chapter turns its focus on a few relatively simple concepts related to optimizing performance. It should be understood that these three areas are intertwined and that Treasury groups that have success in one area should be able to enjoy success in the other areas more easily. The reverse is true, too. If an organization does not put the team together in a complementary way, it is more difficult to optimize the results. When a process and mindset is in place that drives individual performance, the result is generally a positive outcome for the entire team's performance.

A primary role of Treasurers is to make sure that their team has the right team members. Having the right team members is rarely a single event that will not need adjustments at certain times in the life of an organization.

Putting the Puzzle Together

Certain romantic notions can develop in one's mind about a blank piece of paper. This is regularly true when a Treasurer is new in a role or has inherited staff for various reasons. However, not everyone can start with a blank sheet of paper when looking at her Treasury organization. Indeed, there are many times when moderate change is needed, and it helps to make adjustments to something that is reasonably well constructed that simply needs some modifications.

Every Treasurer will need to keep a mental picture of what her team should look like to meet the firm's current needs as well as needs it will have in three years. Few organizations remain stagnant for long, and the Treasurer needs to think ahead as to how the group will fulfill its mission in light of various changes.

No Treasurer can be a Strategic Treasurer who does not think deeply and act wisely when it comes to her team.

Quality of Team Members

Paul Greenhalgh, Head of Sales for North America at IT2 Solutions, has worked with many organizations. For Treasurers, he says, a crucial and essential action that they must perform relates to the team. "The Treasurer is only as good as the team they have around them. Those Treasurers that have the highest level of success have put really good people in place around them." Treasury organizations tend to be smaller than other areas, so each person has a bigger impact on the overall success of the group.

Making the Pieces Fit

The pieces of the puzzle need to fit together well. It may seem easier if only one lens or perspective is necessary to have an effective and complementary team. However, reality is a bit more complex. For most organizations, three types of fit must be examined carefully when forming or reorganizing the team.

DIVERSITY OF THOUGHT, SKILLS, AND EXPERIENCES   The unique set of positions, education, and responsibilities that each person has contributes to the value he can offer any organization. However, that value is not a single sum that is good for every organization. Linda Cascardo, a Senior Vice President and Wholesale Sales Executive at Wells Fargo, who has vast experience observing Treasury groups, provides some guidance: "When a Treasurer or other financial professional puts together their team, they have to understand their own strengths and weaknesses. It is very easy to hire somebody who is just like you. That is the wrong answer. Treasurers should hire someone who has something they do not have so they will be a complement."

She further states the problem of hiring people with near-identical professional backgrounds: "...those [Treasurers] who hired a bunch of people who have the exact same skill set will find that they have the exact same type of shortcomings."

Hiring people with the same type of background is a common occurrence and is justified in various ways. The typical justification made by the hiring manager is manifested in conversations about the benefits of having a cohesiveness of opinions and the value of having a particular background. When hiring people with the same skill sets and experience, it is duplicative or, at best, marginally additive. Adding individuals with complementary skill sets and thoughts provides the opportunity for the value to be multiplicative. While many jokingly articulate a desire to have a clone made of themselves, this is neither possible nor lawful. Perhaps the common occurrence of hiring someone with nearly identical experiences and professional background is in some way a type of skill-set cloning.

For example, peering into a handyman's tool bag one should see a range of tools for different tasks. If, instead, you observed it contained six hammers, four handsaws, and 11 flathead screwdrivers, you would have some serious questions about the handyman's ability to complete a variety of tasks. You might even wonder what he was thinking. People are not like hammers or screwdrivers, of course. However, one should question the lucidity of hiring managers if they need a range of skills and experiences that are complementary to complete their mission but choose instead to hire based upon similarities.

CULTURAL FIT AND BENEFIT FOR THE EMPLOYEE   The need for an organization to have employees with the right type of experience and skills must not make hiring managers forget that employees have career needs also. Treasurers should ensure that the professionals they bring on board will perform best if their position is a good fit for them. IT2 Solution's Greenhalgh provides advice for Treasury professionals as they look at positions: "Finding an organization where you can grow and thrive based on what your goals and personal needs are is pivotal. You can get a great job with wonderful compensation and everything else that seems good. But, you would become miserable if it is not a good fit. If it is a bad fit for the professional, it becomes a bad fit for the organization."

INTELLECTUAL CURIOSITY AND BROAD THINKING   Treasury work is often about magnitude and direction of numbers when performing analysis. It is also steeped in risk management generally and about identifying risks and opportunities specifically. Treasury must be able to provide rapid analysis and guidance at an order-bounded level versus to-the-decimal calculations. These demands should have an impact on the selection process as a Treasurer builds and changes her team.

The requirements of Treasury should drive Treasurers to hire those who are intellectually curious, creative, and able to think about matters on a macro level.

Elyse Weiner, Managing Director, Global Product Head, Liquidity & Investments for Citibank, comments on how intellectual curiosity can be fostered and improved by building a diverse team: "There is a great need for Treasury departments to accommodate a diversity of skills, abilities and experience on their team across financial, technical and market disciplines. Differences in perspective will challenge the Treasurer to step back and look at things from fresh perspectives and chart new and innovative courses of action, rather than pursuing the status quo."

Developing the Team

The term *human resources* can sometimes seem cold and calculating. The development of staff may have some consistent patterns, but since people are unique, some modification in their training and development will be necessary and natural. The Treasurer has strategic human-resource management as a responsibility and, therefore, he plays an important role in setting the tone and driving development that is good for the Treasury staff and for the organization. Staff development must be done in a manner that supports the organizational objectives.

Defining a Pathway

Treasury organizations vary in size, even if most are relatively small. A larger organization provides more flexibility to move and train staff. And often more specialization is possible. Smaller organizations tend to offer broader responsibilities because each role must cover more activities and functions. Whatever the size of the organization, thinking through the development process and career paths is valuable to both the team and the organization.

Vice President and Treasurer for Honeywell International Inc. John Tus enjoyed seeing his group recognized for "excellence in Treasury" when the firm won the Alexander Hamilton Award for Overall Excellence for two consecutive years. Different leaders within his organization won different individual awards both years, demonstrating a deep level of bench strength. Honeywell is not positioned with a few strong leaders in Treasury who did all of the hard work; it has a culture and a methodology that brings on talent and develops those people. The particular process it uses is specific to Honeywell. However, there are some principles and perspectives that are recognized and followed that many Treasurers would do well to analyze.

- **The best and brightest will move on.** They will move, either within the organization or externally. Keeping talent in the firm tends to be very valuable to the organization. Honeywell seeks to foster movement to other areas that can benefit from the skills and abilities of their best and brightest talent.
- **Move high-potential people up as fast as possible.** Within as few as three years, a high-potential person may move from senior analyst to manager to director. Keep them challenged.
- **Cross-training is essential.** Moving up into different roles develops staff. Also, moving to other areas will broaden their skills and abilities. For example, someone may move from being a corporate finance analyst to a risk-management analyst to the manager of Foreign Exchange and then to director of all risk management for the organization.
- **Flexible and responsible—two essentials.** Assign specific accountability to staff. They do not need to be left without resources or input, but they will have accountability for executing, planning, and improving on their plans. Honeywell leverages the group's knowledge to challenge and vet ideas. By pushing people hard and giving them experience, these people can move up and on when they want to, since others are being groomed and can fill their role.

Career Communication and Perspectives

John Tus outlines some key activities performed at his firm that help ensure employees know what is expected and how the organization can help develop them and further their careers. The Treasurer and senior leadership in Treasury will work toward the following:

- **Partner with the people.** Discuss their careers. How can we help them to be successful? Talk to the person and don't just talk about people.
- **Set high expectations.** Make it clear that they need to perform at the highest level. Have an environment of success for the group. Teamwork is essential, and at Honeywell teams are the way things get done.
- **Organize Treasury by process.** Organize the activities and responsibilities into a process like a cattle chute. Almost everyone likes to work in silos, but a lot of work happens between the silos. Treasury must think about broad impacts outside of the individual silos. Chapter 8 discusses the ramifications of this in detail.
- **Provide opportunities and allow people to take initiative.** Too many people wait for things to happen versus making things happen.

Questions That Make Connections

Every organization needs a Treasury group that can make a clear connection between activities and the organization's objectives. Asking questions is an excellent method to get people thinking so that they can make the necessary logical connections.

Tim Hart, Senior Vice President and Treasurer of the First National Bank of Nebraska, regularly thinks about making connections between events and how that impacts his organization. He asks a few key questions to get the synapses firing along the lines of external implications to a Treasurer's organization:

- **Normal?** Can you recognize something as abnormal? Am I in the relative range of what makes sense, or is this outside that range? What are the implications of this nonnormal situation or event?
- **Diversified?** Are you diversified enough to take the first hit and survive? Hart restates this question as, "What deductible can you take?"

Tus makes a point of asking his Treasury staff questions in order to make sure the connections between what they are doing and what the organizational goals are, can be clearly understood. Among those questions are:

- What is new? And what are the implications of this?
- What are you working on? How do those tasks help accomplish the CEO's and CFO's goals?

- Does it drive an increase in ROI on the capital side? Does it help with the growth of margins? Does it reduce the weighted average cost of capital?
- If management thinks these things are important, how does what you are doing help the organization achieve those objectives?

Summary

Due to its limited size and critical roles, the Treasury team requires more careful formulation than many other areas. The team must be formed and then reformed as organizational needs change. It is often easier for a new Treasurer to form his team properly at the start rather than to make needed adjustments later on, as certain people who have served the organization faithfully in the past may no longer be a good fit.

Optimizing the overall performance is possible only when the responsibilities are delegated and regular dialogs with the team about the approach, results, and goals are communicated clearly. Holding each leader up to accountability and transparency makes each professional improve. This is a requirement if Treasury is to fulfill its mission.

CHAPTER 14

Understanding and Maximizing the Use of Treasury Technology Tools

When selecting a technology tool, Treasurers must make sure they get the right partners because selecting a technology tool is a long-term choice. You'll probably have it for seven years, not just a few years. Therefore, make sure that the partner firm that you are going to work with has plans to advance the product into areas you can use. They should be able to explain how they are addressing your needs and where they expect to take the product in two or three years. What resources will they need to accomplish this? Their product map needs to be clear and must make sense to you.

—Jean-Luc Robert, CEO, Kyriba Corp.

It is a great time to be a Treasurer for a variety of reasons that go beyond the experience and joy of turbulent and uncertain markets. Developments in technology and the addition of some greatly needed services can make the people in Treasury far more focused on tactical and analytical items versus spending excessive energy on operational matters. This is good news. However, being able to take advantage of the technology that is offered by banks and technology vendors does not just happen automatically. Like becoming accustomed to many good tools, planning and understanding are required in order to leverage those capabilities for organizations.

The entire landscape of Treasury technology tools can best be described in a book rather than in a single chapter. And, due to the rate of development in this area, such a book would need to be updated on a monthly basis. Thus, this chapter will focus on several major items as well as provide some advice on moving forward that will remain current even as the technology tools advance and progress.

The following sections will first focus on the principal perspective that technology tools are a business-process enabler and then will examine various software and service categories.

Technology Supports the Treasury Role, and Treasury Supports the Organization

Technology tools are not the focus of the Treasurer. No matter how elegant or effective, the tools merely support the Treasurer or Treasury processes as they help the organization fulfill its mission. The goal is the proper use of technology. As Jeffrey Wallace, Managing Partner of Greenwich Treasury Advisors, says, "The objective is world-class use of technology, not the use of world-class technology."

Indeed, while there is quite a bit of excellent Treasury technology purchased by the marketplace, the amount of acquired Treasury technology that is effectively put to use amounts to a surprisingly small subset.

This basic concept about the role of technology tools and the overall technology landscape has implications that matter for the Treasurer. The following should provide a basis for a discussion within Treasury departments:

- Role of Relationships and Partners
  - **Bank-specific services.** Many services are available through banks directly. Some of these services tend to be oriented solely or primarily toward their products and services. Other banks provide more open platforms, which allow organizations to use information or execute transactions with other institutions.
  - **Customer-base advantages.** When large banks make a decision to move forward with a particular technology and service, they can normally add hundreds and thousands of customers to the platform. Their ability to leverage their franchise and distribution channel is a tremendous advantage over technology vendors.
  - **Lending.** Banks, in normal environments, lend money. Vendors do not. This fact will need to have some bearing on the decision process. *Note:* if the purchasing department can decide who provides certain services—whether it be purchasing card programs, Treasury, travel

and entertainment cards, invoice printing, and so on—then purchasing will need to be responsible to secure credit from those firms at affordable rates. If the difference in services is relatively minor, for most organizations it will make sense to secure those services from their bank.

- Vendor Systems
  - **Bank agnostic.** Vendor systems, when they interface with banks, tend to tout their bank agnosticism. They have historically oversold the ease with which data can be connected to anyone. They will almost always blame the bank. New offerings are making the sales pitch of easy connectivity more closely aligned to reality.
  - **Less than 100 percent replacement.** Some vendor systems don't have the current ability to replace a bank system (for instance, which Treasury workstation allows you to view paid check or lockbox images? Or place stop payments?). Some don't even plan to do this. And some services may always be delivered better through the bank portal.
- Changing Technology
  - **Changes to technology.** Technology platforms change from time to time. Treasurers need to live with decisions about a partner for many years. Accordingly, Treasury must ensure its technology plans look five to seven years in the future. Does the potential partner perform the functions you need right now? Will they be able to add what you need as your need emerges?
  - **Process and technology decision.** Deciding on the technology to use in support of a business and its Treasury responsibilities is about both the process and the technology. It is not an either/or proposition. If the technology is outdated, you will have a harder time supporting constituents and the financial process.

Treasury Technology Landscape

There are multiple ways that Treasury technology can be grouped or categorized. Many of these methods have merit. Exhibit 14.1 provides one such categorization and shows the landscape of corporate Treasury technology systems and supporting tools.

The left section of the exhibit covers core Treasury activity related to bank information, cash positioning, forecasting, debt and investment management, and core financial risk management activities. The middle section groups the various services and software that a company may employ in its effort to optimize working capital and to leverage the assets of and drive efficiency through the financial supply chain. The right section of the exhibit touches on core compliance-related systems that are dear to

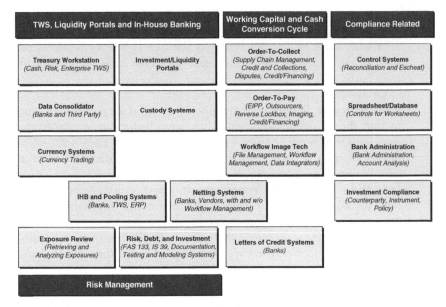

TWS, Liquidity Portals and In-House Banking	Working Capital and Cash Conversion Cycle	Compliance Related

Treasury Workstation (Cash, Risk, Enterprise TWS)	Investment/Liquidity Portals	Order-To-Collect (Supply Chain Management, Credit and Collections, Disputes, Credit/Financing)	Control Systems (Reconciliation and Escheat)
Data Consolidator (Banks and Third Party)	Custody Systems	Order-To-Pay (EIPP, Outsourcers, Reverse Lockbox, Imaging, Credit/Financing)	Spreadsheet/Database (Controls for Worksheets)
Currency Systems (Currency Trading)		Workflow Image Tech (File Management, Workflow Management, Data Integrators)	Bank Administration (Bank Administration, Account Analysis)
	IHB and Pooling Systems (Banks, TWS, ERP)	Netting Systems (Banks, Vendors, with and w/o Workflow Management)	Investment Compliance (Counterparty, Instrument, Policy)
Exposure Review (Retrieving and Analyzing Exposures)	Risk, Debt, and Investment (FAS 133, IS 39, Documentation, Testing and Modeling Systems)	Letters of Credit Systems (Banks)	

Risk Management

EXHIBIT 14.1 Landscape of Treasury Technology Systems

the Treasurer—from spreadsheet compliance tools to bank account management and additional visibility tools to counterparty exposures.

This exhibit is not an exhaustive list of the technology landscape categories. Visually showing the landscape requires some measure of perspective, since many products grow their capabilities from one of the designated categories into other areas requiring some adjustments that are not easily created in a two-dimensional drawing. Accordingly, when seeking to match up needs with various technologies, providers must review and modify the landscape picture in order to relate it directly to their specific needs.

Extension and Visibility Services

Banks provide an entire range of what would be considered traditional banking services. These include all types of cash management, card services, foreign exchange, custody, and investment services. Many of those services have been in place for decades with enhancements in delivery methods and features being added at regular intervals.

Beyond the traditional services, there are several categories of services extending deeper into the financial processes with the goal of improving efficiency, optimizing working capital, or facilitating better visibility and transparency to your investments and cash. These services are offered by banks as well as third-party vendors.

Outsourcing Services

Banks in particular are offering useful outsourcing services. These services move further up the cash conversion cycle. Outsourcing the payment creation process and even the invoice creation process are essential services for many leading Treasury banks. A bank that can create and deliver the invoice can have an advantage in the cash application rates as funds and information are collected either through the lockbox or electronically. The outsourcing options include the order-to-pay and order-to-collect sides of the cash conversion cycle.

These services should be considered as they are often run more efficiently than an internal process and provide superior capabilities from the segregation of duty and contingency-planning perspectives. They will often be selected due to the additional benefit of being able to provide greater and more consistent fee income to the banks that lend your organization funds.

Financial Supply Chain

Accounts receivable securitization programs represent a traditional source of borrowing against one current asset. Accounts receivable and accounts payable can both be leveraged with a range of supply chain financing services offered by both banks and technology vendors. Some of these services provide a far more cost-beneficial method of securing funds, using a process that is highly efficient. The technology can help support a clean process that will allow for financing to be executed quite simply. These changes can be made and performed without causing financial or relationship harm with a firm's vendors and customers.

Liquidity and Money Market Portals

Banks and technology vendors have begun offering money market and liquidity portals as a way of creating an extremely sticky client relationship. A client has access to a single portal where decisions about investment activity can be executed simply against multiple options. This information is open and creates a level of transparency that was not available until recently. Being able to see counterparties, instruments, balances, and maturities in a simple manner through a single site serves to make the daily life of a Treasury manager easier, while still providing competitive rates. These benefits make the decision to leave a particular bank or vendor more difficult.

Data Consolidators

Accessing the data that is necessary in order to perform proper analysis and make useful projections and forecasts has long been a thorn in the side of Treasury. Data consolidators can aggregate rates, yield curves, bank balance, and transaction details. Problems with securing, validating, and organizing needed data can become an enormous time-absorbing process for a Treasury group. Data consolidators can also act as a conduit for various transactions that must be initiated, such as wire payments or drafts. Not all data consolidators or networks perform all of the same functions, but many organizations greatly benefit by outsourcing—one of the biggest headaches in Treasury. The category of data consolidators includes banks, Society for Worldwide Interbank Financial Telecommunication (SWIFT), and other consolidators, which include several levels of service bureaus.

The use and value of data consolidators are discussed in more detail in Chapter 17.

Treasury Workstation and the Technology Landscape

The environment of broad Treasury technology has changed due to a convergence of technology and capabilities as well as the emergence of data consolidators. Technology shifts have made it far more affordable to develop, deploy, and support various services generally and Treasury workstations (TWSs) specifically over the Internet. And data consolidators can take care of most problems related to gathering data and executing transactions and confirmations.

This is encouraging news for Treasurers. It is appropriate to have a realistic view of the landscape to analyze these changes and a firm's needs based upon current rather than historical information. Using the term *historical* in this context refers to out-of-date information that, if used, can lead an organization to improper conclusions.

With emerging developments across the broad spectrum of Treasury technology, a major competitive conflict is brewing in the middle-market space between banks and Treasury workstation providers.

Treasury Workstations and Bank Systems Converge

There is a strong perception that banks, as a group and in certain respects, have long been laggards in developing and deploying new technology. Their focus is often about initiating transactions or providing bank information or images that customers demand. Value-added services, such as tools to aid in forecasting, accounting, or tracking debt and investments, are not normally provided. Every firm needs to create accounting entries and needs a consistent and comprehensive view of its liquidity. Few banks provide any tools, portal, or offering that helps customers achieve this goal.

Perception differs from reality in some respects, however. Banks as a group moved to web-based solutions before Treasury workstation providers. They could not support the number of clients required when they were using the installed software approach, and the numbers grew to the thousands of clients. Treasury workstation providers were slow to move to the Web via a hosted or Software as a Service (SaaS) model, due largely to the investment in the previous technology and the addiction to licensing revenue.

Convergence between Treasury workstation providers and bank systems is occurring in the "cash" space between these two types of providers. Many banks are adding capabilities to their information-reporting and transaction-initiation systems. Some are also adding liquidity portals, allowing an improved and integrated view and process for executing investment actions. These banks are moving up the capability scale and leveraging their large client base in the process.

Treasury workstation providers are targeting smaller clients for two primary reasons. They are offering their system via a more affordable Web-based model, which allows them to achieve a profit at lower cost levels and addresses the needs of smaller clients.

Also, smaller clients are demanding more services as they are becoming more complex and international in nature and thus increasing their needs and expectations. The needs and expectations of these smaller organizations currently are equivalent to much larger organizations in the past. Technology is making it easier for banks and Treasury workstation vendors to level the playing field somewhat.

There has long been a gap in the capabilities and customers that use bank information systems and those that use Treasury workstations. With the new technology offered via the Internet, convergence is occurring. Bank systems are adding capabilities and features and moving upstream into larger organizations. Their more robust features and greater global capabilities are allowing them to act more workstation-like. Treasury workstation providers are taking advantage of the development and distribution cost advantages of their subscription models and are targeting ever-smaller firms. The cash systems are making inroads into firms at the $100 million-plus in annual turnover level. Previously, Treasury workstation vendors targeted firms with $2 billion-plus.

Exhibit 14.2 shows the area of convergence between cash systems offered by banks and cash Treasury workstations. The area of convergence is shown conceptually and would generally represent target companies with annual revenue of between $100 million and $2 billion.

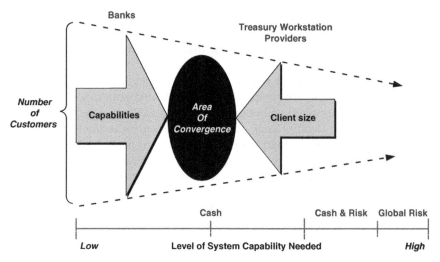

EXHIBIT 14.2 Bank Information and Treasury Workstation Convergence—Area of Convergence

Movements on the Treasury Workstation Landscape

With a shiny hammer in hand, everything starts to look like a nail that you just want to hit with your new tool. A bronze plaque at the American Saw Co. notes the firm is in the "product-separation business." Most thought that the company makes saws. However, American Saw recognized that people do not want saws; they want their material or products separated. Perhaps cutting is the best way to do that today, but there may be other and more improved ways of accomplishing one's objectives.

BEST OF BREED VERSUS INTEGRATED SYSTEMS In the Treasury technology space, technology vendors have realized that some of their customers need other capabilities or results. Accordingly, the vendors have added capabilities to their systems and expanded into other product areas. Some other Treasury workstation vendors have shifted their focus at being the broadest integrated system and have partnered with other specialized vendors to offer a more integrated best-of-breed approach.

For example, Wall Street Systems and Reval have a formalized arrangement where the Wall Street Suite uses Reval for the hedge valuation and accounting activity and has built connections and processes between the different products. Considerable growth of cash-oriented Treasury workstations connecting to risk management systems on a client-by-client basis is happening under the heading of "best of breed." This concept is shown

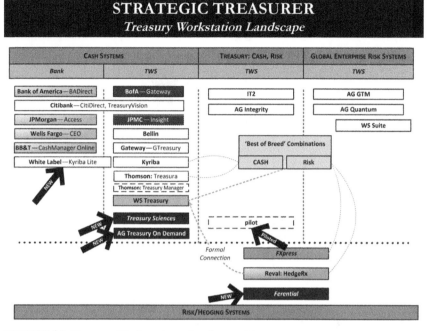

EXHIBIT 14.3 Treasury Workstations: Landscape Movements

in Exhibit 14.3 with the lines connecting to a box titled "Best of Breed" Combinations.

Exhibit 14.3 details a sample of some of the players in this space along with some of the movements and new entrants. This exhibit is intended to show basic product position by system capabilities along cash and risk-management drivers for Treasury workstation providers. Factors such as scalability for high-volume activity, market position, reporting flexibility and dashboards, implementation methods and product development commitment, and roadmap are not shown on this two-dimensional chart. This chart also does not provide a price scale or show the distinction between technology platform and distribution model. These other factors can be quite important to many organizations based on their critical needs. Additional charts and analysis must be made for an organization to make an appropriate decision about its technology needs. Exhibit 14.4 shows a sample scoring continuum for some of the other attributes that are not fully captured in the two-dimensional chart in Exhibit 14.3.

NEW ENTRANTS   There are movements on the landscape based on capabilities and features. There are additional movements on the landscape when

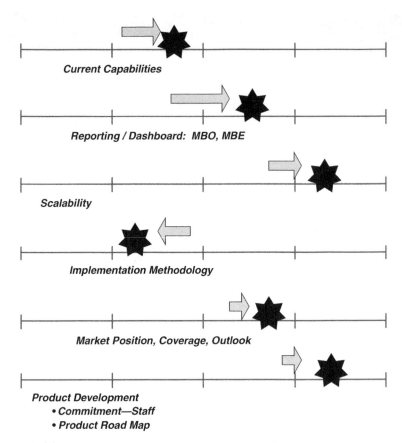

Current Capabilities

Reporting / Dashboard: MBO, MBE

Scalability

Implementation Methodology

Market Position, Coverage, Outlook

Product Development
  • Commitment—Staff
  • Product Road Map

EXHIBIT 14.4 System Considerations: Position and Trend

using a geographical lens. A regular and consistent movement of technology vendors from one region of the world to another is always being attempted. Many meet with failure. For those that successfully move across oceans, it is important to observe and note that this journey takes significant time to succeed and achieve critical mass. For example, for vendors that move to North America, from either Europe or Asia—if they are focused and committed—it will normally take three or four years to get a handle on North American cash management and build up enough clients with name recognition to be considered "established" or "mainstream." The longer these vendors deny or minimize the differences and their inability to meet them properly at the outset, the longer it takes for them to achieve success.

Other entrants have emerged by adding cash capabilities onto their risk-oriented system (such as FXPress Corp.) or by developing a system with an intensive cash-oriented client (Treasury Sciences).

The Order of Activities

To avoid buying the wrong technology or partnering with an organization that will not be able to address an organization's needs requires a logical process. Calling first for a sales demonstration or embarking on a "free" try-before-you-buy trial may seem like a fairly harmless approach. Writing out your goals, critical needs, and overall structure without the pressure and soothing words of the salesperson will help Treasurers remain focused on what is important to their organization.

Just because staff views a demonstration of how you can control the space shuttle with this new piece of Treasury technology does not mean your firm has the need for that feature. While an actual, specific, unneeded feature may be more impressive, it may also be just as impractical for an organization. Determining where you want to go first and then selecting the path and your travel companions is appropriate.

When selecting a technology partner, an erratic process will usually lead to undesirable results. The following represents a series of logical steps that an organization should take to select the proper technology partners.

- **Understand the environment.** Maintain a reasonable understanding of the technology landscape, developments, and resources.
- **Document critical needs.** Document critical needs in an informed manner with awareness of your firm's future needs and the technology landscape.
- **Create the design.** Create a working design structure for Treasury information and Treasury processes; using resources to aid in this process is reasonable.
- **Select solution and partners.** Undertake the proper solution-selection steps and select the proper partner or partners.
- **Implement completely.** Implement quickly and thoroughly.
- **Continuous improvement.** Engage in continual system optimization. This allows you to protect your investment and achieve your objectives. It is a process and not an event.

Respecting Your Time: A Tale of Dashboards and Reports

Information overload. The phone rings. Someone is standing outside of your office. E-mails pour into your mailbox relentlessly. The smartphone attached to your hipbone buzzes with nonessential and important items that can be ignored or assigned, or scream for attention.

While the author has stated that the BlackBerry is probably the single best productivity tool created to date, it, like other technologies, must be mastered, or it will be a major distraction.

The Treasurer and Treasury staffs all have the need for information. This information should ideally be delivered in the proper format, in the proper manner, and at the right time. System reporting, dashboards, and alerts can all serve as distractions or as useful information sources. Making them highly effective requires a combination of world-class technology put to world-class use.

Across the Treasury technology spectrum exists a significant gap related to capabilities. It is useful to have just the right information delivered where it is needed at the proper time. Too much information is detrimental. Since different roles require different information, flexibility is important.

Many banks and technology vendors provide dashboards that can provide much summary information on a single screen or report. The need for information and reporting centers around two concepts and various types of information-delivery methods. The two concepts are management by objective and management by exception.

1. Management by Objective
   - Daily activities
     - **Actions.** These represent events and activities that need to be performed or transfers that need to be executed. This might be a request for a wire transfer that is pending approval. The dashboard or alert may indicate that a specific item needs to be performed in a certain period of time.
     - **Process documentation and workflow management.** Various processes need to be performed, and ensuring that the order is done properly and/or that the steps are all completed is key. Tools can enforce workflow discipline and completeness.
   - Information needed
     - **Company-specific information.** Reports on daily balances or holdings may need to be reviewed or confirmed. This type of information can be either operational or management-oriented. This could include a covenant compliance report, holdings by currency, and a cash forecast by region.
     - **Market information.** Observing market information related to interest-rate yield curves or foreign exchange rates can help both a trader as well as a Treasurer.
2. Management by Exception
     - **Violation.** A notification that a limit is being approached or breached allows senior management to get involved at the time of their choosing. These violations could relate to counterparty risk that a Treasurer would be concerned about.
     - **Error/exception.** Notification of a delay in a transfer approval that the Treasury manager can pursue or information that your primary

European bank has failed to report balances can aid the right person to either resolve the issue or be made aware of the event and avoid making a faulty decision.

Other Treasury Systems

Treasurers should understand that there are several other systems that perform functions supporting Treasury or Treasury-related processes. When needs arise, knowing that there are various systems that have been designed to handle different functions or perform various types of analysis is useful background. Many Treasury groups will not have staff members with extensive, current experience with all types of systems or vendors. This knowledge and experience gap needs to be closed.

Addressing the Knowledge Gap

There are four alternatives for addressing this knowledge gap:

1. **Hire someone with that experience.** This usually ends up very costly as the organization must pay a full-time person for specialized experience that is needed only over a short period of time.
2. **Have someone learn about the offerings.** Many organizations use this approach. It is quite enjoyable for the staff member or members to gather as much information as possible through research and demonstrations. This method is viewed at the outset as inexpensive. However, it normally requires substantial time and cost to go through this process. That cost is usually dwarfed when an error is made in the selection process due to inexperience.
3. **Hire experts on an as-needed basis.** While consultants can be expensive, and some can lack knowledge of the overall landscape or of particular vendors, others will save a firm time, money, and pain. Avoiding pitfalls, speeding the selection process, and ensuring a better solution for the organization can make this cost a worthwhile investment. As in other activities, perform due diligence carefully.
4. **Assume every vendor is about the same and just make a selection.** The top 10 common pitfalls to selecting and implementing Treasury technology should give every Treasurer pause before choosing speed of selection over a thoughtful effort. *Thoughtful* is not a code word for "a long and painful process."

Exhibit 14.5 lists 10 common pitfalls that organizations experience in the selection and implementation phases of a Treasury project that includes automation.

10. Alice-in-Wonderland disease . . . or "Just ask the Cat"

"Would you tell me, please, which way I ought to go from here?"

"That depends a good deal on where you want to get to," said the Cat.

"I don't much care where—" said Alice.

"Then it doesn't matter which way you go," said the Cat.

"—so long as I get *somewhere*," Alice added as an explanation.

"Oh, you're sure to do that," said the Cat, "if you only walk long enough."

From Lewis Carroll's 1865 novel, *Alice's Adventures in Wonderland*

How many projects start in this fashion? Everyone knows that we need to automate . . . so automate. Without a vision for the future, the plan will surely get somewhere . . . as long as you implement long enough.

9. "As-is" blindness

If you don't know what is available, and if you don't have a vision for the future, you see things as they are and fail to realize what a good automation tool set can allow you to be.

This is similar to Alice's issue. In this case, Corporate Treasury moves forward to automate existing processes without fixing or changing the broken or antiquated ones.

8. Overeager expectations

Software rarely lives up to the demonstration. Every system has problems or areas for which it is not optimized. The "Big Bang, Go-Live, That-will-change-business-as-you-know-it" is an almost impossible task.

This is also known as "The Halo Effect," "It will be perfect when we implement___," or "All we need to do is___."

If only the world were that simple.

7. Lack of formal team structure

Every project requires a formal team structure—even if you have a small Treasury.

There are three basic reasons for this: communication, accountability, and authority. Someone needs to be in charge. Someone needs to

EXHIBIT 14.5 Top 10 Automation Pitfalls

communicate the goals, responsibilities, needs, timelines, and milestones. Someone needs to be able to hold others to the task and to be accountable for moving the project forward. And, lastly, someone needs to have the authority to break the logjams.

If the project is worth doing, it is worth having a project plan and a team. There are no projects that can be done successfully by a single person in Treasury.

6. Kicking the tires

"Kick the tires and light the fires."—A Military Aviation definition of an inadequate aircraft preflight inspection.

Poor preparation ends up with tragic results. Similar results will occur when poor due diligence is applied to a Treasury automation selection effort. Many vendors can appear to be exactly what you need with an unscripted demo of their best features.

It is what is under the hood that matters.

5. "Everybody's doing it"

This typical-teenage comment covers the concept that it is safe to follow the crowd. Of course, where others are going may be based upon their standards and needs—and have nothing to do with your organization. Just because others have done something doesn't make what they have done a good decision by itself.

Make decisions based upon your needs and what makes sense for your organization. What others have done may provide information and insight into your situation but should not be the guiding factor.

4. "Get it up and running, and then we'll fix our problems"

Somewhat akin to "as-is blindness," this usually strikes after a project has been initiated. In this case, a mad rush is made to get software up and running so someone can say, "It is up and running." Often this results in little usable functionality and a product so completely foreign to the user that it is not productive, or it results in automated processes that were broken in the beginning. Now they are just broken automated processes.

EXHIBIT 14.5 (Continued)

3. "We can do this completely on our own"

Pitfalls include making hasty decisions or bad assumptions. Sometimes critical capabilities in one system are incorrectly assumed to be in another system and that error is discovered late in the process. Preparation for testing is treated as an afterthought and that mistake is apparent in production. There is value in avoiding selection and implementation pitfalls. Often, simple tasks are complicated because of incomplete information about all of the related subtasks. Someone who has been through the process multiple times brings insight and knowledge to avoid the traps along the way.

2. Wandering Around Due Diligence

"What you don't know *can* hurt you." The lack of a structured plan for checking references, pursuing necessary functionality, and vetting critical claims of a vendor can have dire consequences. Although the sales team (usually) does not intentionally lie to you, they may be talking around a significant weakness in the product as it relates to your needs. It is better to know about a shortfall before you buy and before you implement.

1. Setting a Deadline—Then Figuring out Your Project

Calling a deadline "aggressive" may simply be a code word for "arbitrary." Deadlines are set for multiple and various reasons. A project does need clear goals, expectations, and deadlines to be accomplished effectively and with satisfaction to the client. However, a deadline that is created before the problems are understood and the scope is defined will ultimately result in failure.

Setting a timeline is an iterative process that requires some degree of give and take. You must quantify the real problem(s), define the scope of what you desire to address, and define realistic timelines and expectations. If outside factors are driving the timeline, limit the scope of the project by more clearly defining the essential project goals and moving additional functionality to a later date or different project. This is the iterative part. A few well-defined goals and a realistic plan can be accomplished crisply and on time with dedication and the right resources.

EXHIBIT 14.5 (Continued)

Reconciliation and Spreadsheet Compliance Systems

All Treasury departments rely quite extensively on spreadsheets for ad hoc analysis, which is understandable. And most Treasury departments use spreadsheets for recurring reports and analytics. Since spreadsheets are fraught with control problems that spawn errors and lack an audit trail, many Treasurers, Controllers, and others are exposed far more than necessary. Based on recently revised studies of spreadsheet errors, the percentage of spreadsheets with errors has averaged 88 percent with some studies showing 100 percent error rates.[1] Based on the number and significance of errors in spreadsheets, more caution is needed. Additionally, major problems caused by spreadsheet issues are detailed in an article entitled, "Eight of the Worst Spreadsheet Blunders."[2]

The issues from spreadsheet errors can be minor, embarrassing, or career-altering. Many repeated activities that are performed using spreadsheets should be evaluated to determine if change is required. When changes are necessary, this typically requires one of two actions:

1. **Move the activity into a system or process** (information-technology developed, bank system, Treasury workstation, risk-management system, and so on) that has built-in quality controls, an audit trail, and documentation.
2. **Use a spreadsheet compliance tool** that enforces version control, documents changes, and supports testing and debugging. For a current list of spreadsheet compliance tools, refer to the resources tab located on Strategic Treasurer's website at: www.strategictreasurer.com.

Reconciliation represents an important control in all organizations. It also represents an area of risk for organizations and for careers. Reconciliation is not on the list of functions that helps Treasury professionals advance their careers. This role has significant downside potential as people regularly get fired or have their careers sidelined for having less-than-adequate results with regard to reconciliation.

Treasurers are responsible for owning cash, as indicated in Chapter 5. That chapter further describes types of reconciliations and proofs that are done in an organization. In the following list, several types of reconciliation systems are described. Exhibit 14.6 provides a view of these systems that perform reconciliation functions in relationship to one another. This exhibit makes a clear distinction between the real-time reconciliation systems that are necessary for financial institutions and nonbank financial organizations and batch-reconciliation systems that are needed by many other nonfinancial firms.

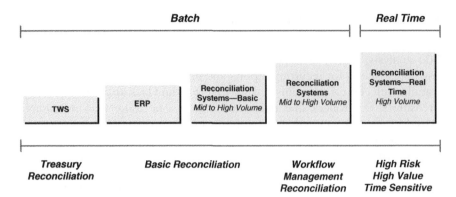

EXHIBIT 14.6 Reconciliation Systems

- Treasury Reconciliation
  - **Treasury workstation.** This reconciliation is usually best performed with a Treasury workstation. This system helps to identify the causes of differences in today's opening cash balance at the bank versus what was expected after the Treasury manager finalized the firm's cash position yesterday.
- Reconciliation (Bank, Transaction)
  - **Enterprise resource planning systems (ERP) and basic reconciliation tools.** Integrated accounting and production-oriented systems often provide the ability to perform disbursement and bank reconciliation up to a competent level. Available software packages and database add-ins provide fairly simple matching algorithms. Both of these systems may or may not provide a complete workflow mapping and management set of tools necessary for larger volume or more complex reconciliation efforts.
  - **Reconciliation systems (workflow routing).** There are several highly capable reconciliation systems that can handle high volume and complex reconciliation activity. These systems support reconciliation policy compliance by managing the timing of follow-up and distribution of work and escalation notifications. These are highly capable systems. All have a client-server version. Some vendors have written their software in new Web technology and offer the service on a hosted (SaaS) basis. These systems tend to be used in organizations where a batch-mode process is acceptable.
- Reconciliation (Real Time)
  - **Real-time reconciliation systems.** Financial institutions and non-bank financial firms are often executing enormous financial trades throughout the day. Being able to confirm this activity through a

reconciliation and matching process is essential on an intraday basis; a process designed around a nightly batch-mode process would leave their organization exposed. These systems help mitigate many risks and are the most costly. They are designed to handle a large volume of items on a real-time basis.

Select Miscellaneous Treasury Systems

There are numerous systems that could be categorized as belonging to Treasury. Exhibit 14.1 (page 168) provides a larger list of the primary and secondary Treasury systems. On this list are two systems that merit some descriptive commentary: the system that helps manage the bank invoices, called "analysis statements," and the bank account administration tools that support correspondence about account changes and signer management.

- **Account analysis systems.** *Account analysis* is the term that refers to the bank invoice for Treasury services. It is suspected by some that a secret society exists that is bent on making bank invoices as complex and confusing as possible.

  In addition to their complexity, these invoices are normally approved outside of the normal accounts-payable process, which creates an exposure. Systems that manage the allocation, price and volume accuracy, and compliance are sometimes referred to as "bank relationship manager" (BRM), after the name of the largest provider of this type of software. This software is designed to take electronic feeds of the bank invoices to make the allocation, analysis, and review process easier.

  Organizations that spend more than $300,000 in bank fees per year with three or more banks will usually benefit from this type of automation tool.

- **Bank account management.** There are only a few dedicated systems that give an organization the ability to manage all account and signer change processes systematically. Knowing what accounts are opened and closed, what controls are active, and what controller signs for every financial account seems like a rather simple administrative function for an organization. Yet, a majority of mid-size to large organizations do not manage this process effectively or accurately.

  New accounts and accounts that were supposed to be closed are found or discovered to be active at a surprising frequency. Each account represents a point of exposure that needs to be controlled. The level of capabilities of these systems varies. In addition to the items shown in Exhibit 14.7, there are several Treasury workstation vendors that have developed a module or partnered with a bank account management

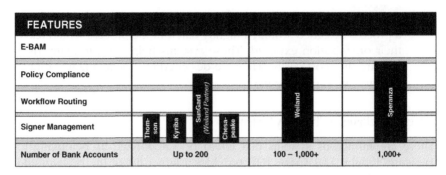

FEATURES				
E-BAM				
Policy Compliance				
Workflow Routing	Thomson	Kyriba	SunGard (Weiland Partner) Chesapeake	Weiland	Speranza
Signer Management				
Number of Bank Accounts	Up to 200		100 – 1,000+	1,000+

EXHIBIT 14.7 Bank Account Management Landscape—Technology Vendors Dedicated

firm to offer some capabilities in this area. Banks began adding this type of capability recently. The push by SWIFT to offer electronic bank account management (EBAM) will make these software tools more efficient because they will be able to interface through their network to execute corporate actions.

All organizations with 100 or more bank accounts at 8 or more banks will benefit greatly by using this type of service to manage their accounts, services, and signers on their financial accounts. It is inappropriate to try to build this functionality internally.

Managing Financial Processes

Throughout this chapter a number of Treasury systems have been examined that help to manage financial processes on an ongoing basis. The controls in most of these systems are built into the process, making the management reasonable once all of the data is established in the system. This is particularly true of data and processes that reside within Treasury.

There are two challenges that most Treasury groups face. Exhibit 14.8 provides a landscape of tools that are used for inventorying and those that provide an ongoing monitoring role. This exhibit further shows how these specialized tools interface with the core Treasury systems. These systems were created and continue to develop in a difficult environment. Treasurers regularly minimize the challenges of assessing and implementing technology services. These are hard lessons. They are lessons that can be avoided or learned through the experience of others.

The first challenge relates to the inventory process. The initial inventorying of core data related to assets and liabilities is crucial as this data must be gathered and organized for several purposes. This data is usually analyzed, and structures are rationalized. This analysis typically supports

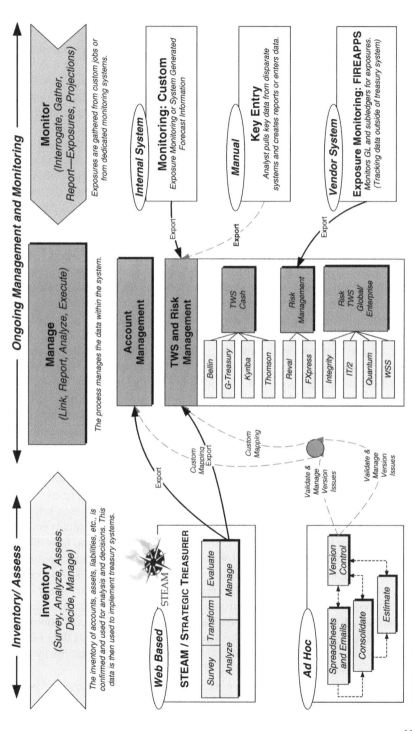

EXHIBIT 14.8 Financial Inventory and Management System Landscape

185

the financial model where investments are made in new systems. Once the analysis has been made and software solutions have been purchased, the data that was originally gathered must now be entered into various systems. Unfortunately, this data was incomplete and is also impure, usually suffering from version control issues if the inventory effort was the traditional process centered around e-mailing spreadsheets and then consolidating the data.

Not only does this process typically jeopardize the accuracy of the analysis, it also harms internal relationships. Very few people in the field enjoy seeing a second and third survey covering much of the same data. Most will not carefully review that data unless they happen to report directly to the Treasurer. While it is inefficient to gather and review the same data multiple times, it also becomes frustrating to spend so much time validating the same data simply to move it into the technology tool you acquired to make everyone's life easier.

Under the Inventory section there are two types of tools listed. The Ad Hoc systems are generally the spreadsheet and e-mail combination approach that, while fraught with terrible problems, remains the dominant method of gathering and analyzing the data. The second tool is a Web-based service that allows all data to be managed in a single location across the globe leveraging current technology. There are several survey tools in this category that range on the low end from providing a simple Web information-gathering tool that does not interface with other technology providers to the higher end where there are tools, STEAM for example, that not only will provide workflow support for the information-gathering process, but also will provide some online analytical capabilities that can enable more rapid and accurate decisions. This data can then be used to feed into some of the core setup tables of Treasury workstations, bank account management tools, and other systems. It can also provide feeds of the inventoried items right into the management system. The level of work required by the ad hoc systems is enormous and seems unbelievable until it has been experienced.

The second challenge for these systems and these processes relates to the need to secure data from systems outside of Treasury's direct control. In this chapter we have discussed several sources of bank data and how this can be managed. The next challenge for most Treasuries relates to forecast data and managing exposures. Forecasting cash flows can progress to a certain level using data that resides within Treasury. Increasing the accuracy of the forecast requires gathering data from other external systems on a manual or automated basis. The processes for gathering this data are commonly performed by either automating the forecast methodology, and then making it available to the Treasury system, or having various areas manually enter the data for Treasury using a variety of tools.

For capturing certain types of exposures, foreign exchange exposure for example, the data may sit in a number of financial systems that are often outside of the Treasury department. Vendor-provided exposure monitoring systems will query the various systems and bring this data back to Treasury. Treasury can then execute the proper hedge activity based on this data. These systems can serve as useful monitoring tools enabling Treasury to better observe the actual exposures their organization is facing.

Summary

Treasury systems must support Treasury processes in an efficient and well-controlled manner. There has been an increasing level of change in the Treasury technology landscape. That change has been a vast improvement.

Banks and technology vendors have been able to take advantage of an environmental change in technology. Better technology has allowed better tools to be developed more quickly and supported and delivered through better channels.

Data consolidators manage the movement of management of data and transactions and represent an ability to shift the headache of this effort to an external provider.

Hosting Treasury technology over the Internet by SaaS providers has become a dominant force in the delivery of Treasury technology, which has helped bring higher-end capabilities once available solely to large organizations to the low end of the middle market.

Outsourcing various components of the cash conversion cycle allows Treasury and other areas of the business to focus on activities where they can add value. This provides another avenue where an organization can give banks additional fee-based business, which can better support a strong appetite for credit. Finally, outsourcing various components of the cash conversion cycle now allows for more flexible management of capital without harming vendor and client relationships.

Treasurers must be able to grasp the current landscape of Treasury technology and the opportunities that may be available. The resources available are significant, and they are constantly changing and growing. Accordingly, Treasurers will need to ensure that their organizations have access to internal and external resources that will help to properly design their Treasury information structure and make partnership and selection decisions that match their firm's needs.

Notes

1. Raymond R. Panko, "What We Know About Spreadsheet Errors," *Journal of End User Computing* (Special Issue on Scaling Up End User Development) 10, No 2 (Spring 1998, revised May 2008):15–21.
2. "Eight of the Worst Spreadsheet Blunders," *CIO*, August 17, 2007.

CHAPTER 15

Advice from Various Treasury Leaders*

If someone accuses me of being a conservative Treasurer I say "thank you" and take it as a compliment. You hope for the best and prepare for the worst. Be flexible.

—John Beattie, Vice President, Treasurer, Spectrum Brands

An oft-repeated piece of advice for Treasurers is to seek advice from other Treasurers and senior people within Treasury. This chapter captures some of the people and some of the conversations that were held for the purpose of providing specific input for various sections of this book. Not every great piece of advice fit nicely into a particular chapter. However, since there were a number of concepts and quotes that will be of use to other Treasurers, some of them have been placed in this chapter.

Change Management

Communication

Communication is important, and Joni Topper indicates that Treasurers may need the ability to communicate like Alan Greenspan.

---

*All quotes in this chapter are from personal interviews.

In today's world with the unbelievable turbulence that we're experiencing, Treasurers now are challenged on a communication front. In the past, they might have been able to submit their numbers and walk through some items at a very high level about risk. Now, a Treasurer almost has to be an Alan Greenspan.

They have to have some way of helping people feel comfortable about not just the Treasury piece but also the debt side. They must have time and the competence to get to know various situations, stay on top of them and then be able to turn around and communicate well with people. Communicating well requires a good team to help prepare and bounce your ideas off.

—Joni Topper, SVP and Regional Director—Government and
Institutional Banking, Wells Fargo

Managing Change

The most successful things that we've done are those that we didn't just decide to do on the fly, even if we knew it was the right answer at the outset. When we stop, crack it open and build consensus around it, it becomes everyone's solution. It's just a completely different outcome than when something is forced upon an organization. The consensus solution is superior because it is accepted and better understood.

—Ted Hanson, CFO, Apex Systems

Organizations may be defined differently, but a Treasurer who is strategic, no matter how their box has been defined, thinks past their area of control. They understand and are aware of various interdependencies whether they own them or not. They influence different parts of the company and impact the finances of the organization positively. Ineffective people are exactly the opposite—they don't think beyond their box.

—Linda Cascardo, SVP Wholesale Sales Executive, Wells Fargo

Building back-channel communication can help organizations move forward more nimbly. Topper says:

In observing some organizations the Treasurer learns from staff coming in from other departments and has people they have sent out that provide them with back-door or back-channel communication. These informal communication channels work very well. So much gets done that way, even in lightly or moderately political organizations.

—Joni Topper, SVP and Regional Director—Government and
Institutional Banking, Wells Fargo

As Assistant Treasurer, Crista Binder has a significant role in helping the City of Los Angeles move forward by making critical changes. Once change starts, it cannot be stopped.

Adopting a philosophy of change is important because it's a new world and change is constant. We live in a world where you implement a solution and tomorrow the environment has changed. So you're never going to have it right all the time. In order to make change or implement solutions, you've got to realize going forward that you've started a perpetuating cycle of changes and once you jump on the train, the train's going to move forever no matter what.

—Crista Binder, Assistant Treasurer, City of Los Angeles

Conflict

Crista Binder (on keeping focus in chaotic times and when conflict arises) relays principles she learned from her boss as they have been applied to her position:

Leadership during a time of change requires a person who enjoys chaos and conflict. Set the overarching vision right up front. Make it clear. Then as you move forward and resistance arises, point out that it is no longer about whether this is where we want to go, it is where we must go.

—Crista Binder, Assistant Treasurer, City of Los Angeles

Changes in Treasury

Jiro Okochi notes that the role and skill set required of the Treasurer have changed over time, and differences exist regionally:

I've seen more and more, year after year, change in the required skill set of a Treasurer. It has moved away from a focus on cash management and liquidity. This change is dramatic in the United States. Globally, now the Treasurer is more focused on the marketplace; financial risk, credit risk, and even enterprise risk is now the top concern. In Europe, there was an earlier move toward risk management since they were always trying to understand how 15 different currency pairs moved. Treasurers are becoming more mini-CFOs, where CFOs in the United States were twenty to thirty years ago. CFOs moved on and Treasurers picked up more of the strategic activities that CFOs weren't focusing on. Treasury staff that came in over the last two decades are coming up the curve quickly and come from different backgrounds and are risk savvy.

—Jiro Okochi, CEO and Co-Founder, Reval

Okochi continues to note some specific risk activities Treasurers are assuming:

Treasurers are using commodities' volatility and the need to control and hedge that risk to become more strategic. Before, procurement departments would manage that risk by embedding it in the contracts or hedging it with a futures contract. Treasury wasn't involved. Treasury had its own set of disciplines on FX and IR hedging. As hedge accounting developed, Treasurers became more well-rounded and [now] are getting more involved across the business lines.

—Jiro Okochi, CEO and Co-Founder, Reval

In the case of governance, some departments may not be able to have a high performing organization without some people having spent time in Treasury. Treasury really helps people to understand the whole notion of risk assessments. This is even more important now, because risk assessment in the past for Treasury was always risk of the transaction. Now there is a concern over headline risk and governance risk in addition to transactional risk. Treasury has the ability to look at what's happening and do more than just assess that transaction risk. This is really valuable for people who are working their way through an organization and want to come out of it with a terrific perspective about all sorts of risks.

—Joni Topper, SVP and Regional Director—Government and Institutional Banking, Wells Fargo

Amy Kweskin comments on the broader responsibilities of the Treasurer that require a broader perspective:

The Treasury role has changed over the past few decades. It used to have more of a focus on cash management and debt management. Now, Treasurers are responsible for a much broader picture and more of the total risk for the institution. Therefore, people who are going into this role need to have a broader perspective.

—Amy Kweskin, Treasurer, Washington University in St. Louis

Risk Management

Managing Risks

Having regular discussions with other areas about their needs can turn up an important discovery of where Treasury can help. For example, we were talking to the facilities people at one point and we found out that they were purchasing natural gas and experiencing the impact of price fluctuations. This provided an opportunity to discuss how Treasury could help manage that volatility with hedges. This was not something that they would normally think to approach Treasury about for a solution.

—Amy Kweskin, Treasurer, Washington University in St. Louis

No matter what the company's position, the Treasurer needs to make sure they manage the one or two things that can sink them. They need to know where their key risks lie. Then, they need a good external sounding board to vet their approach since Treasurers rarely get that from within their own organization. And, Treasurers shouldn't rely on advice from someone who makes money based upon that advice.

—Mark Henry, Senior Vice President of Global Tax, Treasury, and Risk Management, Infor Global Systems, Inc.

Regarding the risk management and hedging: the only reasonable objective should be to remove or reduce volatility. To make it work, you need to have a concerted commitment to it. You can't jump in and out of it, just like you shouldn't jump in and out of the stock market, because you will do more harm than good. You either don't hedge at all or you commit to a hedging program to reduce volatility. It has to be a multi-year horizon or you will create more volatility to your financial results than had you not hedged at all.

—John Beattie, Vice President, Treasurer, Spectrum Brands

Beattie further discusses risk management and why Treasurers must take a fiscally conservative approach:

An extension of risk management is always to have a back-up plan whether about cash or liquidity. You need to have a rainy-day fund set aside. If you wait until you need it, you will probably be too late.

—John Beattie, Vice President, Treasurer, Spectrum Brands

Cash Is King and Visibility Is Essential

Cash is King. Risk management helps you realize that cash is King. Cash is your best insurance policy.

—Amy Kweskin, Treasurer, Washington University in St. Louis

Now more than ever it is critical that Treasurers have a holistic view of their liquidity situation at different institutions and with different instruments and be able to react on a daily or even intraday basis to major changes in the marketplace. Having a tool which can aggregate your positions across banks and then put it into an application that allows you to make transactions is essential. That allows you quickly either to just move money from an account to another account or to have the ability to then invest directly into other types of investment instruments.

—Mike Berkowitz, Market Manager, Citibank

Diversification

Diversification is critical and you can never fully anticipate what's going to be the next investment class or counterparty to have severe issues. First, auction rate securities issues emerged and created problems for liquidity. Next, there were issues with some banks and broker dealers as counterparties. Then money market funds faced a challenge with the Reserve Fund breaking the buck. Since you are not always going to be able to predict the next issue, one way of ensuring your company's future is to diversify so, if any single asset class or counterparty is hit, you can survive.

—Mike Berkowitz, Market Manager, Citibank

Elyse Weiner comments that the underlying reason for diversification requires broader preparation than counterparty and instrument diversification alone.

In the end, diversification is not just about spreading your investments between firms, it is also about having the proper infrastructure. By having standard processes and fewer locations and systems to monitor, changes are much easier to implement. If an issue begins to develop with a counterparty, it is far easier to make an orderly change.

—Elyse Weiner, Managing Director, Global Product Head,
Liquidity & Investments, Citibank

Relationship Management

Bank Relationship Management and Using Advisors

Ted Hanson takes a strong position that his bankers and consultants need to be part of the team and provide useful insights:

If I get a relationship banker where I feel like I'm just part of their services quota for the year and I'm really not getting any thoughtful input—I work really hard to change those.

—Ted Hanson, CFO, Apex Systems

Good Treasurers expect the same kind of integrity from the bank that they would expect from their staff. They are not shy about giving feedback.

—David Hurt, Treasury Management Sales Consultant, M&T Bank

Use your advisors, your bankers, and consultants. They can add significant value. Pay attention to those partners and use them as a secondary piece of your Treasury staff. We operate pretty leanly and our partners provide us with more resources.

—Ward Allen, Vice President Finance, WinWholesale

Allen comments about the importance of ensuring access and availability to his partners.

I instruct my admin that if a banker calls up, find me, get me, or interrupt me. I want to talk to them. It's that simple.

—Ward Allen, Vice President Finance, WinWholesale

You can't wait to develop relationships when you have to have them; you need to begin developing those relationships earlier. Having an idea of what your balance sheet needs to look like 36 months in the future will help you better prepare.

—Tim Hart, SVP and Treasurer, First National Bank of Nebraska

Hart comments on the fact that relationships can change and Treasurers need to prepare for this:

Understand that banks change people and strategies; you need to find out where they are and where they're going.

—Tim Hart, SVP and Treasurer, First National Bank of Nebraska

Thick Skin

[The] Treasurer, more than many other roles, requires a thicker skin. Treasurers have a responsibility to say no when that is the right thing to

say. Treasurers need to plow new ground and that can meet with active resistance.

—Joya De Foor, Treasurer, City of Los Angeles

Treasurers, Controllers, and Others

A Treasurer has to look forward and prepare for the future. But they have to do more than that. As a finance professional, a Treasurer, you need to forge new ground. A Controller records and there are myriad rules on how to record and when to record and why to record. A comparable set of rules doesn't exist to that extent in the Treasury world. There are Best Practices, but then those are very fluid and more varied organization by organization.

—Joya De Foor, Treasurer, City of Los Angeles

Controllers look historically and focus on compliance with various rules that are defined. They have schedules that will tie out to the dollar. They provide and prepare the same monthly reports. Treasurers are different from Controllers, and Treasurers are forward looking and per-form a lot of ad hoc and one-off-analysis. Their numbers are typically approximations, and schedules don't cross foot because they are pro-viding a positional number. The Treasurer is concerned about future investments. Their responsibility is to frame the idea of the project and of the concept, taking in high-level considerations of tax, legal, and various projections. They will talk to the vendor community which may be sales leaseback, investment bankers, etc. to vet the assump-tions.

—Tom King, Treasurer, Progressive Insurance

King further explains how these differences can play out in terms of temperament:

If the numbers don't add up, the Controller gets nervous; whereas the Treasurer is comfortable with estimates. Broader ranges are part of the Treasurer's role.

—Tom King, Treasurer, Progressive Insurance

Other areas of the organization have different responsibilities from the Treasurer. King comments:

No one is afraid of the Treasury group. They are more fun since they look at opportunities. Treasury isn't viewed as Dr. No.

—Tom King, Treasurer, Progressive Insurance

Mindset and Perspectives of the Treasurer

Reinventing the Role and Understanding Expectations

Mark Henry emphasizes: *Understand and help set the proper expectations*:

You need to have a practical viewpoint of the value that you're expected to provide in the organization and the value that you can provide, given the environment in which you're working. I think that has a lot to do with sizing up your colleagues, as well as understanding the knowledge of your boss, as well as the knowledge and emphasis of the Board. One of the most immediate tasks to do when you step into a job is to figure out from everyone what other people think is important and understand from a risk management perspective where you think you can add value to the organization. You will then need to be effective at fleshing out those concepts with individuals in Treasury and with the leadership of the organization.

—Mark Henry, Senior Vice President of Global Tax, Treasury, and Risk Management, Infor Global Systems, Inc.

This is not a one-time event. Henry goes on to explain:

You have to reinvent yourself. Organizations are constantly changing. They get different leadership, and it will change direction on what they find important. You have to adapt and react to that in an appropriate value added fashion.

—Mark Henry, Senior Vice President of Global Tax, Treasury, and Risk Management, Infor Global Systems, Inc.

Grey Matter as One Weapon

Find an analytical tool that can get you the data you need. They are paying Treasurers for the gray matter between our ears. It's not about sitting down and putting spreadsheets together and saying, "Wow, isn't this pretty?" Data gathering should be an ancillary part of the duty.

—Ward Allen, Vice President Finance, WinWholesale

The gray matter between your ears is the primary weapon of the Treasurer. Approach issues as you would a general in battle. You need to be strategic most of the time and tactical when you must.

—Joya De Foor, Treasurer, City of Los Angeles

Accomplishing changes in an organization requires allies. De Foor indicates a thoughtful approach to alliances:

I build allies by starting with those that others can't object to. I try to make the auditors my first allies.

—Joya De Foor, Treasurer, City of Los Angeles

Perspectives on: Roles and Your First Days as Treasurer

When you join an organization, understand the financial history of the company before you start making changes to how things are put together and reported. Your company may have 50 years of built-up experience that you can leverage.

—Ward Allen, Vice President Finance, WinWholesale

To ensure you are doing the right things for the organization, Allen comments further that the fastest way to accomplish that is to:

understand most Treasurers report to CFOs. Get to know your CFO and understand what's driving the driver.

—Ward Allen, Vice President Finance, WinWholesale

Our Treasurer has instilled in the organization the mindset that when we're working on improving a process we want to employ leading and best practices. And, to do that we have to look outside the organization and outside our "industry." Nothing is really unattainable. There may be a particular solution that the City can't utilize now, for whatever reason. Those items will be on the parking lot list and it becomes something we will get to down the road.

—Crista Binder, Assistant Treasurer, City of Los Angeles

Binder further describes the mindset that helps move the organization forward without unnecessary detours:

We fixate on the end result and work backwards from that perspective. We think about everything from the end result and try to make every change in a way that moves us closer to that point.

—Crista Binder, Assistant Treasurer, City of Los Angeles

Avoid falling into a conventional wisdom trap. The organization has a particular view of how things work and the decision rules that must be followed. Treasury has more access to outside perspectives and can shake up an insular view that can act like a bunker of conventional wisdom.

—Tom King, Treasurer, Progressive Insurance

Hart outlines six questions and perspectives about and for Treasury:

1. *Treasury is the easiest place to make money and Treasury is the easiest place to make your company fail.*
2. *If everyone is wrong, what must then be true?*
3. *The Treasurer needs to know how many hits they can take.*
4. *How do you know you are okay with counterparty risk?*
5. *Can you deliver your balance sheet 36 months into the future?*
6. *When you most need your models to work, it is then that they fail.*

—Tim Hart, SVP and Treasurer, First National Bank of Nebraska

King describes what he refers to as five key Treasury ideas:

1. *Treasury has much to do with thinking at the margins, including opportunity and costs.*
2. *Some risk can be mitigated with diversification and some cannot.*
3. *Net present value has to do with the amount, timing, and certainty of cash flow.*
4. *The Treasurer must have a feel for statistical inferences and how much data is needed to be comfortable with the future.*
5. *Seeks external sources of input.*

Investment bankers call on Treasurers. They hear lots of examples of war stories, tons of data, and ideas of various levels of quality. This provides Treasury with additional inputs and a point of view that may be different from of the rest of the organization. The additional perspectives help with critical thinking, which is crucial for the organization.

—Tom King, Treasurer, Progressive Insurance

One thing that has helped me and others in the role has been a willingness to take on projects that may not necessarily fit the typical analytical activity that Treasury is known to perform. Take on the task that will allow you to use your skills to think through all these other areas of Treasury, too. The Treasurer will be doing something different every day and sometimes even from minute to minute.

—Amy Kweskin, Treasurer, Washington University in St. Louis

Developing Treasury Staff

Respect your staff's time. Instead of issuing a broad directive to prepare a presentation and then reviewing a 50-page presentation that took hundreds of hours of work, outline the broad categories first. This saves a lot of iterative activity.

—John Tus, Vice President and Treasurer, Honeywell

And

Every job has a daytime and nighttime component for Treasury. The daytime component is keeping the operations going. The nighttime component is looking at things differently. Determining where we are headed. Avoid being caught off guard.

—John Tus, Vice President and Treasurer, Honeywell

Linda Cascardo on great Treasurers:

They develop people and identify who has talent. Developing talent isn't simply encouraging someone or saying "go to a conference," it's about creating an expectation and providing opportunities.

—Linda Cascardo, SVP Wholesale Sales Executive, Wells Fargo

Building a team with different competencies is a terrific plan because you don't have to be everywhere to get the job done. You just need the right face there and the right approach. Trying to be everywhere limits you to a great extent and you can't be an effective Treasurer. You would also limit the effectiveness of the Treasury organization if you try to center everything on yourself. Sometimes Treasurers do this early in their career because they're so concerned about errors.

—Joni Topper, SVP and Regional Director—Government and
Institutional Banking, Wells Fargo

In addition to benefitting the organization by building the team with different competencies, there is great value with proper leadership.

Topper relays more principles drawn from her observations of an exemplary Treasurer from a major city.

Every terrific person has some areas that need some work. If you are looking for people with strengths on one side of their puzzle piece and some weaknesses on the other, you're really offering to them the ability to work on those weaknesses. If you're a Treasurer and understand that people come together with a positive and a negative charge, you're going to do everything you can to help them achieve their objectives on the negative side and really give them career opportunities by doing that. In the meantime, you have the chance to leverage their strengths. The Treasurer who understands that you can have some very strong personalities in the room when you do that had better be ready. But, the risk of strong personalities is overshadowed by the great return they achieve.

—Joni Topper, SVP and Regional Director—Government and
Institutional Banking, Wells Fargo

Vision, Strategy, and Execution

Excellent Treasurers all seem to have a mindset that they have to build an organization where they can delegate the tactics down and the operations so that they can think about the strategic issues. If they do that, then they have a chance of being a Strategic Treasurer.

—Jiro Okochi, CEO and Co-Founder, Reval

Great Treasurers and leaders are forward looking. They drive their organization by looking through the windshield. Reactionary Treasurers try to drive by looking in the rearview mirror.

—Linda Cascardo, SVP Wholesale Sales Executive, Wells Fargo

Daily	Periodicals—Business	Periodicals—Treasury/Finance	Industry-Specific
Finance Oriented: *Wall Street Journal* *Financial Times* General: *New York Times*	Business: *The Economist* *Harvard Business Review* *Forbes* *BusinessWeek*	Treasury and Risk: *CFO* *AFP Journal of Treasury Management* *GT News* *Journal of Accountancy*	Most Treasurers read at least one publication about their specific industry or business.

EXHIBIT 15.1 Treasurer's Reading List

Reading List

In speaking with dozens of people on what they read to stay current and to learn, some basic trends emerged. Treasury leaders read broadly. They read daily. And, some plow through a lot of material on the weekend.

Exhibit 15.1 shows the most frequently appearing list of materials by category.

The *Wall Street Journal*, *The Economist*, and *Treasury & Risk* were staples among almost every Treasurer. A number of Treasurers read the *New York Times* for the primary reason that their board members read this paper and it is advisable to know what they might be thinking and asking. Headlines and articles in the *Journal* and the *Times* can often trigger questions from the board. Treasurers like to be prepared.

The book reading list covered a wide range of leadership, sports, history, hobbies, and other topics. It appears that most Treasurers have a liberal arts reading program when it comes to books. Some Treasurers, however, when looking at a new topic search for all of the books on the topic on a Web bookstore. They purchase three to five of them and read one thoroughly and reference the others. For specialized subjects such as derivatives and macroeconomics, and rule management mathematics, one Treasurer indicated that he will go to top universities and look at the books that they are using and purchase them.

Summary

One of the best methods of learning in Treasury is to talk with smart Treasurers and those in the Treasury field who have a record of significant accomplishments. By asking questions and listening there is much to learn.

Smart Treasurers will surround themselves with great staff and will ensure they can exchange ideas with other Treasury leaders.

The best Treasurers exhibit a tremendous amount of intellectual curiosity, which shows in the variety of ways that they ensure that they and their organization can learn. They put themselves and their organizations into situations where they will be stretched and will be better able to serve their organizations.

It should come as no surprise that great Treasurers have a fairly heavy and deep reading list. But the key factor is how wide they read to fulfill their organizational purpose and role.

CHAPTER 16

Volatility and Liquidity Management

In theory, reality is just like theory. In reality, theory is nothing like reality.

—*Anonymous*

P residents, potentates, and kings all need protection. This requires knowing where the king is and where he will be in the future. To protect the king requires knowing what the main threats are to the king. Threats change over time, and sometimes they change quite rapidly. Understanding these threats and being able to plan and react promptly and properly requires a regular threat assessment.

Protecting the King

Cash, or more specifically liquidity, is King. To protect this type of King requires a similar type of planning and work to guarding a flesh-and-blood potentate. The Treasurer must understand the current state of the organization's liquidity and what it is expected to be in the future. Especially important, numerous threats to liquidity exist that must be understood and assessed at various intervals. Protecting organizational liquidity is a key responsibility of the Treasurer. This includes insight into how different sources of volatility impact liquidity. Understanding the crucial steps to achieve improved visibility and identifying potential impacts to liquidity is rather simple. Actually achieving visibility is far more challenging.

This chapter will explore some general types of issues that threaten liquidity. The severity of the recent financial crisis is instructive about the magnitude and rapidity of changes the market can bring and about government actions that impact Treasurers and challenge their ability to properly prepare for and respond to many rapidly developing events. This chapter is designed to convince both a new Treasurer and the board of directors of the level of volatility that can occur and to emphasize the need for proper preparation.

In identifying and preparing for volatility, this chapter highlights three critical components of managing liquidity, which include achieving visibility to the firm's liquidity, assessing various impacts to liquidity, and acting to protect liquidity during turbulent times.

Volatile Times

During times of extreme volatility nearly everyone supports the idea of managing liquidity thoroughly and diligently. Providing the funding to achieve a certain level of visibility and preparation is viewed as prudent and necessary. During times of relative stability, the voices calling for the steps necessary to prepare for more volatile times tend to be singing solo.

Treasurers are told various stories about how it is not a priority at this point in time or that it would not be a prudent use of resources. The people that fight the effort and cost necessary for proper preparation are the same people that will accuse the Treasurer of not being prepared if things go awry. The Treasurer must be prepared and must continue to deliver consistent messages about the impact of volatile developments on liquidity and the need to be properly prepared to manage liquidity during both good and challenging times.

Good times do not always last. Treasurers know this, but others may not. Treasurers must fight and defeat arguments that say, for example, "We are in a long-term or permanently stable period that won't or can't change dramatically." Treasurers must be prepared because other challenges to protecting organizational liquidity will arise from some source at an inopportune time. And while some challenging situations may be predictable they are usually not preventable. However, preparations can be made and the impact usually can be minimized.

Financial Crisis of 2007+

From 2007 and into 2009, Treasurers saw tremendous dislocation of the markets, financial instruments, rating agencies, banks, and government intervention and policy. Exhibits 16.1 (a) & (b) show select events of this financial crisis. The extent and causes of this volatility and dislocation appear to be wholly unprecedented as to scope and speed. Some of the areas saw rapid change, and discussion of these matters is instructive for Treasurers. These events included:

- **Financial instruments:** rapid degradation and a stampede toward perceived quality
- **Counterparties:** from blue-chip to high risk
- **Foreign exchange rates:** extreme volatility of various currency pairs
- **Commodities:** volatility and redirection at unprecedented levels
- **Rating agencies:** untimely downgrades
- **Banks and insurance companies:** failures and credit issues
- **Governments:** unpredictable actions, rescues, and course changes

For many organizations, most of these areas had a substantial impact on their liquidity. The volatility and impact of any of these would be substantial. The fact that many of these have interconnections, and they happened at the same time created an extremely volatile situation. Treasurers who can learn from history and adjust their responses to current events are invaluable to their organizations.

Financial Instrument Risk

Financial instruments can move rapidly from a position where they are favored by many organizations to one of disfavor. Recent events have emphasized this point again. Astute Treasurers understand that changes with instruments and markets can happen quickly, and as a result they must stay alert to any indicators of a change. They also seek to learn from other people's experience.

Auction-Rate Securities

Many net investors used auction-rate securities (ARSs) to increase their yield on short-term assets. While ARS instruments are long-term debt, the active market allowed them to be traded as short-term items. The intent was to allow borrowers to access more affordable short-term cash for their long-term debt.

For the investor, ARSs earned a higher return for these investments with an instrument that was supposed to act just like other short-term instruments. Investment policies in organizations were sometimes changed to allow for this type of investment; and sometimes, even though the policy

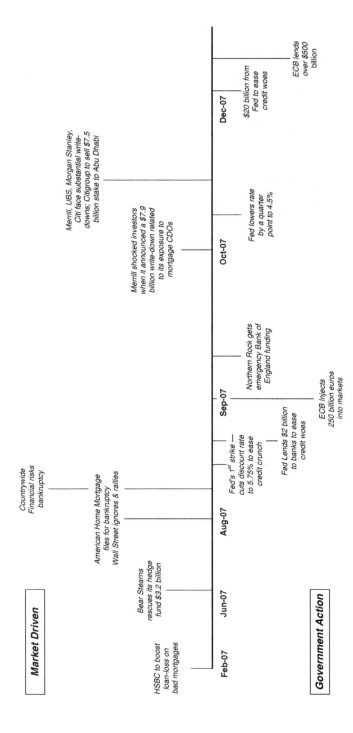

EXHIBIT 16.1 (a) & (b) Financial Crisis Timelines 2007–2008

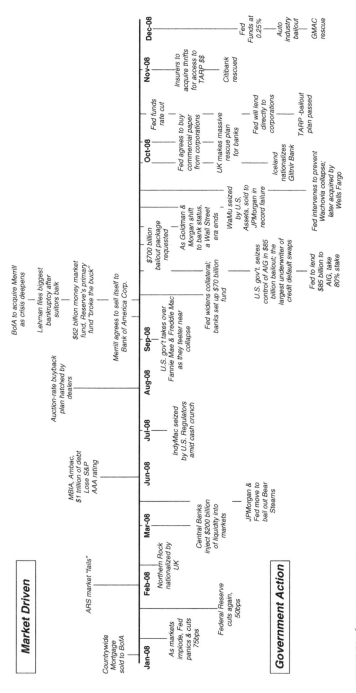

Market Driven

Jan-08
Countrywide Mortgage sold to BofA
As markets implode, Fed panics & cuts 75bps

Feb-08
ARS market "fails"
Northern Rock nationalized by UK

Mar-08
MBIA, Ambac, $1 trillion of debt Lose S&P AAA rating
Central Banks inject $200 billion of liquidity into markets
JPMorgan & Fed move to bail out Bear Stearns

Jun-08
IndyMac seized by U.S. Regulators amid cash crunch

Jul-08
Auction-rate buyback plan hatched by dealers

Aug-08
$62 billion money market fund, Reserve's primary fund "broke the buck"
U.S. gov't takes over Fannie Mae & Freddie Mac as they teeter near collapse

Sep-08
BofA to acquire Merrill as crisis deepens
Lehman files biggest bankruptcy after suitors balk
Merrill agrees to sell itself to Bank of America Corp.
$700 billion bailout package requested
As Goldman & Morgan shift to bank status, a Wall Street era ends
Fed widens collateral; banks set up $70 billion fund
WaMu seized by U.S. Assets, sold to JPMorgan in record failure
U.S. gov't. seizes control of AIG in $85 billion bailout; the largest underwriter of credit default swaps

Oct-08
Fed funds rate cut
Fed agrees to buy commercial paper from corporations
UK makes massive rescue plan for banks
Iceland nationalizes Glitnir Bank
Fed will lend directly to corporations
Fed to lend $85 billion to AIG, take 80% stake
Fed intervenes to prevent Wachovia collapse; later acquired by Wells Fargo
TARP-bailout plan passed

Nov-08
Insurers to acquire thrifts for access to TARP $$
Citibank rescued

Dec-08
Fed Funds at 0.25%
Auto industry bailout
GMAC rescue

Federal Reserve cuts again, 50bps

Government Action

EXHIBIT 16.1 (Continued)

was not changed, investments were made in these types of securities nevertheless.

Retrospectively, after the ARS markets froze up, it is easy to observe the obvious problem of investing short-term liquidity into a long-term asset. Things can go wrong, and they did. It is important to note the key prospective views on these instruments. Many of these instruments were triple-A-rated, overcollateralized, and backed by insurance. Additionally, the brokers were active market makers, buying any instruments that were not repurchased by the market if the overall liquidity was low that day or week. Those four protective measures convinced many to proceed with their purchase, especially given the increased yield they offered. The instruments were largely deemed to be well worth the slight additional risk, given the generous increase in yield.

By February 2008, as ARS markets were failing, the rating agencies finally adjusted the ratings downward. Timing is everything, and this belated adjustment represented a substantial failure on the part of these agencies. The insurance component that backed these instruments became insecure as the firms backing this insurance became financially unstable, given the size of the claims coupled with other financial disruptions that impaired insurance companies' strength.

And what appeared to be overcollateralization rapidly became undercollateralization as certain asset classes traded significantly below par, if at all, due to dislocation in the marketplace for these instruments. The market makers—nearly all at once—stopped acting as a backstop due to overall softness of the market and their own liquidity and balance sheet concerns.

Thus, short-term assets changed rapidly from stable investments with an improved yield, to long-term illiquid assets. As this mess of ARS failures unwinds, certain brokers have stepped forward as bargain hunters, creating a secondary market for these instruments, and issuers have stepped up and replaced them, along with various regulatory and government groups working settlements to allow firms that invested in these instruments to get more of their money out in the near term.

Money Market Funds

Money market funds, long considered a stable principal investment, suffered a great loss of confidence and an uptick on withdrawals after the Reserve's primary fund "broke the buck" (meaning the fund fell below $1) due in large part to the Lehman Brothers meltdown. Indeed, this $62 billion fund's net asset value fell below $1 in September 2008 and was forced to put restrictions on participants' ability to withdraw funds to allow for a more orderly withdrawal and liquidation of assets. Losing principal on this type of fund, coupled with the inability to withdraw money, was deeply disconcerting for many Treasurers and the market in general.

Seeing the loss of principal and restricted access to "highly liquid funds" created a movement to funds that were viewed as providing a greater level of stability and a superior protection of principal. This movement, to some extent, was a stampede to Treasury bills. Movement for the sake of simply acting is not without its own risks and errors.

The fund size and diversity of the portfolio are some of the considerations Treasurers have. Making movements from one fund to another may create a different set of issues, and rapid reaction does not trump thoughtful actions. Elyse Weiner, Global Product Head Liquidity & Investments of Citi, advises:

> *As you're reviewing the money funds in which you invest, consider the size and diversity of the portfolio as important determinates of the fund's ability to withstand volatility. Is the fund big enough to handle large-scale redemptions and market moves? During the height of the economic turmoil in 2008, a number of organizations reacted in very rapid fashion to events and changes in the marketplace. But moving for the sake of moving, or moving to what's generally perceived as a lower risk option, does not necessarily achieve the desired end result. For example, many companies moved out of money-market funds, regardless of the underlying portfolio or other relevant factors, and invested directly into Treasury securities, to ensure safety of principal and absolute access to funds when needed. Not only did they experience a loss of yield, but there were liquidity issues associated with direct securities of which they may not have been aware. This market risk element was a surprise to some that made the move.*

Making any movement—or remaining in an existing fund or with a counterparty—requires a rational approach that considers both the organizational goals and the various risks that are being reduced or exchanged. Additionally, a movement of the herd can by itself increase the risk of counterparties and funds. These events may happen very quickly, and the Treasurer must pay attention to those events and activities in order to be prepared to respond.

Exhibits 16.1 (a) and (b) show the beginning of the Financial Crisis of 2007–2008. The first part of the timeline shows a financial crisis that was international in nature. The effects were first identified and felt in the United States and then recognized internationally. This timeline of events identifies some of the key features of market events above the line and government interventions below.

Counterparties

Managing counterparty risk represents one of the basic requirements of effective liquidity management. The first steps are knowing who your counterparties are and making sure they have a high rating that proves their strength. The Treasurer further ensures diversification among counterparties because this protects the organization from failing due to a single event or counterparty in the midst of financial turmoil.

During the financial crisis, some of the historically top-rated financial counterparties were gravely damaged and needed repair. The dramatic and rapid fall of some storied institutions with unblemished histories of more than a century was shocking. Firms such as The Bear Stearns Cos. Inc., Lehman Brothers Holdings Inc., and Merrill Lynch & Co. all succumbed.

In a matter of months, the four largest investment banks were either bought or recharted as commercial banks with the help of the U.S. government. A massive insurance company of the reputation, size, and breadth of American International Group Inc. was supported by, and essentially forced to sell itself to, the federal government for access to $85 billion to stabilize the firm. The rules of the stabilization were later made less onerous, but the government ended up providing the firm with more than $150 billion to steady the firm while an orderly disposition could take place. AIG was the largest issuer of credit default swaps (CDSs).

As a result of the financial crisis, many company board members began asking if their organizations had any counterparty exposure to the firms that seemed to appear in the headlines almost daily. Treasurers needed to respond to these queries with alacrity. Depending on what systems and processes had been established, firms could find it rather simple or incredibly challenging to answer this legitimate question.

Given the volatility and rapidity of change during this crisis, this question often needed to be asked and answered multiple times in the same day. Some firms that were intellectually and systematically prepared to identify direct counterparties found themselves playing catchup as they found they needed to see indirect counterparties as well. They may not have had Merrill Lynch as a direct counterparty, but may have found that they participated in a fund that had Merrill Lynch as a counterparty; and this meant they did have exposure to Merrill.

Foreign Exchange Rates

Most U.S.-headquartered companies with more than $750 million in sales/turnover have found a significant and growing exposure to various currency rates from one source or another. Volatility of numerous markets and currencies will have a positive or negative impact on liquidity. The discussion that follows does not contemplate all of the various hedging and risk-management scenarios a company may employ. Nonetheless, the point is made of how volatility of exchange rates can impair an organization's liquidity if they are not properly managed.

In finance, knowledge of history is useful. At the same time, history is not always a good predictor of the future. However, memory tends to be the worst predictor of the future since it tends to focus on the stable recent periods and forgets times of rapid change. The Treasurer must understand both historical volatility and possible events that may chart a new trail.

By managing risks according to the organizational risk framework and policy, the Treasurer reduces volatility and can provide a more stable liquidity picture. The change between two currency pairs will be discussed as a way of showing foreign exchange (FX) volatility.

USD/EUR

From July to November 2008, the exchange rate between the U.S. dollar and the euro went from nearly $1.60/euro to $1.25/euro. This represents enormous volatility. This swing of more than 20 percent between two of the world's largest economies and currencies was unprecedented. The movement of the exchange rate between these two currencies has generally been a gradual increase in the valuation of the euro with some periods of notable volatility. During the recent history of the euro there was a long buildup over years, with fluctuations, from a low point of $0.88/euro to the peak of more than $1.60/euro with a rapid give-back of more than 20 percent over a period of weeks. The magnitude of the recent fluctuations was startling for many in the Treasury field. This created some unexpected winners, and losers who were not hedged as much as they might have wished. (See Exhibit 16.2.)

JPY/AUD

While not all U.S.-based firms have exposure to this particular currency pair (Yen and Aussie), the level of volatility serves as an additional warning and example from a liquidity management perspective. (See Exhibit 16.3.) During a five-year period (the rise is also apparent over approximately seven years beginning with 2000), the rise of the Aussie dollar—and its complete reversal—can be seen in a period of weeks. Dramatic changes can create significant losses and unexpected results.

Commodities

Commodities are no stranger to significant volatility. Commodities of a variety of sorts are used in various products or may be used in the creation or delivery of services and may touch many organizations. Dramatic movements in commodity prices not only have an impact on the profit or loss of

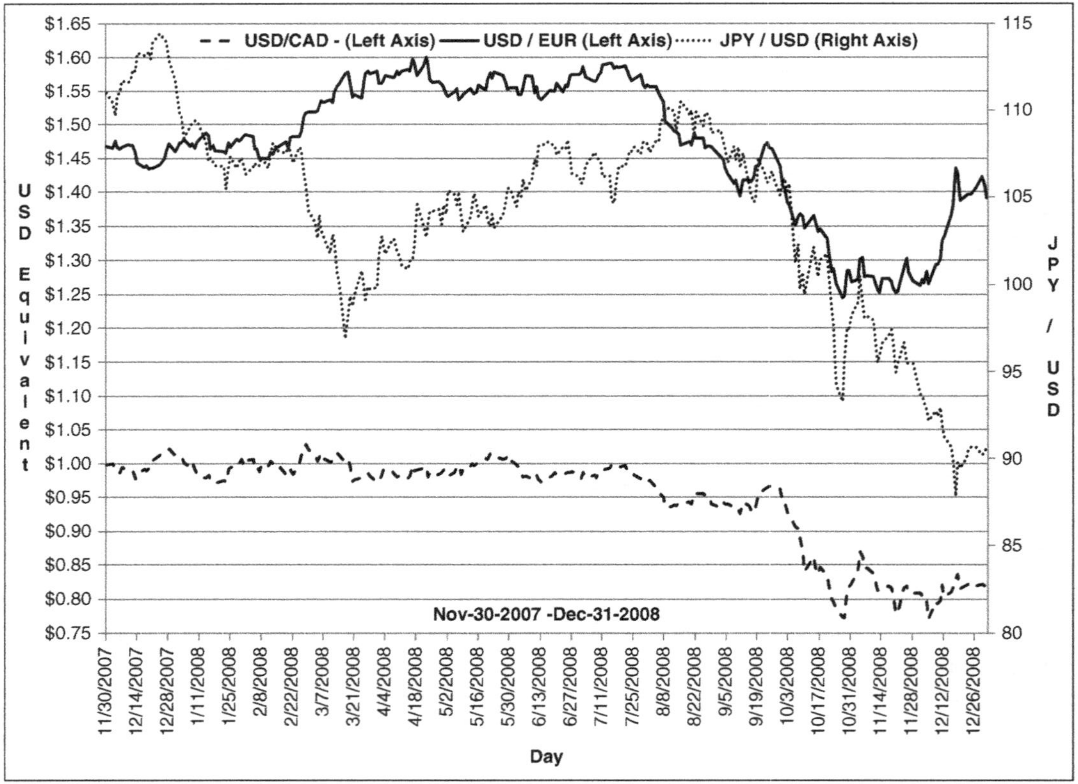

EXHIBIT 16.2 Foreign Exchange Rates—USD/Euro

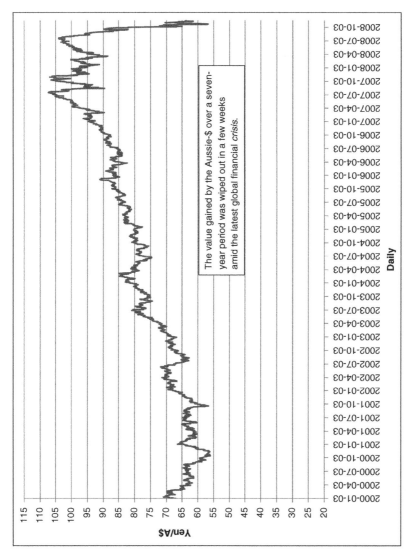

The value gained by the Aussie-$ over a seven-year period was wiped out in a few weeks amid the latest global financial *crisis.*

EXHIBIT 16.3 Foreign Exchange Rates—JPY/AUD

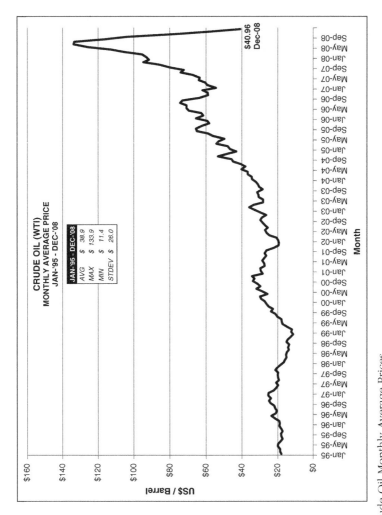

EXHIBIT 16.4 Crude Oil Monthly Average Prices

This chart shows the average monthy price of crude oil. The average price over a month provides a much less dramatic view compared with daily price volatility.

Source: Energy Information Administration.

an organization, they also impact liquidity. During the financial crisis, there was a long and significant run-up in the price of crude oil, impacting the price of various oil products.

After exceeding $150/barrel for crude oil, much of the global economy sputtered hard, and expectations of use and actual use of oil plummeted. For the first time in 25 years, global oil use decreased. Even before that result was known, the market began to believe and then saw the slowdown. Prices fell to below $50/barrel, less than one-third the price just a few months prior. See Exhibit 16.4. Even with the Organization of Petroleum Exporting Companies (OPEC) cutting production, the demand was declining faster than the supply.

The runup and drop of oil prices impacts transportation, travel, and many businesses directly and indirectly. Other commodities may not have as broad an impact, but can affect particular organizations deeply. Treasurers of those firms need to give special focus to these commodities.

While some people outside Treasury—with the benefit of hindsight—will often comment about what should have or should not have been done and how much the action or inaction cost, the Treasurer needs to be vigilant in making the organization understand the importance of risk management and how that can reduce the volatility of income and liquidity.

Rating Agencies

Firms have long relied on rating agencies as a major component for dealing with counterparty risk and fund/instrument risk. The magnitude of agency failures to downgrade securities, insurance companies, and banks in a timely manner left Treasurers with an impaired measurement tool. Not being able to discard rating agencies from the mix, Treasurers saw the need to base their credit risk and counterparty risk parameters on additional sources of data and monitoring.

Banks and Insurance Companies

Exhibit 16.5 shows failed U.S. banks brought under receivership by the Federal Deposit Insurance Corp. in 2007 and 2008. Prior to 2007, the last bank failure had occurred in 2004. From October 2000 through 2004, there were 24 bank failures. In 2008 alone, 25 banks failed. Other "forced" mergers have occurred as well. The largest failure in U.S. history, IndyMac Bank, occurred during this timeframe. It was alarming to have Charles Schumer, the senior senator from New York, declare on June 26, 2008, that he was "concerned that IndyMac's financial deterioration poses significant

Bank Closings	
Bank Name	Date
Miami Valley Bank, Lakeview, OH	4-Oct-07
NetBank, Alpharetta, GA	28-Sep-07
Metropolitan Savings Bank, Pittsburgh, PA	2-Feb-07
Douglass National Bank, Kansas City, MO	25-Jan-08
Hume Bank, Hume, MO	7-Mar-08
ANB Financial, NA, Bentonville, AR	9-May-08
First Integrity Bank, NA, Staples, MN	30-May-08
IndyMac Bank, Pasadena, CA	11-Jul-08
First Heritage Bank, NA, Newport Beach, CA	25-Jul-08
First National Bank of Nevada, Reno, NV	25-Jul-08
First Priority Bank, Bradenton, FL	1-Aug-08
The Columbian Bank and Trust, Topeka, KS	22-Aug-08
Integrity Bank, Alpharetta, GA	29-Aug-08
Silver State Bank, Henderson, NV	5-Sep-08
Ameribank, Northfork, WV	19-Sep-08
Washington Mutual Bank	25-Sep-08
Meridian Bank, Eldred, IL	10-Oct-08
Main Street Bank, Northville, MI	10-Oct-08
Alpha Bank & Trust, Alpharetta, GA	24-Oct-08
Freedom Bank, Bradenton, FL	31-Oct-08

Bank Closings	
Bank Name	Date
Security Pacific Bank, Los Angeles, CA	7-Nov-08
Franklin Bank, SSB, Houston, TX	7-Nov-08
The Community Bank, Loganville, GA	21-Nov-08
Downey Savings and Loan, Newport Beach, CA	21-Nov-08
PFF Bank and Trust, Pomona, CA	21-Nov-08
First Georgia Community Bank, Jackson, GA	5-Dec-08
Sanderson State Bank, Sanderson, TX	12-Dec-08
Haven Trust Bank, Duluth, GA	12-Dec-08

Other Financial Institution Events		
Institution	Event	Date
Bear Stearns	Acquired by JPMorgan	14-Mar-08
Lehman Brothers	Bankrupt	15-Sep-08
Merrill Lynch	Acquired by BofA	15-Sep-08
AIG	Nationalized	16-Sep-08
Wachovia	Acquired by Wells Fargo	28-Sep-08
Royal Bank of Scotland	Nationalized	12-Oct-08
Citigroup	*Rescued*	23-Nov-08
GMAC	*Rescued*	30-Dec-08

EXHIBIT 16.5 Bank Closings and Other Financial Institution Events

Source: FDIC.

risks to both taxpayers and borrowers," and that IndyMac "could face a failure if prescriptive measures are not taken quickly." The IndyMac Bank seizure occurred on July 11, 2008. And that was not the end.

Wachovia Corp., the fourth-largest bank in the nation at the time, was suffering significantly from its exposure to mortgages in Florida and California. They acquired a California bank with an enormous portfolio of mortgages that allowed the mortgagee to have payment flexibility. This acquisition brought troubled assets onto Wachovia's balance sheet and created tremendous financial pressure. Based on pressure from regulators and from depositor action, Wachovia was pushed into the arms of Wells Fargo & Co. rather abruptly.

In an effort to provide liquidity and ensure major banks remained adequately capitalized, the government injected them with massive cash infusions and capital. Some, including the mammoth Citibank, in November 2008, received a second round of funding and additional guarantees on some assets by the federal government to stabilize the institution against any future issues that might arise.

Banks were not lending to banks, and the Federal Reserve loaned record-breaking and ever-greater amounts of funds to provide liquidity in the system. The lending was made to U.S. banks, and liquidity was also pumped into other central banks on both a bilateral and coordinated basis. And, for a while, the reported London Interbank Offered Rate (LIBOR) was called into question when it became obvious that banks either were not lending to other banks or were not lending at the rates being reported.

Banks earn much of their money on the difference or spread between the rate at which they borrow funds and the rate at which they lend. In times of great turbulence, an interesting situation occurs often where numbers indicative of short-term bank borrowing and lending cross. Since this spread remains pretty consistent over time, it is notable anytime the numbers collapse or cross.

Exhibit 16.6 shows two of these crossings. During the recent crossing, the prime rate (the rate that the largest U.S. banks charge their best customers) went below LIBOR (the rate at which banks reportedly borrow from one another for short time periods).

While banks raise capital and also borrow for longer terms than one-month LIBOR rates, the crossing of these curves is indicative of dislocative events. These rapid and intersecting changes in rates indicate broader liquidity issues. During the crisis, many uncommitted lines of credit were pulled or reduced. Much activity between banks and Treasurers occurred in efforts to shore up access to credit. Some of this activity was done gracefully, with some companies given months to locate other sources. Other banks were more abrupt and pulled corporate lines instantaneously. Some committed lines were also frozen during this event.

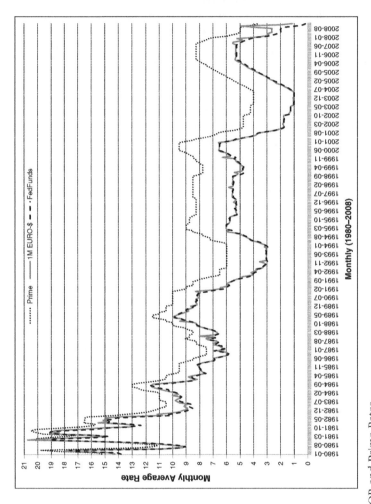

EXHIBIT 16.6 LIBOR and Prime Rates

This chart uses a proxy for LIBOR—the one-month euro-dollar deposit rate—given the two rates' high correlation and to ensure consistency in data sources.

Source: All data was sourced from the Federal Reserve Staistical Release: H.15 Selected Interest Rates.

With the failure of IndyMac, individuals and companies lost money above the insured limits. During times of rapid and dramatic dislocation in the markets and uncertainty about counterparty and bank viability, a flight to quality takes on new meaning.

In the past, moving funds took hours and days. By the late twentieth century—with electronic banking and the democratization of information—funds can be moved almost instantaneously based on real news or even speculation. Banking with strong and relatively stable institutions came back in vogue during this crisis and is likely to fall out of vogue over time as memories fade. Wise Treasurers know history and are watchful of current events.

In the midst of the activity surrounding the crisis, much uncertainty existed. There was no handbook for handling the crisis of 2007+. While the experiences and select principles from the Great Depression were at the forefront of the Fed and Treasury, there were also many differences. This uncertainty among those handling the situation created additional volatility in the reaction of the government.

The government decided whom it would rescue or force to be acquired. The direction was changed, it seemed, almost daily. A staggering $700 billion was allocated for the investment in troubled assets with the Troubled Asset Rescue Program (TARP). Not long after this program was approved, the U.S. Congress was informed that troubled assets would not be purchased, but that investments in banks and guarantees would be made. In time, entire books will likely be written about the government movements and counter-movements during this time.

Insurance companies faced challenges with regard to their assets and liabilities. They had exposure to liabilities related to credit default swaps, counterparties, and market volatility (through their market exposure via annuity products). To counter these challenges many insurance companies raised additional capital at less-than-favorable terms and sought additional funds through the TARP by buying troubled thrifts. Treasurers who relied on a credit default swap as a type of insurance could have faced situations where the counterparty that protects them from the downside is not there when they need that insurance.

Governments

In addition to the rapid course corrections and adjustments by the U.S. government, other central banks were making dramatic changes, too. While there were many movements by Japan, China, and Western European central banks, Iceland stands out as an extreme example. The government nationalized its three largest banks and shut down its stock market for a period of time. It then sought capital from other countries and from the International Monetary Fund to reopen its markets.

This type of credit crisis provides Treasurers with a refreshed reason to ensure that country financial system risk is considered. The negative impact on liquidity for an organization can be dramatic. And it requires diligence to monitor such developments.

Summary

Treasurers must ensure that their organization has adequate liquidity. Liquidity can be impacted by numerous causes. Each of these causes can create strong or extreme volatility to the liquidity of the organization. As the protector of cash and liquidity, the Treasurer must stay current and fully aware of the various threats to the firm's liquidity.

This vigilance in protecting the King (cash or liquidity) depends upon ongoing education and communication to others in the organization. When the market is in turmoil, everyone understands how important the Treasurer is in protecting liquidity. By proactively educating the organization, the Treasurer will be more easily able to take adequate steps to protect the organization's liquidity during the periods where there is relative calm.

While events cannot necessarily be predicted or avoided, their impact to the firm can be mitigated by having an action plan in place. For that, the Strategic Treasurer needs to be well-organized and able to act, and react, prudently and promptly.

CHAPTER 17

Achieving Visibility to Your Liquidity
Visibility and Process-Automation Requirements for the Strategic Treasurer

I will gladly pay you Tuesday for a hamburger today.

—Wimpy, character in "Popeye" cartoons

A key component of liquidity management is having a clear and accurate view of your assets and capital. There are numerous structures, services, and activities that must be employed in order to manage liquidity effectively and efficiently.

Chapter 16 emphasized the level of volatility and various sources where issues of volatility can arise. Once those areas are understood, other actions need to be completed. These include reviewing direct and indirect activities such as banking structures, securing lines of credit, employing an optimal capital structure, managing working capital, and others. Many of these components are covered in other chapters. This chapter emphasizes three key steps necessary for managing organizational liquidity during turbulent times. All three components are preparatory in nature, the third relating to being prepared to react to changing events. For the Treasurer, preparation for liquidity challenges is, in its essence, an exercise of organization. During times of stability, there will be great pressure on Treasury not to spend the time or money on organizing for events that are deemed highly unlikely, given the current state of affairs, controls, or regulations.

The message that what happened in the past will not occur in the future is as common as it is inappropriate. While exact situations and triggering events are unlikely to mirror history, the Treasurer must ensure that the organization will be ready for similar events that may come about or be exacerbated by other actions or regulations. While it may be possible to predict some of these turbulent events, it may be impossible to prevent them. However, the Treasurer can ensure that her group is organized and prepared to address events as they unfold with a much higher level of data, analysis, and confidence than would otherwise be the case.

The Treasurer must guard the organizational cash and liquidity with vigilance. Failure of Treasury to be prepared for liquidity challenges at a level appropriate for the organization represents a clear abdication of duties. Preparation can be at different levels, and the needs of different organizations regarding liquidity can vary greatly, given their net borrowing or investing position, exposures, geographical reach, current structure, and so on. The three steps related to preparation and response build on other work for which the Treasurer is responsible, including capital structure, Treasury structure, and relationship management.

Step 1: Achieving visibility to the firm's liquidity. Since the Treasurer must guard cash and sources of liquidity for the organization, achieving clear visibility to these assets and components is essential. Timeliness matters. It is important to note that visibility to liquidity components that comes too late or at an inappropriate level is almost useless.

Step 2: Assessing threats and impacts to the firm's liquidity. Astute and Strategic Treasurers understand the need to perform a regular review to identify and measure organizational liquidity and the various factors that impact liquidity in a negative direction. A regular review of liquidity is necessary for every organization. When there is great market disruption and significant events, all Treasurers must reassess where they are in light of new, emerging, and possible events. This is a time when Treasurers earn their keep.

Step 3: Execution—making rapid (workable and prudent) decisions according to plan. As worrisome or unexpected market and government events unfold or threats to the firm's liquidity arise, the prepared Treasury group will be able to reassess or react quickly according to plan. This can contain components that are the Treasury equivalent to medical triage.

Achieving Visibility to Liquidity Requires Internal and External Data

To gain an accurate picture of the firm's liquidity position requires visibility to the data and forecast information that resides in multiple locations. This data—which may vary depending upon a company's particular situation—will be typically found within Treasury systems or databases, in the financial records of the organization, within the Treasurer's mind, or in a spreadsheet controlled by a particular operating area.

The need to view data that provides a picture of the organizational liquidity can be seen as a progression of data. Exhibit 17.1 shows the Treasury department-oriented data. This level of data is focused on cash balances, investment information, and debt and credit facility data along with any hedges that exist. This provides the essential first level of liquidity data that can be summarized or grouped as desired.

The items listed in this exhibit provide Treasury with a baseline of available cash and investments as well as a view into the use and capacity of credit. Cash is typically a current balance figure, while the investment, debt, and hedge components have cash flows with dates associated with each item.

The next two levels of data that is gathered are shown in Exhibit 17.2. These include the high-value items that often need to be reported separately. Forecast data derived from historical information is normally gathered from the financial statements or from Treasury's information database. This data is used by the operating area or Treasury department to help create short-term forecasts.

Exhibit 17.3 shows how some organizations may gather data from external partners. This type of visibility is extremely challenging and rare. Most organizations achieve superior benefits by building out their capabilities in

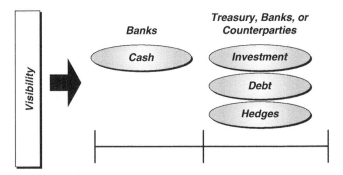

EXHIBIT 17.1 Visibility to Treasury Items—Level 1

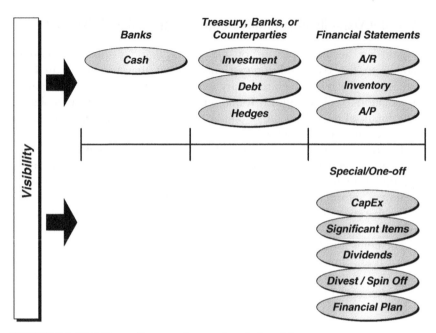

EXHIBIT 17.2 Visibility to Treasury Items—Levels 2 and 3

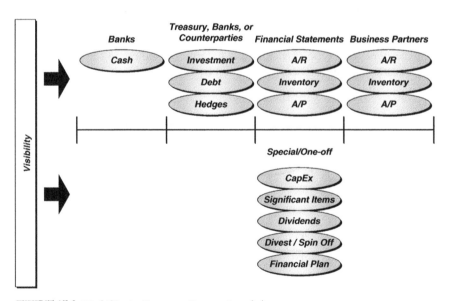

EXHIBIT 17.3 Visibility to Treasury Items—Level 4

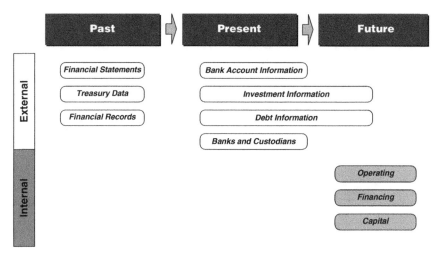

EXHIBIT 17.4 Achieving Visibility to Your Liquidity

the first three areas before doing much work in the fourth area. Nonetheless, the fact that there are tools that help with this type of visibility, financing, and liquidity planning is important to certain organizations. There are times when Treasurers need to leverage tools and services that help in these areas from a forecasting and flexibility standpoint.

The previous three exhibits looked at data needed to manage liquidity from an ordered priority perspective. Exhibit 17.4 looks at the data needed to ensure adequate liquidity from a broad-timeframe perspective. This shows current information, historical, and future forecast and planning data.

- **Past.** Historical information is used for creating forecasts with the assumption that for many lines of business, the past is a very good starting point when trying to determine future cash flows. This category includes financial statements and records that are external to Treasury. Treasury data may be internally or externally stored, depending on the company's situation. It is shown here as external data.
- **Present.** Bank and counterparty information is shown as a current source of data. Banks hold balance and transaction data for cash, custody/investment, as well as debt information. Additional information about hedges and investment portals is available, too, from external sources. Many organizations pull this information into their own Treasury system(s) to better analyze their activity.
- **Future.** Investment and debt information extends from the present into the future category since either category may not have fixed

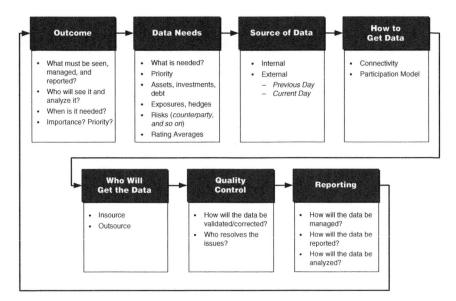

EXHIBIT 17.5 Achieving Visibility to Your Liquidity

and unchangeable rate components. Debt or investments can have their cash flows influenced by various forces. A change in cash flows could be the result of a change in the yield curve on which the debt or investment is based. Furthermore, the change could be based on prepayment or restructuring activities. Additionally, corporate action related to operating flows, refinancing, and capital expenditure plans can create significant adjustments to the forecast and actual cash flow.

Exhibit 17.5 diagrams a chart for determining information needs, sources, methods, and controls at a process level. Data needs differ based both on the organization and on what type of information is sought. This chart is meant to be a general guide for achieving visibility to the organization's liquidity through various sources of data that exist.

The following provides a more detailed description of the process:

- **Outcome.** Determining what needs to be known and seen, and by whom, sets up the first questions that must be answered. Concurrent with those activities are the issues of timing and priority. Both of these influence the cost.
- **Data needs.** Once the macro outcome is determined, more details about what data is needed must be listed.

- **Source of data.** This is an inventory function. Where does this data reside? Inside Treasury? In the organization? At a third party such as a bank? At a client or vendor site?
- **How to get the data.**
  - *Connectivity.* This process identifies the preferred method to use when connecting to get data for each source identified in the previous step.
  - *Participation model.* This refers to how one might participate in a network such as SWIFT (Society for Worldwide Interbank Financial Telecommunication). For example, corporations can connect with various participation models such as a bilateral arrangement cleverly named MA-CUG (Member Administered Closed User Group) or a more network-friendly model, SCORE (Standardized Corporate Environment).
- **Who will get the data?** Many organizations have historically run the hardware and processes of gathering all types of Treasury data themselves. Outsourcing the hardware and management of this effort is becoming far more popular. Service bureaus and data consolidators are two types of organizations that outsource those activities for corporations and businesses of all sizes.
- **Quality control.** For firms that outsource various components of the data gathering, key questions must be answered about where control resides and where responsibility rests in order to ensure accuracy. Data validation refers to the process of file control where files must be in balance, the mathematics must be correct, and files are not duplicated. The correction component refers to how information that is duplicated, wrong, or incomplete is fixed. Missing information, as well as incorrect data, must be resolved and not merely reported. Resolving many of these issues can be outsourced or handled in-house by Treasury or Information Technology. There are numerous models and services that exist and represent a key set of decisions for Treasury.
- **Reporting.** This section answers a number of questions, including: Where will the data be processed and stored? How will this information be reported and analyzed? Will reporting be made on a time basis or on an exception basis? How will the information be summarized, or detailed, and provided to users who have a need to know and see this information?
- **Loop back to outcome.** The process begins again. Data access and management is not inexpensive. Regularly asking the ultimate questions of what is needed, who needs it, how do they use it, and what is the priority and value of that data/analysis is appropriate. This saves money and ensures that the overall organizational and informational needs are met.

Prerequisites to Achieving Visibility

Rationalizing banking relationships and banking structure is the first pre-requisite to achieving visibility. While a clean account structure helps with visibility, it often contains other benefits for efficiency and control. Every bank account represents a point of exposure and cost. It also represents a hurdle or impediment to clean visibility.

Optimizing the number of counterparties that you do business with, beyond commercial banks, also will help improve visibility. It is important to remember that the goal is optimization, not minimization. The problem with minimizing banks and other counterparties is that while visibility to a firm's bank accounts may improve by having a single bank, it may increase risk by overly concentrating exposure to one financial institution or counterparty.

External Information

There are many sources of external information that may be needed. While determining the necessity and priority of each component is of top concern, the practical matters must also be addressed. Addressing the practical aspects of gathering external information requires being able to answer a number of questions about the data itself. These items require resources with a strong understanding of the subject matter. The Strategic Treasurer will ensure that he has access to professionals who understand the issues and can ensure that the organization forms an appropriate Treasury information plan and executes on that plan. When choosing an external source of information, the following issues must be considered:

- Location of data
- Formats available
- Connectivity needs, options, and security
- Frequency data is needed and available
- Cost of various connection and information options
- Level of support needed for implementation and ongoing purposes

Internal Information

A critical need for Treasurers is direct and clear visibility into various parts of their organization. One key component is seeing their liquidity. Liquidity for a Treasurer is made up of several major pieces. These include balances in various bank accounts, activity held at custodians related to investments and holdings, as well as debt instruments and lines of credit held by banks and other providers of credit. Also included in this view of liquidity are the hedges attributed to interest rate, foreign exchange, and commodities. Additionally, a fair amount of internal information is needed for good visibility into liquidity—some related to the operating flows that are part of the cash-conversion cycle, which include capital expenditures and large items, such as tax payments or proposed purchases or divestitures.

The Treasurer needs to have clear visibility into these various areas, particularly into those activities that will happen in the near term. This requires access into accounts, investments, and debt when looking at the short-term cash forecast. Access and visibility require a number of things: knowing where the data is, how to get to it, and how to analyze it.

The organization needs to be able to focus on both strategy and analysis, and not spend all its time on operational activities, such as connecting to and managing data from every point. Additionally, the Treasurer needs clean Treasury processes, meaning that they are efficient and elegant, and that data is not reentered. Where appropriate, straight-through processing should be pushed, particularly for trades and various transactions in the Treasury model.

Being able to see where the firm's funds are coming from and where they are going both in the present and in the future requires a multipronged approach. Examining today's information requires access to several types of data and information. Pulling items such as balance information and debt and investment activity for many organizations means connecting to a number of different organizations, systems, and networks. There are certainly challenges in making these connections—such as the cost of each connection where payment is required for that service. There are overhead fees required to establish the connections, maintain them, have the ability to change passwords, to resolve and restore differences when they occur, and to monitor when there are problems.

Connecting Through Networks

Thankfully, Treasurers do not need to be IT professionals. Yet, almost all Treasurers will benefit themselves and their organizations by understanding some of the basics of the technology of Treasury generally and connections specifically. Making and maintaining direct connections to all of the banks and counterparties for all of the firm's activities become increasingly difficult as the number of banks and counterparties grows larger. Establishing and maintaining a host of bilateral connections can be an enormous hardship for midsized and large corporations as passwords change and encryption demands adjust. They almost always create a problem at the most inopportune time. Also, the staff required to maintain and provide backup coverage is costly.

Many organizations find that connecting to banks and other counter-parties through a network is prudent and far less stressful. Two types of networks are covered in the following sections: the SWIFT network and con-solidators/service bureaus. Using these types of networks and services is an essential requirement for many Treasurers to achieve visibility and resiliency of their financial processes and information. Please note that other Treasury professionals may categorize differently the features and organizations that provide these services.

SWIFT Corporate Access

The Society for Worldwide Interbank Financial Communication, known as SWIFT Corporate Access, refers to using the SWIFT network to make connections with banks. SWIFT supplies secure messaging services and interface software to wholesale financial entities. While SWIFT was originally designed for bank-to-bank communication and messaging, the network has been open to corporations for some time. SWIFT is a network for banks that many corporations can join. The following list shows the main rea-sons for corporations to access SWIFT and provides some details about the information that is used to achieve specific efficiency goals.

- **Visibility.** Visibility is important to liquidity management and risk man-agement. Basically, visibility means being able to see where funds are coming from and where they are going—today and in the future. This requires access into several different types of data and sources of infor-mation.
- **Efficiency.** Clean and efficient processes reduce risk and remain impor-tant to nearly every organization. *Efficiency* basically refers to doing things right and avoiding problems. A typical prescription for efficiency is straight-through processing (STP). SWIFT provides an avenue into a number of key processes—which allows a company to connect into more processes. The degree of detail, or visibility, SWIFT provides includes:
  - **Balance information.** Where is your money? If you have accounts all over the globe at various banks, you need to access that information. This can be difficult with all of the connections that must be set up, managed, and monitored. SWIFT allows Treasurers to use their infor-mation network to get all or a majority of that information centrally and securely. However, this requires some measure of effort. There are ways to make this process somewhat easier. This topic is covered in the following section on consolidators and service bureaus.
  - **Investment, debt, and hedge information.** The organization's cus-todian or loan information will typically represent a fair amount of its

cash flow. Access to that data can come from the custodian or from the company's records. SWIFT may be a channel for some of this data as well.

- **Bank Account Management.** The opening and closing of bank accounts and signer adjustments can be managed via the Electronic Bank Account Management messaging process.

Being able to connect to a single source, which is highly secure and is the top priority connection for the company's banks, can make life a little easier for the Treasurer. The focus can move off of operational activities and onto analysis.

Consolidators and Service Bureaus

Consolidators act as private networks that connect to numerous banks and other financial counterparties on the corporation's behalf. The consolidator establishes a single connection (or limited number of connections) to the corporation and handles the data transfer, data transformation, and transaction movement activity on an outsourced basis. The value of many networks lies in the number of participants and the services that are provided. Regarding the number of participants, it is helpful to understand that the many consolidators connect to other consolidators and to networks such as SWIFT. Chapter 14 provides additional information on the options for how organizations may gather necessary data. Bank systems and Treasury workstations can often be very useful tools, if they are selected properly and used appropriately.

Organizations that deal with multiple financial institutions and counterparties can benefit from using consolidators to gather and purify data, and deliver banking transactions. In the world of SWIFT, the terms *service bureau* and *service bureau plus* refer to organizations that perform the task of consolidators. For simplicity's sake, the term *consolidator* is being used here while the different levels of services that are offered by consolidators are further categorized later in this chapter.

The information necessary to achieve appropriate visibility requires a fair amount of operational and technical resources. The responsibility for gathering this information and ensuring its accuracy and timeliness is the role of either the company or an outsourced party. Few organizations really need that level of expertise, contingency infrastructure, and service level support internally. Some organizations can be an exception, and they may fall into the Treasury-intensive organization list, which would include banks, nonbank financials, and companies with enormous Treasury needs. However, it almost always makes sense to connect through some sort of consolidator rather than maintain a dozen or more different connections for account information, custody information, and so on. For many organizations, out-sourcing these activities is justified for the following reasons:

- **Connection overhead.** Establishing and maintaining connections requires significant effort and yields little joy. Rarely does it make sense for Treasury to maintain staffing to support all this effort. Treasury-intensive organizations (for instance, banks and nonbank financials such as insurance firms, brokerages) can fall into the exception category and have their own support staff. Eliminating all the overhead of making these connections, translating the data, and pulling it into the system is helpful for Treasury staffs that have been stretched thin and need to focus on performing additional analysis and items of a more strategic nature.
- **Costs.** Among the costs for running this activity internally are hardware, software, and IT staffing. The setup and recurring costs are substantial for the hardware and software, even if the IT technology group indicates, at first, that it is not. Equipment and software needs include:
  - Servers: production, test, and development
  - Communication hardware
  - Security hardware
  - Software: communication, translation, schedulers, and so on
- **Problem reporting and problem resolution.** Resolving differences or determining when there is a problem with data is a crucial require-ment for Treasury. Daily information is usually the basis for decision making of different types for that organization. Obviously, it is a big problem if some data has not come through, if it is old or dated, if it is missing several countries' worth of information, or if it does not contain certain balances that are needed to determine the company's cash position, make investment or borrowing decisions, or move funds across the border. Large problems can result in not knowing, detecting, or resolving these items.

There are three levels of using an outside data aggregator—defined as firms or services such as SWIFT Corporate Access, Fides, Broadridge Ser-vices, and so on. These services pull data in and provide it to organizations as a Treasurer connects through a workstation or in-house accounting pack-age. The system pulls this information in according to levels of services that need to be performed. Whether these are performed by an outside con-solidator organization or in-house is a question that organizations need to answer. The available levels include:

1. **Simple consolidation (aggregation).** At this level, the consolidator will retrieve data from various sources and return it in the format needed.

Similarly, for transactions initiated in-house, the consolidator sees that they are properly formatted and securely delivered as instructed. If the data is not available when it is supposed to be, the consolidator often makes several additional attempts to pull the data. For example, SWIFT acts as a network and ensures that all files it has received are delivered. It does not track files that should have been sent but are not.

2. **Consolidation and exception reporting.** The next level of service has the firm doing everything that a simple consolidation service does with extra attempts at resolution and communication with their clients about what data has failed or is missing. The fact that they will notice and tell when there are items that are late or do not exist is quite valuable. Achieving visibility to the firm's liquidity includes knowing when the data the Treasurer has is complete or incomplete. The consolidator is responsible for those activities and notifications. Additional problem resolution is then the responsibility of the client.

3. **Consolidation and problem resolution.** The third level represents very active notification and resolution. In addition to notifying their customers of any problems, some consolidators offer a higher level of service where they will take all necessary steps of resolving the problem and reporting to the client firm when it is complete. For instance, if a bank has failed to report balances by a certain time, you receive notification that you are missing that bank's information. The consolidator contacts that bank to determine what the problem is and how and when it can be fixed.

Most banks offer some type of consolidation services at very different levels. Many banks leverage other consolidators to make their offering more complete. This is an area of great distinction between banks. Only a few banks have an offering that is robust enough to allow for all three levels of service.

Technology firms also offer consolidator services, either as their sole offering or as part of a suite of products that a firm may employ. SWIFT has allowed corporations to access its network for some time now. The participation models have become increasingly less cumbersome. Physical connections require approximately the same level of technical resources, as always, with the exception of the SWIFT Alliance Lite offering that was released in 2008, which is a Web interface for low-volume transactions using a USB stick for security. Most firms will want to leverage a consolidator to access the SWIFT network, banks that are not part of SWIFT, and other sources of data.

SWIFT has some characteristics that show shortcomings as an entire solution but has strengths when used properly. Many banks are connected to SWIFT. However, there are many banks all over the world that are not part of that network. SWIFT is a very reliable network and ensures that every piece of data that is received is delivered to its destination. However, it does not recognize if information that is supposed to be sent to it is not. It also cannot recognize if information is late. The service is not designed for those types of functions. Consolidators can help with the missing and late information and can also aggregate data from banks that are not part of SWIFT.

Some consolidators offer a service that schedules and keeps track of what data is supposed to be received and delivered to whom, by whom, and when. Knowing your needs and matching those with the capabilities of the various consolidators is important work. Some consolidators connect to SWIFT and also connect to banks that are outside of SWIFT. Still others connect with other parties where the client firm trades or sends/receives information.

The purpose of having visibility to the firm's liquidity is to ensure that the Treasurer can accurately see where it is and then make good decisions. This requires information to be complete, accurate, and timely. If the information is not meeting all three requirements, Treasury needs to know in order to be able to act properly. There are several characteristics to contemplate when selecting network(s) and data sources:

- **Resiliency of the network.** A chain is only as strong as its weakest link. More links in the chain may indicate less reliability and most firms are making thousands of multimillion-dollar trades every minute that require constant real-time connections. SWIFT, as a network, has a 99.95 percent uptime record. Additionally, it sits on a secure network that is not part of the Internet (although SWIFT Alliance Lite does provide a link into the network via the Internet). It is extremely resilient. Organizations should ensure that if they use a consolidator, they are aware of the consolidator's uptime and resiliency. Some of a firm's information counterparties distribute their data and manage transactions through different channels. Knowing the priority of those channels is crucial to the goal of ensuring reliable access to the data the Treasurer needs.
- **Participant match in the network.** Part of the value of a network relates to the participants in that network. When selecting networks and consolidators, the Treasurer must know: Do they have the connections his or her organization needs?
- **Uptime of transaction and information partners.** If information partners do not get information to the location needed and when it is needed, you will be disappointed. The data they provide may have to be run through their systems in real-time or via a nightly batch process. Then data or transactions are delivered or received through their own proprietary reporting database, communication hub, or via other channels, such as their SWIFT connection. Their level of uptime and ability to recover is important to organizations needing good visibility

to their liquidity. A bank, for example, should be able to explain how it ensures the highest degree of information availability through design, monitoring, and recovery processes.

Assessing Threats and Impacts to the Organization's Liquidity

Being well-organized and prepared is essential to making appropriate and quick decisions—and, most particularly, when difficult financial times arise. Being able to see your firm's cash, investments, debt, and other related items efficiently and in a timely manner is the critical first step. The second step is to regularly assess the challenges and risks to that liquidity. Knowing the items that can impact your liquidity becomes extremely important when the markets get volatile. The magnitude and impact of various events can be significant and may be felt both directly and indirectly. Exhibit 17.6 describes the impacts and how to mitigate.

All of the preparations the Treasurer makes to allow for visibility into the organization's liquidity allow it to move quickly when unfortunate events arise. During turbulent times, questions arise that must be answered, or events occur that require a response. Exhibit 17.7 provides a planning guide for gaining visibility to your organization's liquidity. The preparatory work will allow for faster analysis and response. The work includes these steps:

- **Communicate to senior management and the board.**
  - In stable times, ongoing communication with senior management and the board is always appropriate. Management and the board should be kept apprised of issues and actions related to liquidity management and how Treasury is reducing organizational risk.
  - In volatile times, recognize that the board must stay current on news and will have questions. The board should be kept informed on a proactive basis by the Treasurer; don't wait to be asked first.
- **Maintain clear reporting.**
  - Bank balances and activity should be reviewed daily.
  - Debt, investment, and hedge data should be reported for exposure and against compliance levels.
  - Counterparties' ratings should be monitored. Direct and indirect counterparty exposures should be reported on systematically.
  - Do not make assumptions about entities related to counterparties (i.e., a bank affiliate in another country). The financial strength of the firm may be substantially different from the past.
- **Keep policies current.**
  - Policies should be kept current, reflecting rapid changes to various counterparties and instruments. Since banks or other counterparties may be downgraded too slowly to be considered timely, ensure that

Impact	Possible Preventative Steps or Reaction
Trapped cash. Cash can be trapped in various accounts or institutions for reasons beyond a design flaw or execution error. While cross-border tax issues can create costly fund transfers, other situations can restrict cash movements for a period of time. For example, if the firm's financial institution is seized, a financial instrument becomes insolvent or a liquid fund "breaks a buck."	▪ Rationalize account structure. ▪ Diversify relationships. ▪ Actively monitor and report.
Tightened liquidity. In highly volatile times, liquidity in short-term credit markets can become overly tightened or "frozen." This can impact a bank's willingness to lend. Uncommitted lines can be pulled, commercial paper markets can become inaccessible, and even some committed lines may be impacted. In times of extremely tight liquidity, firms can be forced into finding and using alternative sources of funding.	▪ Diversity of investment maturities, instruments, and counterparties. ▪ Diversity of debt sources, instruments, and renewal dates. ▪ Level of liquidity in excess of what is needed during the times of calm seas. ▪ Active relationship management at all times.
Fewer capital raising options available. During times of financial crisis, equity investors may be unreceptive to any new issues of stock amid historic volatility and depressed values.	▪ Proactively make and take conversations even before capital is needed.
Bank constraints. Capital constraints at bank partners can impact bilateral arrangements as well as the syndicated loan market. The strength of a firm's bank partners can provide the key to whether a successful deal or loan rollover is consummated in this type of environment.	▪ Monitor bank ratings and strength. ▪ Ensure constantly active relationship management. ▪ Maintain a bias to work with stronger banks. ▪ Have a strong bias to banks with a deep relationship mindset.

EXHIBIT 17.6 Assessing Threats and Impacts to Liquidity

■ **High volatility and uncertainty.** When the markets go sideways, the volatility can spread to other financial areas. For example, volatility can grow with interest rate swings and foreign exchange and can further impact both the cash flow as well as the predictability of a Treasurer's planned liquidity and cash flow.	■ Hold treasury debriefs on a frequent basis. ■ Seek external input from bankers and other professionals. ■ Speak with finance thought leaders and other Treasurers. ■ Look for abnormal actions and causes. ■ Educate senior management on volatility implications.
■ **Rating agency reliability.** Many organizations have historically relied upon the ratings created by several of the larger rating agencies as a key component for their investment and counterparty risk policies. The experience of firms holding very high ratings up until the time they file bankruptcy or become insolvent and impaired has diminished the amount of trust financial professionals place in these firms and their ratings. The rating agencies are now simply one component an organization will tap as they perform their ongoing diligence in the protection of their assets.	■ Perform due diligence with your own firm's counterparties. ■ Monitor other proxies for a rating as one component.
■ **Rules are not clear or changing.** When the financial markets are extremely turbulent and the violent actions are causing significant dislocation, the government will often act. It usually will not know exactly what to do since there is no textbook. Thus, its actions will vary and may shift directions quickly. Rules may be changed multiple times in midstream, which can either be helpful or harmful. A key concern is that your firm may get caught with negative rule changes that were impossible or nearly impossible to adapt to as rapidly as you wish.	■ Monitor events and reports.

EXHIBIT 17.6 (Continued)

Know the Outcome: What Do You Need and Want?

Determine the Best Source of the Data: Where Is the Data? Determination Includes:

- Look at the present and past: What is necessary?
- Make and examine the forecast: What is changing and why?
- Prioritize those needs: Is it critical or something that is *nice* to have?

Rationalize Information and Relationships:

- Create a treasury information plan and road map.
- Determine the value (*cost/benefit of the data*) comprising both a short- and long-term perspective, including during times of high volatility.
- Select external and internal partners for the data and analysis.

Implement the Plan

Review and Optimize Plans as the Situation Progresses

Challenge the Assumptions:

- Determine what risks need to be removed.
- Volatility exists and it can cloud visibility.

EXHIBIT 17.7 Treasurer's Planning Guide for Gaining Visibility into the Firm's Liquidity Status

> your organization is watchful for potential downgrades or increased concerns about other parties.

- **Ensure resiliency of treasury.**
  - Treasury has helped prepare the overall organization to be more resilient. The firm can withstand multiple hits from a variety of sources due to diversification and other risk management activities.
- **Establish an early warning system for volatile and abnormal activity.**
  - The area where business and finance is played out must be carefully monitored for volatile and nonstandard activity. This is monitored via reports, data, news, and industry and market dialogue. It also requires being intellectually alert. This is important in so many ways. Tim Hart, Senior Vice President and Treasurer, First National Bank of Nebraska, advises, "In a period of information overload, it is important to know what is normal so you can focus on the non-normal and what has changed. Can you recognize something as abnormal? The Treasurer must be able to determine if they are experiencing events that fall within the relative range of what makes sense or if it is outside that range."

- **Engage in constructive conversations.**
  - Information and understanding are crucial. There are several different ways this could play out. Getting good quality input from various sources is crucial for the Treasurer, and this response must be almost reflexive. Ted Hanson, Chief Financial Officer of Apex Systems, says:

    > *When new or challenging situations arise on important matters, we normally take three steps to address this situation. First, internally we share what we know and discuss the matter. Second, we lean on our bank relationships and ask them for as much information and advice as possible. Third, we use other experts in the area we are focusing on. By using these resources, we can then better determine if we are covering all of our risks properly and then move forward with greater confidence. This helps avoid large mistakes that could be prevented by tapping the right resources for information and advice.*

Summary

The Treasurer must ensure that the organization has adequate liquidity. This requires that the Treasurer have visibility into the organization's liquidity. Achieving that visibility requires a good structure, an excellent Treasury information plan, appropriate Treasury technology, and diligence in execution. There are many factors that can threaten liquidity, and the Treasurer must ensure that those risks are assessed, mitigated, and reviewed.

After all the preparation is completed, the Treasurer must still be able to act and react properly to rapidly changing events. Successfully performing this function is, after all, how the Treasurer protects the organization.

CHAPTER 18

Envisioning Treasury in the Future

In the future, packages will be digitized and transmitted as beams of light. . . .

—Audio message playing on the Space Mountain
ride at Disney World

In any prognostication, the more dramatic the pronouncement, the more airtime it may receive, along with a fair bit of criticism. Making a prediction that is only marginally different from the present is usually greeted with jeers and comments about how uncreative and safe the author decided to be. Those who commented about packages—physical packages and real items—being converted into beams of light and transferred almost instantaneously and then being reassembled in some distant location certainly took the road of being dramatic.

There are many exciting happenings in Treasury that are associated with technology, finance, and management. The following represents the musings of one who enjoys pondering a number of different data points and who hopes to come up with a new idea by putting some old ideas together. There will probably be many more misses than hits, but if the following causes readers to think more broadly—and with more creativity—then this chapter will have served its purpose.

Treasury's Role in the Corporation

In the past, too many Treasurers labored in obscurity. They secured funding for the organization, ensured that proper services were available to support the business, and quietly worked to protect the firm against great loss. Increasingly in the future, Treasurers will work less and less in obscurity. Rather, they will work more in the open with their opinion, insight, and financial analysis sought out by those on the board and in senior management. This expansion of the perception and even the role emerged partially as a result of the 2007–2009 financial crises. The items previously thought of as tactical or operational, such as managing bank partners, securing credit facilities, or layering on a floating-to-fixed swap, have gained more visibility at the upper levels of an organization for a variety of reasons.

Few other areas can have such a rapid impact, positive or otherwise, on an organization as Treasury. Board members will recognize the fiduciary responsibility they have to the shareholders or owners of the business to ensure an adequate level of business resiliency. And achieving a high level of resiliency means that Treasurers need to have regular face time with other senior leaders. Their work and input will rarely be ignored. Those who ignore a Treasurer's strong advice and counsel will have themselves to blame and will be accountable to those whom they serve. They do so at their own peril.

Directors will want to ensure that the Treasurer is well heard in the company and has an effective plan to ensure that the organization can take multiple hits and remain standing. To accomplish this, future Treasurers will ensure their organization's resiliency by taking a number of prudent steps to make certain that they are protected and can act and react quickly and appropriately when situations arise that were not contemplated and may have never occurred before.

Stewardship: Technology Developments and Green Treasury

Treasurers have a responsibility to be good stewards of the assets entrusted to their care. Exciting technology developments will continue to allow Treasurers to enhance critical business processes and provide data more quickly and accurately, as well as perform richer analysis more rapidly. Many of these technological developments will help Treasurers serve their organizations more effectively and efficiently. This will result in the interesting situation where Treasury will help financial processes become more "green"—even if this is not an articulated goal.

The movement to electronic processes from paper processes, and the movement of electronic processes that require human intervention to straight-through processes (STP), will reduce the level of energy and time necessary to accomplish key tasks. In addition to the environmental benefits of moving to better business processes, the layering in of new technologies that better utilize hardware and software will decrease the level of energy necessary to support a greatly increased need of computing capabilities.

Everything as a Service: Cloud Computing Comes to Treasury

To explain cloud computing and how it will come to Treasury requires a few other descriptions first. Software as a Service (SaaS) became increasingly popular in the early 2000s. This functionality allowed software to be delivered over the Internet (versus stored at a firm's location) and was typically accessed by a browser. Not needing hardware or having to upgrade systems brought great relief and hope to Treasury departments.

Grid computing is, essentially, the process whereby hardware is shared by different areas and entities. This saves the cost and trouble of owning and managing hardware, cooling, and other costs, as one organization's peak time is another firm's slow time.

"Cloud computing," by one definition, is the concept and practice where hardware and software are shared and can work together exceptionally well. Exhibit 18.1 shows a conceptual view of a Treasury cloud computing environment. Databases sit on one tier, and the business processes interact with the databases according to a set of rules. The overall interface is controlled, and security is layered on. The concept of cloud computing is in some ways like Software as a Service on steroids. Of course, SaaS usually employs much of what was just described as part of cloud computing. Here is where Treasury cloud computing will develop.

- **Best-of-breed solutions.** The choice between using a more comprehensive and integrated solution versus multiple types of software that must then be integrated has been a dilemma in the past. In the future, it will become increasingly easy to select several finance or Treasury best-of-breed solutions and connect them together for your solution. The Treasury cloud will eventually allow Treasurers to more easily and quickly connect the solutions that best fit their needs.
- **Common development architecture.** This concept has begun to grow in popularity among large software firms. Since they often must develop similar sets of functions and capabilities for their different applications, they seek a better way.

   This better way is the *common development architecture* or *modular development*. This allows one development effort to create

TREASURY STACK

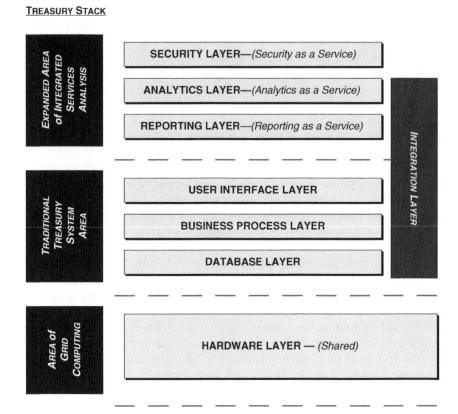

EXHIBIT 18.1 Treasury Cloud Computing Conceptual Environment

a service that can be used by multiple products. This quickly morphs into an internal best-of-breed solution model for large Treasury software firms and banks that offer multiple software platforms.

Being able to focus development efforts will allow software firms to more nimbly come out with more robust and useful tools. Theoretically, this would allow them to be nearly as responsive as the single-solution vendors but have the added advantage of being able to use that tool for multiple products.

■ **Reporting as a Service (RaaS) and Analysis as a Service (AaaS).** The more information an organization needs to access to provide needed electronic reports, the greater the range of data sources or systems that will need to be accessed. Within firms this is often accomplished by moving information into data warehouses that are then queried and reported on. Over time, data will be moved to the cloud, where various types of reporting can be performed efficiently and simply. This may include data necessary for accurate forecasting, covenant compliance tracking, and various other standard and nonstandard reports.

Analysis as a Service refers to the ability to easily create ad hoc analytics for a one-time use and to be able to repeat this process on an automated or scheduled basis.

Wide Area Netting Groups

- As efficiency gains are realized and additional improvements are sought, banks and a major enterprise resource planning (ERP) vendor will build a network of companies that have significant trade among themselves. This facilitated trade network will be supported and backed by a bank or banks. Once the ERP vendor and a few Treasury workstation providers join the group, it will grow along with the efficiency based on the scale of this network. Such an initiative will serve to help firms decrease settlement exposure and reduce costs. (Exhibit 18.2 shows a hypothetical netting group.)
- Supply chain and settlement financing will be connected later on as an add-on service as banks recover their strength.

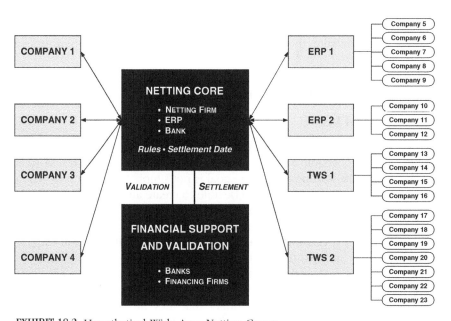

EXHIBIT 18.2 Hypothetical Wide Area Netting Group

SWIFT as a Network/Data Consolidators

- The Society for Worldwide Interbank Financial Telecommunication (SWIFT), which supplies secure messaging services and interface software to wholesale financial entities, will grow as a network along with corporate use of this network. Eventually, corporate-to-corporate transactions may be allowed on this network for the largest organizations to further drive down costs and meet the demands of SWIFT's owner-banks' top clients.
- Extensible markup language (XML), which is created to structure, store, and transport information, will dominate all new message types using the ISO 20022 standards to make the format more or less standard.
- Data consolidators and service bureau plus models will continue to allow more firms to connect, and the level of additional services they perform will add significant value to the corporate access ecosystem. Certain banks will use technology vendors to offer these services to their clients, since many banks will not be able to compete directly on a technological basis.
- In the future, there will no longer be a need for finance areas of corporations to attend SWIFT events. SWIFT will be treated like the telephone network that is used by everyone—either directly or through banks or other service bureaus. Just like the telephone, it will be expected to work, and users will be loath to discuss using other "phone systems." They will also be loath to discuss the network, viewing it as part of the financial network plumbing. Instead, Treasury groups will focus their efforts on meeting the business needs, managing risks, and performing analysis.

Visibility and Risk Management

War Gaming and Analysis

Testing the organization models and assumptions for the once-in-every-100-years flood will become a common occurrence. Testing of known historical issues will be the starting point. The goal is not simply to predict if or when this rare event may happen, but to be able to create an action plan that can be utilized if this unfortunate situation arises.

Additional modeling, analysis, and war gaming will be performed and reviewed. The expectation of ensuring organization resiliency will require astute Treasury groups, timely data, current technology, and well-utilized and solid analysis. All of this creates a future Treasury group that is prepared to act, prepared to protect, and prepared to analyze.

Future Treasuries will be confident that they are resilient enough to withstand a few hits if necessary. And they will take the steps necessary to ensure their survival and sustenance.

War Gaming: Risk Management

In the past, many firms would perform only minimal analysis of various risks and threats to their organization. For Treasurers this might mean looking at changes in interest rates, currency fluctuations, and various commodity price shift potentials. The majority of this analysis would look at single events and try to determine the total impact to the firm. This analysis rarely looks at a broad range of events occurring either at the same time or in rapid succession. Performing more extensive analysis of multiple issues with a war game mentality will become much more common given the more realistic view of rare and previously unexpected and interrelated events happening in rapid succession, combined with the level of emerging capabilities. The war games will include a designated enemy who throws the situations at Treasury. The designated enemy will likely alternate from one within Treasury to one outside. A formal debriefing of the scenarios will occur, action plans will be created and executed, and the next game will be scheduled. Some of the characteristics of war gaming will include:

- Actual war gaming created by various Treasury data warehouses
- Using historical data and projected trends
- Using supplied high-stress scenarios
- Modeling multiple years of the balance sheet

Dashboards, Management by Exception, and Ad-Hoc Analysis Will Mature

More complete and timely data, pulled in automatically, will allow Treasury to finally perform substantial analysis. Technology-based tools for risk, Treasury, and account management will offer dashboard and exception reporting that will actually be used by Treasurers. Events and triggers will alert Treasury to pending, imminent, and broken covenants and policies. Senior members of Treasury will rely on this capability rather than the standard monthly reports. These alerts and information will be pushed to the proper person for action.

Ad-hoc reporting, when deemed to be of repeat value as either a standard or an exception report, will be incorporated into the Treasury system on an automated basis.

Forecasting Will Finally Work for Most Firms

Short-term forecasting (the traditional Treasury forecasts) will be very accurate and will be fully supported by Treasury workstations. Enterprise resource planning (ERP) and bank systems will have basic forecast capabilities, but will continue to play catch-up for more than a decade.

Balance-sheet forecasting will be in vogue, as tight integration of the financial planning data (emphasizing the income statement) will be used by Treasury to model the future needs of the organization as far as the balance sheet is concerned.

Robust and Well-Understood Risk Management Framework

Treasuries will be in regular communication with their boards of directors during periods of relative calm, signaling a change from the past. A robust risk management framework will have been established and be well understood and regularly reviewed. Senior management will rarely second-guess the results of hedging programs, as they will understand the purpose, value, and cost of stability.

Treasury departments will continuously educate management. Boards will demand that Treasuries have clear visibility to liquidity and threats to liquidity. They will not tolerate the answer that it will take a few days to figure out "who our counterparties are," or "why the cash balance is off by $25 million from what was expected." Effective technology tools will be key to this new enhanced visibility.

Achieving Visibility to Liquidity and Threats to Liquidity

Near-total visibility to the firm's liquidity position will be available to senior management 24/7. While the special gloves that allowed Tom Cruise's silver-screen character to move and organize data by working with a holographic image in the movie *Minority Report* may not exist for decades, there will be increasingly powerful analytical tools that will provide for excellent ad-hoc analysis.

Achieving visibility to an organization's liquidity only in time to produce the financial statement will be unacceptable for future Treasuries. Treasuries will know exactly where their liquidity is on a real-time or daily basis. This view will cover all cash, committed and uncommitted lines of credit, debt, investments, and any hedges. Some of the actions they will take to accomplish this are:

- **Data consolidators.** They will use data consolidators, including bank data consolidators and SWIFT corporate access, to have visibility into all bank accounts.
- **Software as a Service (SaaS).** Most will deploy Application Service Provider (ASP), the technology solution that organizes all necessary data for a comprehensive view of the firm's liquidity picture from all financial institutions. The ASP market will dominate, with some exceptions for cash conversion cycle solutions for accounts payable and

credit/collections activity. Installed solutions will still have a significant role with Treasuries that have high-end requirements.

- **Forecast feeds.** Forecast data, at various levels, will be fed automatically from internally developed systems to facilitate the short-term forecast view.
- **Investment and exception management reporting.** Diversification reporting will exist from within the organization's Treasury workstation and liquidity portals.
  - Instrument, counterparty, maturity, and other base reports and management by exception reports (e.g., you are approaching your policy limit) will be pushed as necessary within the organization.
  - Broad diversification (counterparties, instruments, and maturities) will be standard, and Treasurers will ensure they are complying with their risk management framework.
  - Investment management will no longer be taken for granted—that is, managed by stale policies and poor reporting and performance measurement. Management of excess cash will be pushed up the chain to a higher-level Treasury officer, such as the position of senior Treasury manager, who will have the necessary investment-management skills and experience, or the function will be performed by outside managers.
- **Account management.** No more Parmalat SpA or Satyam Computer Services Ltd. examples of missing cash or missing accounts will be tolerated. Every organization with more than 100 bank accounts and six or more banks will use a bank account management tool enforcing compliance and control on a system-wide basis.
- **Regular assessments.** Treasury teams will regularly and on an as-needed basis assess the risks to their liquidity and plan accordingly. Treasuries will stay alert to market conditions and, if they show signs of rapid change, will take appropriate action.

Relationship Power Shifts

Extensive and easy relationship reporting will exist with the largest firms (those with large levels of cash and investments first, then spreading to other large firms). This reporting will allow senior management to see an internally generated risk-adjusted return on capital (RAROC) model that will help a firm gauge how important it is to its key bank relationships. Achieving this goal quickly will require advances in visibility technologies.

In the future, credit will be almost always able to stand alone, based on the pricing level. The connection of fee-based business, by banks and companies, to those that offer credit will certainly continue. Relationships

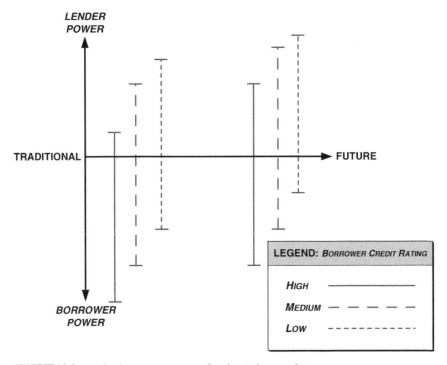

EXHIBIT 18.3 Lender/Borrower Range for the Balance of Power

will be formally managed, and ideas and value-added services will continue to set apart a firm's financial partners.

The balance of power between lenders and borrowers will move in a tighter band reflecting a more reasonable and sustainable relationship model. While, over time, the balance of power may broaden some, it will not return to its former level. Exhibit 18.3 provides a visual of the new range of power levels between banks and borrowers.

Liquidity and Balance Sheet Management

Resiliency requires more than a large pile of cash and a plan to manage counterparty risk. Future Treasuries will project their balance sheet needs out multiple years. Their needs will be communicated with relationship banks by a Treasury that uses a formal bank relationship planning process that senior management understands. This will be similar in scope and focus of the income-statement-oriented corporate planning projection.

Chairing the Working Capital Council and Advising Business Areas

The Treasurer will chair the working capital council in his or her organization. This group will educate the organization about drivers of working capital usage and the impact on organizational performance. It will publish metrics and drive balanced behaviors throughout all areas of the cash conversion cycle.

Some Treasuries will do more. In addition to improving the financial performance through the working capital council, they will also be systematic in helping their departments accomplish their objectives by bringing business acumen and intellectual rigor to the process. They will leverage their access to external parties to challenge the insular approach that develops in many organizations.

Cash, Checks, and Miscellaneous Projections

Congressional Financial Expert

A provision in the Sarbanes-Oxley Act of 2002 requires that a financial expert sit on the board of directors of public companies. A similar type of requirement will be placed on the U.S. Congress. One or more financial experts will be required within congressional subcommittees that deal with budgeting, banking, and so forth.

Check-Stopped Society

Predictions that once abounded about how we would become a paperless society are viewed as laughable today given the ability and proclivity of everyone everywhere to print a hard copy—and to do it in color. The predictions that were made about a checkless society were laughed at, too, until the check volume in the United States actually started to decline. With the decline, the common expectation is that we are becoming a less-check society, not a checkless society. We will become a check-stopped society, meaning that even as paper check volume declines, the ability to stop the physical item at an early stage in the collection process will increase. The following show some of the detailed predictions or estimations related to the replacement of the physical clearing process with other methods.

- Postage in the United States will grow too expensive for checks to be mailed. (Well, at least one can hope!)
- Physical check-clearing will cease before 2020 as Image Cash Letter and Check 21 services wipe out the process of business checks.

- Availability float will still exist in some areas for years, but will eventually become de minimis. Banks will succeed in fighting the disappearance of float for many years despite its inevitability.

Some Things Will Not Change

Some Treasury perspectives and activities will not change significantly over time. However, since this chapter focuses on future Treasury, the commentary is biased toward changes within Treasury.

Cash Will Still Be King

- Some things just won't change.
- Some will still say "credit is king" or "risk management is king."
- They will still be wrong. Cash will still be King!

Webinars and Seminars

- The popularity and use of webinars will increase, as will their effectiveness. However, nothing will ever fully replace conferences and seminars with direct interaction with peers and professionals as learning and networking experiences.
- Smaller regional Treasury associations will be challenged to maintain their conferences in the present form.
  - Those adopting newer technologies will perform better and be more useful for users.
  - The first projected live Treasury presentation (projected to multiple locations) will allow for higher-quality presentations at leading local Association for Financial Professionals (AFP) groups and other professional Treasury organizations.

Summary

Future Treasurers will not work in obscurity. They will be viewed as critical leaders by their boards of directors and senior management.

Their organizations will be far more resilient and more fully automated from a visibility and risk management perspective. Operationally, they will enjoy processes that much more closely mirror the promise of straight-through processing (STP), but that will become an assumption, not a goal.

Even mediocre Treasurers will make sure that their organizations can take multiple hits and remain standing. However, leading Treasurers will be able to handle new experiences and previously unheard-of crises by ensuring that they have a resilient organizational, informational, and technological framework that will allow for rapid analysis and informed decision making while under attack.

Relationships will be formally managed, and ideas and value-added services will continue to set apart their financial partners. The balance of power between lenders and borrowers will move in a tighter band reflecting a more reasonable and sustainable relationship model. While over time the balance of power may broaden a bit, it will not return to its former level.

The future of Treasurers who have a strategic mindset and relentlessly pursue the objectives that will take their organizations where they need to go is indeed a bright one.

CHAPTER 19

"Not-to-Do" List for the Treasurer

Here is Edward Bear coming downstairs now, bump, bump, bump, on the back of his head, behind Christopher Robin.

It is, as far as he knows, the only way of coming downstairs, but sometimes he feels that there really is another way. If only he could stop bumping for a moment and think of it.

—A. A. Milne, *Winnie-the-Pooh*

In many organizations there are distraction-generating machines that create the bumping that makes it hard to focus effectively. These distractions do not announce themselves as such. Rather they are often presented as "urgent issues that won't take much time to complete" or they'll be tenuously linked to the organization mission but will not achieve what is promised.

Like *Winnie-the-Pooh*'s Edward Bear, many in finance know that there is a better way of doing things. However, the distractions of the urgent, if not eliminated and managed effectively, will be the largest hindrance to achieving Treasury's goals and helping the organization fulfill its mission.

To be a Strategic Treasurer, having a "what *not* to do" list will provide a complement to the mindset of all the key functions that do belong on the to-do list. The "not-to-dos" are not always transferable between firms and Treasurers. To that point, the reader should proceed with discernment. Learning even one applicable pointer on what not to do or what to avoid should make the time spent on this chapter worthwhile.

Relationship Management

Consultants

Do not hire to teach or train the consultants. It is natural that they will learn from each project; however, they should bring with them the ability and knowledge to significantly contribute to your organization's success. Remember the fact that a consulting group has finance experience doesn't necessarily mean it can assist with Treasury activities. Due diligence is in order here.

Conversely, do not take inappropriate risks to help save costs by avoiding consultants altogether. Increasing the risk of failure by depending on internal resources for one-time events can produce the opposite effect and cost more than expected.

If the consultants you have hired or are planning to hire cannot explain the differences between system capabilities, or internal processes, or why something is a leading practice for your organization, why are you paying them? Don't accept constant equivocation from consultants. You are paying for their guidance, advice, opinions, and decisions. Their advice and guidance need to be given in the context of your firm's specific needs—or it is time to move on to perhaps another consultant or firm.

Bankers

Bankers who offer good ideas and advice that you can trust are rare. Do not let your bankers get away with agreeing with all the ideas offered by you or your staff or reasons for a project or for postponing important work. If a banker never challenges assumptions or reasons, it is likely he or she is not a very good adviser. The corollary to this, of course, is: don't be overly defensive when your thinking is challenged.

Bank Relationships and Relationship Management

Do not ignore the value of your credit relationships by failing to support them. By securing operational services from banks that put their balance sheets to work for your organization, you strengthen the economics of those relationships. No vendor will lend your organization money. And, if you want to remain important to the bank, it is advisable to be among the clients that generate a profit—a practice that is generally good business for both sides.

Do not let purchasing, accounts payable, accounts receivable, or other areas ignore the bank's offerings, unless they will provide the funds your organization needs; then they should be challenged. Do not be afraid to escalate this issue if another area decides it wants to move forward without what Treasury deems an adequate cause or reason.

Request for Proposal

When sending a request for proposal (RFP), do not simply copy an old RFP and add a few questions as an update. Every question in an RFP must be understood by the firm issuing it and needs to relate to something of value based on the firm's critical-needs document. The argument "We might as well ask additional questions so we have the answers" rings hollow. There is no problem with asking for a bank's or vendor's responses to an organization's standard RFP. This can be electronically generated in minutes and can act as a reference document without wasting hours and days of a potential business partner's life.

Do not issue an RFP if your pricing is too high and you simply want better prices. The first step for saving money is often found by designing a better financial process and bank structure. The savings achieved by ordering your side of the equation will usually dwarf the savings achieved by pressuring your banks and partners to shave some costs and profits off the bill.

If you are paying too much, make an effort to indicate you know that that is the case. Then, if you are confident you wish to continue service with the same institution or vendor, have a specific price discussion. You can also request that the party issue a new pro forma based on guidance you provide.

Finally, if you ask your bank partner to give guidance on how you can lower your firm's bank fees, the bank will often willingly oblige. Be prepared also for suggestions the bank will probably make on how your firm can improve its operations.

Do not ask for new ideas in an RFP if you won't share anything of substance about your process with the bank or if you are not truly open to new ideas. And note that not being open to new ideas is not a leading practice. However, there are times when a Treasurer has to limit the amount of input he or she actively receives.

Do not rush into a "try before you buy" sales model. Vendors can offer this model for a variety of reasons. The result can simply be enticing a company to shortchange an orderly due diligence process before the hard work of matching up critical needs with the various services that exist. That is not to say to avoid performing "proof of concept" when appropriate. Using a proof of concept approach is relevant in many instances after the fit between your needs and the particular vendor services appears to be superior. The proof of concept approach can serve as a final due diligence step in the selection process.

Technology Decisions and Perspectives Don'ts

Since technology supports the vast majority of Treasury transactions, activities, and risk management activities, it is a very important part of the solutions that Treasury must deliver. Technology decisions last for a long time, and it is important to make proper decisions with regard to many aspects of the technology life cycle. The following list highlights some of the major don'ts of technology decisions.

- Do not buy the same technology or service merely because a firm you respect has acquired something.
- Do not buy or lease technology based on a fantastic demonstration that shows your staff wonderful things that may have very little or no bearing on your organization's critical needs.
- Do not shortchange the due diligence work on the selection process. Reference checking is typically done in a perfunctory manner, either focusing on a particular capability or wandering around a few topics. Then, based on the findings, decisions are made, with the vendor rarely being given the opportunity to respond to the issues or questions that may have been raised. This is not effective. Setting specific objectives for the reference checking combined with the meeting/call plan needs to have appropriate follow-up with the vendor.
- Do not avoid having someone from information technology (IT) review the underlying technology. Even if the IT department is rarely helpful to Treasury, or has Treasury's interests very low on its list, it should not be kept out of attending the meeting and offering advice and expertise.
- When jobs are being cut, IT has a tendency to backtrack on clear best practices within the IT domain to protect turf. Do not allow a non-responsive IT group to move your applications and services in-house for specious reasons or reasons that contradict the key direction of the industry. During a time of IT job loss, well after the use of application service providers (ASPs) was well established, some IT departments started making the assertion that these applications needed to be brought in-house.
- Build strategic and buy tactical. This old saw holds much wisdom that bears repeating. Despite the fact that building a proprietary system may help an individual feel important and needed, developing and supporting this homegrown system are rarely appropriate. While there may be some minor advantages that can be customized for individual organizations, does it help your organization have a strategic advantage over your competitors? Building tactical usually puts an organization at great risk—being dependent on a single personality. There are ways to provide people with better career security.

- Do not believe that the payment-generation process can be done appropriately only within your organization. Controlling types sit within Treasury and finance, too. This is manifested in many ways, including those who do not want to let any part of the payment-creation process out of the organization. All sorts of creative cost-benefit analyses are generated with a curious set of assumptions that drive to the answer the controlling and defensive person makes about a proposed change. Remind these people about the core business activities that should be their focus.
- Do not underestimate the value of flexibility and business resiliency. The default position for many organizations should be to move these activities externally. The burden of proof will need to fall on the person seeking to keep them in-house.
- Do not manage your investments in-house without serious consideration of the risk and exposure the practice can bring to your organization. Unfortunately, most firms do not have the level of internal expertise necessary to directly manage all investments as effectively as an outside manager. However, to be sure, managing an outside manager is still valuable and engaging work for the Treasury professional.

Staffing, Resources, and Consultants

Hiring people just like you is an exercise in design with a lack of depth perception. Your unique experiences and career path have great value to your organization. Hiring someone else with the same set of skills means you may agree more and can have enjoyable conversations. However, it also will usually mean the organization in general, and Treasury in particular, will suffer from a flatter view. This is a very common mistake that can be rectified rather easily, even if it is a bit less comfortable in the beginning.

Projects and Communication

The Elusive Second Phase of Projects

Do not stop when phase one of a project is complete, but rather build out the later phases. Phase two is not meant to be a dumping ground for items that will not get done or plans that will not be completed. Disappointment is the typical result of an organization that moves items off and never completes them. This often means disappointment with the results or with the bank or vendor—the perception being that Treasury never fulfilled its promise to deliver value.

Do not give in to the concept that your group will redesign the system later and implement according to how things are now. The idea that those changes will be made later in phase two is far more optimistic than is reasonable. While making all process changes may prove to be overly aggressive for the first phase of a project, ensuring that movement toward the future-state process design made in each phase ought to be considered a minimum requirement.

Do not underestimate the amount of work resources needed for a large project. Staff your organization to handle the periods of stability and reasonable volatility. Supplement your permanent staff for changes of a one-time nature such as design or redesign work, testing, connection management, and documentation.

Communication and Training

Do not allow your staff to treat communication and training as a one-time event. Naturally, both communication and training have event components to them. However, what is exceedingly clear to someone steeped in Treasury parlance requires some repetition and reinforcement at regular intervals.

Treasury should not publish metrics and management letters solely for its own consumption. There are metrics that show the value that the Treasury group is bringing to the organization and, as such, need to receive broad exposure. Some of the metrics may require some contextual explanation for nonfinance or non-Treasury staff to make sense of the numbers. The more others understand how their business decisions impact the financials and key Treasury metrics, the easier it will be to encourage better behavior.

Decisions, Debates, and Assumptions

Valuation and Valuing Alternatives

Do not allow a mismatch of rates when calculating benefits of various alternatives to capital structures or working capital movements. The incorrect use of short-term or overnight rates for long-term or permanent changes occurs far too commonly. Staff members make the logical error in the premise of their argument to use lower short-term rates to value changes. This results, frequently, in missed opportunities.

In such cases, the most common defense given by the perpetrator is that he or she was "being conservative." The rates used to evaluate alternatives should be clearly communicated, and staff members should understand when to use each one in their calculations.

Intellectual Curiosity

There is great value in mentally stretching and challenging your staff. Put them in charge of projects or research they either initiated or suggested or that you assigned. Projects can be assigned for several reasons, including time available, previous experience and expertise, and staff development needs.

Every project need not be a monumental intellectual challenge to the leader; however, evaluating the opportunity that each project would present for individual staff members should be factored into the decision process. In such instances, staffers need to be responsible for the outcome and success of the effort and have some freedom in how they approach the issue.

Thus, do not take all personal initiative and responsibility for intellectual growth away from your staff. They are responsible for having active and learning minds, which they should be encouraged to pursue with vigor. Indeed, if you desire leading a group that grows intellectually and professionally, they need to be challenged and given opportunities to learn. Much of the learning will come from the direct work at hand, projects, and research as assigned.

As a leader, it is your role to ensure that there are adequate opportunities for your staff to engage with others outside of your particular Treasury group. This should include other areas of the organization on cross-functional initiatives and with other companies—via events, conferences, and task force teams.

The Crowd: Follow or Take the Road Less Traveled

Do not fruitlessly compare your company with others. An organization that contains a handful or so of Treasury professionals will have a challenge competing for industry accolades against organizations that have dozens of professionals and a dedicated staff of Treasury IT specialists. Use internal and external resources as you would a lever. Your internal resources will be the force acting on the lever. Technology services can act as the fulcrum point. External consultants can help you move the fulcrum closer to the object you are trying to move, improving the effect of your current level of staffing.

Making comparisons with well-respected leaders in the Treasury industry can be both a bit daunting and helpful, regardless of your resource level. Not making comparisons can prevent you from stretching your group and yourself in ways that may not be possible merely by setting goals that are perceived as aggressive.

Seeing where others have been, gives a group that follows the knowledge that it can be done. And, given fewer resources, it can still be achieved by challenging a smaller organization to greater creativity and resourcefulness. Abusing and avoiding comparisons can create suboptimal results.

Benchmarks are very popular. However, do not accept benchmark numbers without understanding all of the assumptions that sit behind them. Is it really true, for instance, that leading Treasuries have 5 to 7.5 people per billion dollars of revenue? Does wrapping and averaging or segmenting responses from a statistically significant or even statistically insignificant survey mean that the other assumptions are true? That the argument is sound?

Far too much information pushed off as benchmark truth or a fact-based approach is unhelpful and oversold. Even if all of the premises or arguments are true, the conclusion can be completely unsound. If either the premise or the conclusion has problems, then the entire argument is unsound.

Do not hesitate to challenge the assumptions and arguments of all those who put forth numbers as a means of aiming to convince you what to do or which way to go.

Some Basics

Do not do something just because you can. You are probably not being paid to do many of those tasks. If you have a problem with delegating, you may want to hire a professional coach, as you will impair your success and the success of your organization if you cannot let go and assign to others.

As a corollary to "do not do something just because you can," just because you can say yes to a request from a partner in your organization does not mean you should answer that way. Declining to do activities or projects is a critical factor in ensuring that Treasury has the capacity to fulfill its mission. There will always be situations where work is requested that neither you nor anyone in your group should perform. The thoughtful Treasurer will respond to such requests with a well-explained no. Answering no is appropriate whenever you cannot be convinced that this activity will help the organization achieve its mission most effectively or that it rightly falls on your area. A polite rejection of the request along with the rationale for declining is a good course of action. When the request comes from the chief executive officer (CEO) or the board of directors, securing intellectual assent that the activity is less productive than other activities is essential for survival.

Creative types sit within Treasury. This is a good situation. However, it can also have very negative consequences. Creative types will want to create something even if it already exists. Do not settle by letting them create something that should be leased or acquired. Rather, channel their abilities into worthwhile projects that help Treasury or the organization fulfill its mission.

Be willing to challenge your own assumptions based on historical norms. Do not maintain a position based solely on old data, old experiences, or old ideas. Accepting new information has a way of messing with one's neatly defined rules of thumb. To wit: "Banks don't offer leading technology" and "Treasury workstations are always cumbersome and disappointing" represent the historical opinions of many that, in many cases, need to be updated.

Do not forget that the type of value you bring to an organization changes over time. When you started your career, your technical expertise played a lead role. Then your ability to lead projects and people was paramount. Your ability to lead people and the organization intellectually must now include the ability to manage multiple groups and expectations.

Summary

The decisions a Treasurer makes about what not to do are extremely important, as they directly impact the ability to accomplish those initiatives that are crucial. Urgent items create an almost hourly pull on the time and attention of both the Treasurer and the Treasury department. Resources are limited. The obviously lower-importance items are easily dispatched. There are numerous good activities that scream to be handled.

The Strategic Treasurer will take steps to eliminate those tasks that are not essential to the mission of the organization. This elimination extends to mean elimination of the task from Treasury and from the organization, not simply removing it from their list.

Delegation and accountability are two other key skills that must complement the elimination-of-tasks skill set. Delegation is effective for freeing up senior staff and training and developing the Treasury team. Direct accountability for achieving the truly important items will help enforce the ability to turn down or delay tasks of lower importance.

Resource Information

In the absence of clearly-defined goals, we become strangely loyal to performing daily trivia until ultimately we become enslaved by it.

—Robert Heinlein

In this Appendix, the author has provided a sample of Treasury-related resources, organized within the following categories:

- Media/Magazines
- Books
- Professional Organizations
  - National Associations
  - Regional Associations of the Association for Financial Professionals
- Treasury/Business Web Sites
  - Information
  - Rating Agencies
  - Treasury/Banking
- Treasury/Banking Technology
  - Cash/Treasury/Risk Systems
  - Account Management
  - Reconciliation
  - Spreadsheet Control and Analysis
  - Escheat/Abandoned Property
  - Trading
  - Data Aggregators/Service Bureaus/SWIFT Corporate Access
  - Other

Note that these resource selections are not meant to be either complete or comprehensive, but rather to aid you in beginning your research quest for further finance-related news, data, professional associations and education, and similar information.

Media/Magazines

To stay ahead of the curve, or at least keep pace with it, entails staying abreast of news and developments across a broad spectrum of areas that can impact current and future Treasury issues.

In addition to the daily financial paper, the following periodicals are helpful in keeping apprised of issues in banking, technology, best practices, and other finance-related news and happenings.

- *American Banker* (www.americanbanker.com)
- *Business Finance* (www.businessfinancemag.com)
- *CFO* (www.cfo.com)
- *FEI/Financial Executives International* (www.financialexecutives. org)
- *Financial Week* (www.financialweek.com)
- *GT News* (www.gtnews.com)
- *International Treasurer* (www.neugroup.com/itreasurer/home.aspx)
- *Risk* (www.risk.net)
- *Treasury & Risk* (www.treasuryandrisk.com)

Books

While this list is far from complete, the author has noted some useful books that the Treasurer may use as primary resources:

- *Accounting for Derivative Instruments and Hedging Activities*, Financial Accounting Standards Board (aka "The Green Book"), February 10, 2004.
- Changes to the February 10, 2004, edition of The Green Book, *Accounting for Derivative Instruments and Hedging Activities*, Financial Accounting Standards Board, January 14, 2009.
- *Analysis for Financial Management*, Robert C. Higgins, McGraw-Hill, 2005.
- *Corporate Cash Management Handbook*, Richard Bort, Warren, Gorham and Lamont Inc., 1991.

- *Corporate Liquidity: Essentials of Cash Management*, Kenneth L. Parkinsons and Jarl G. Kallberg, Association of Financial Professionals, 2001.
- *Essentials of Managing Corporate Cash*, Michele Allman-Ward and James Sagner, John Wiley & Sons, 2003.
- *Options, Futures, and Other Derivatives*, John C. Hull, Prentice Hall, 2008.
- *Principles of Corporate Finance*, Richard A. Brealey and Stewart C. Meyers, McGraw-Hill, 2007.
- *The International Treasurer's Handbook*, www.treasurers.org/handbook.

Professional Organizations

Education is a lifelong pursuit. The national Treasury and accounting associations provide outlets for keeping up with best practices and enhancing one's technical knowledge. In addition, both the national and the regional associations provide opportunities to network with peers, financial service providers, and technology vendors.

National Associations

- **American Institute of Certified Public Accountants (AICPA):** www.aicpa.org
- **American Payroll Association:** www.americanpayroll.org
- **Association for Financial Professionals (AFP):** www.afponline.org
- **Association of Corporate Treasurers (ACT):** www.treasurers.org
- **Chartered Financial Analyst Institute:** www.cfainstitute.org
- **Committee of Sponsoring Organizations of the Treadway Commission (COSO):** www.coso.org
- **NACHA/The Electronic Payments Association:** www.nacha.org
- **National Association of Credit Managers (NACM):** www.nacm.org
- **National Association of Purchasing Card Professionals (NAPCP):** www.napcp.org/napcp/napcp.nsf

Regional Associations of the Association for Financial Professionals

- **Arizona** www.afparizona.org
- **Atlanta:** www.afpofatlanta.org
- **Austin:** www.texastma.org/Austin/
- **Central Ohio:** www.coafp.net
- **Dallas:** www.dallasafp.org

- **Hampton Roads:** www.hrafp.org
- **Kansas City:** www.kcafp.org
- **Mid-Atlantic:** www.maafp.org
- **Mid-South:** www.midsouthafp.org
- **Nebraska:** www.nebraskaafp.org
- **New Jersey:** www.afpnj.org
- **Northwest:** www.nwafp.org
- **Oregon and Southwest Washington:** www.oregonafp.org
- **Philadelphia:** www.philadelphiaafp.com
- **Pittsburgh:** www.pittsburghafp.org
- **Puerto Rico:** www.afppr.com
- **South Carolina:** www.scafponline.org
- **South Florida:** www.sfafp.org
- **Southern California:** www.scafp.net
- **Southwest Ohio:** www.swoafp.org
- **Tampa Bay:** www.tbafp.org
- **Washington, DC:** www.gwafp.org
- **Western New York:** www.afpwny.org

Treasury/Business Web Sites

Information overload can stifle productivity. Nevertheless, for staying abreast of current events/news in the financial markets and current accounting/ regulatory pronouncements or keeping up to date on the financial viability of your customers, suppliers, bankers, and other counterparties, Treasury's appetite for information is large. In pursuit of that endeavor, the author has provided a streamlined list of selected resources.

Information

- **Bank Administration Institute (BAI):** www.bai.org
- **Bloomberg:** www.bloomberg.com
- **British Bankers' Association (BBA):** www.bba.org.uk
- **Econlib:** www.econlib.org
- **Federal Deposit Insurance Corporation (FDIC):** www.fdic.gov
- **Federal Reserve Bank Board of Governors (FRB BOG):** www.federalreserve.gov/Releases/
- **Financial Accounting Standards Board (FASB):** www.fasb.org
- **Fisher School of Business:** www.fisher.osu.edu/fin/overview.htm
- **Hoovers:** www.hoovers.com/free/
- **International Swaps and Derivatives Association (ISDA):** www.isda.org

- **Securities and Exchange Commission (SEC):** www.sec.gov
- **St. Louis Federal Reserve Bank (FRB):** www.research.stlouisfed.org/fred2/
- **Thomson Reuters:** www.thomsonreuters.com

Rating Agencies

- **Fitch Ratings:** www.fitchratings.com
- **Moody's Investors Service:** www.moodys.com
- **Standard & Poor's:** www.standardandpoors.com

Treasury/Banking

- **Lace Financial Corp.:** www.lacefinancial.com
- **Phoenix-Hecht:** www.phoenix-hecht.com
- **UPIC:** www.epaynetwork.com

Treasury/Banking Technology

Technology is at the forefront of an effective Treasury/finance organization. Fortunately, or not, it is ever changing. The following list is a sample at the time of publication, and again, it is not meant to be either a comprehensive list or an endorsement.

Cash/Treasury/Risk Systems

- **Allegro/Commodity XL:** www.allegrosummit.com
- **Bellin:** www.bellintreasury.com
- **Clearwater Analytics:** www.clearwateranalytics.com
- **Concur:** www.concur.com
- **Ferential Risk Systems:** www.ferential.com
- **FireApps:** www.fireapps.com
- **FXpress:** www.fxpress.com
- **Gateway:** www.gatewaysystems.com
- **GTM:** www.sungard.com
- **IT2:** www.it2tms.com
- **Kiodex:** www.sungard.com
- **Kyriba:** www.kyriba.com
- **Quantum:** www.sungard.com
- **Reval:** www.reval.com
- **SAP:** www.sap.com
- **Savvy Soft:** www.savvysoft.com
- **SimCorp:** www.simcorp.com

- **SunGard (numerous):** www.sungard.com
- **Super Derivatives:** www.superderivatives.com
- **Thomson Treasura:** www.thomsonreuters.com
- **Treasury Sciences:** www.treasurysciences.com
- **Triple Point Technologies:** www.tpt.com
- **Wall Street Systems:** www.wallstreetsystems.com

Account Management

- **Chesapeake:** www.chessys.com
- **Speranza:** www.speranzasystems.com
- **Weiland Financial Group (Bank Relationship Manager, Bank Administrator):** www.weiland-wfg.com

Reconciliation

- **Checkfree:** www.checkfree.com
- **Chesapeake:** www.chessys.com
- **Recon Plus:** www.cfacsonline.com
- **ReconNet and AssureNet:** www.trintech.com
- **T-Recs Enterprise:** www.chessys.com
- **Trintech:** www.trintech.com

Spreadsheet Control and Analysis

- **CimCon:** www.cimcon.com
- **ExcelNet:** www.trintech.com
- **Prodiance:** www.prodiance.com
- **Sox-XL:** www.sarbox-solutions.com

Escheat/Abandoned Property

- **APECS:** www.checkfreesoftware.com
- **Fiserv (Freedom Group):** www.fiserv.com

Trading

- **FX-All:** www.fxall.com

Data Aggregators/Service Bureaus/SWIFT Corporate Access

- **Axway:** www.axway.com
- **BancBridge:** www.bancbridge.com
- **Bankserv:** www.bankserv.com
- **Bottomline:** www.bottomline.com
- **Broadridge:** www.broadridge.com

- **Citibank:** www.citi.com
- **FIDES:** www.fides.ch/treasury/indexe.html
- **Kyriba:** www.kyriba.com
- **SunGard:** www.sungard.com/sungard/
- **SWIFT:** www.swift.com

Other Sites for Resources

- **Bobsguide:** www.bobsguide.com
- **Strategic Treasurer:** www.strategictreasurer.com

Index

Printed and bound by CPI Group (UK) Ltd, Croydon, CR0 4YY

23/04/2025

14661000-0001